# PEACE AND THE PLAIN MAN

*By the Same Author*

----

THE GREAT ILLUSION

UNSEEN ASSASSINS

ETC.

Norman Angell

# PEACE

## AND THE

# PLAIN MAN

Harper & Brothers Publishers
New York and London
1935

*This work was originally
published in England
under the title of*
PREFACE TO PEACE

# CONTENTS

[v]

# CONTENTS

The prevention of war has suddenly become supremely important not so much because of what happens in war, but because of what happens in peace
as the result of preparation for war. Under the system of competitive arming the purpose of society is
turned from the ends of welfare to the ends of military victory. In the stress of that competition we
forget the purpose for which society was created.
The kind of nation that can best win wars is the
kind of nation that has sacrificed both freedom and
welfare. What we do about the war problem will
determine the kind of world in which men are to
live and the kind of men that are to live in it.

Wars are not made by governments, capitalists, financiers or armament makers, but by the ordinary man
acquiescing for a variety of reasons in policies that
often suit the ends of predatory governments, capitalists, financiers, armament makers. A few obese
financiers cannot force, they can only persuade, untold millions to do their bidding. It is John Smith's
ideas on such things as the proper method of national defence, internationalism, patriotism, religion,
empire, which made the last war and will make the
next, unless those ideas are changed. War is usually
the last thing that Smith desires but is often inherent
in the policies which he imposes upon his governments.

This subject has become complex and technical and
the specialists differ. So do specialists in medicine.
Nevertheless the layman has so profited from medical
knowledge as to transform the world by the abolition
of dreadful pestilences—bubonic plague, cholera, leprosy—that used to curse it. He has done this by
taking over from the medical expert the few truths
about which no expert differs from another: e.g. To
prevent pestilences sewage must be kept from drinking water. There are a few political and social truths,
no more difficult to understand than the microbic
theory of disease, which would enable the layman to
eradicate the pestilence of war if he could see what
they are. The purpose of this book is to disentangle

# CONTENTS

from specialist knowledge those political truths which correspond in medicine to the transmission of disease by micro-organisms.

## PART TWO

# WHAT WE KNOW OR MIGHT KNOW

Contrary to what seems general belief history gives us numberless examples of war being brought to an end over vast areas in which originally it had raged unchecked for untold generations; the Pax Romana, the Pax Germanica, the Pax Britannica, the Pax Italiana, to cite only a few. Where a group of sovereign and independent units combine into a federation for mutual defence, war ceases. The suggestive difference between the history of the British colonies of North America which learned how not to fight and of the Spanish colonies of South America which failed to learn shows that without certain antecedent political conditions neither psychological nor economic forces could normally produce war.

The War arose because a potential enemy claimed a a preponderance of power that would have left us defenceless. We preferred to possess the preponderance which leaves him defenceless. Each thus puts his power, not behind right, as we may sincerely believe, but behind a denial of right, the denial to the other of that right of judgment or superior power we claim. We used our power of judgment after the war to make the Treaty of Versailles. The Germans now want power to make another treaty which will be worse, compelling us to unmake it, *Da capo,* until civilisation has perished.

Most of the twenty-two states that entered the war had no pre-commitment so to do. Freedom from

[ vii ]

# CONTENTS

commitment (e.g. the United States' position) did not keep them out; commitment *would* have kept them out, since if Germany had known that by following a certain line twenty-two states would range themselves against her, she would not have followed that line and there would have been no war. The lesson is therefore that if states arm they must make known beforehand what will cause them to fight. Unless a state will so commit itself arms can never be an effective instrument of defence.

A state dependent solely upon its own power for defence of its rights must be stronger than any likely to challenge them, which automatically deprives that other of similar defence. The only egress from this dilemma is for the defence of each to become the function of all, which is the method operating within the frontiers of each nation. International relations stumble towards that method, hampered, however by public misunderstanding of the issues. A note on the nature of the police function in the international field, and on grievances as the cause of war.

## PART THREE

# ECONOMIC FACTORS

Instead of conceiving of wealth as based on processes which must be co-operatively maintained, we commonly conceive it as being a definitely limited quantity of land or material which if one nation possesses another is deprived of. This fundamentally fallacious conception largely explains our preference for anarchy over order; for preferring competition for preponderant power to the pooling of power in partnership.

When a Capitalist state has had, and won, its "war for markets," it cannot use victory to get the market, as witness victorious Britain, much less able to dispose of its surplus after its successful war than it was

[ viii ]

# CONTENTS

before. Another war would destroy both markets and capitalism. In promoting war, as they sometimes do, being subject to the same errors and passions as the bulk of mankind, capitalists think and act as nationalists or militarists not as economists. Socialism does not emerge from chaos: Fascism emerges. Socialists and Capitalists have as much a common interest in the creation of an international order as in the maintenance of a sewage system or of rules of the road.

PART FOUR

## PSYCHOLOGICAL FACTORS

[ix]

# CONTENTS

It is not a problem of changing human nature but
human behaviour which can be modified by new
values based on new ideas, new perceptions, new
institutions; as the daily life of the world around us
abundantly proves. The way in which our emotions
are stirred and our nature behaves depends largely
upon the way in which we read facts. One man's
fear may be a wiser man's hope and vice versa.

## PART FIVE

# CONCLUSION

The practical issue is finally reduced to a choice between two courses: to employ force for the purpose
of defence by placing it collectively behind law, or
to use it by the old competitive individual method.
Collective defence can be expressed in actual policy
in many different ways. It need not be a cut-and-
dried plan with ironclad commitments, but a gradual
shaping of day-to-day international policy. How the
present world situation bears upon the development
of such policy; what is essential to it; some of the
arguments usually urged against it.

This chapter is designed to help the ordinary man in
dealing with arguments most current in the daily
talk of train and club and dinner table bearing on
the following points: "War is inevitable," "Human
Nature is naturally quarrelsome," "You cannot
change Human Nature," "War is a Spiritual
Cleanser," "War will continue so long as Man is
selfish," "What would you do if a Brute attacked
your Sister?" "Would you leave Houses unlocked, or
refrain from resisting the Burglar?" "The Strong Man
armed," "Arms are for defence," "Armaments mean
Peace" (Lord Rothermere), "Defence demands that
we should be stronger than any Probable Enemy,"
"Defence must rest upon a Balance of Power," "Isolation is the best Peace Policy," "Our Policy is Defence, so our Armaments need disturb no Foreign
Nation," "Conflict of Ideals, Religion, Race, produce

[x]

# CONTENTS

War," "Marathon . . . the Armada . . . War as a
last resort," "Expanding Populations need Food and
Space," "Capitalism, the Need of Disposing of Surplus Goods is the Cause," "Some Capitalists would
benefit by War," "Armament Makers cause War,"
"Peace would perpetuate an unjust *Status Quo*,"
"Avoid War by removing the Grievances which cause
it," "Armies and Navies are Police," "The Policy of
Commitments failed in 1914," "The League is impotent—a Talking Shop," "The League places British Policy under Foreigners' Control," "The League
costs too much," "What Security have we that Foreign Nations will keep their Word?" "Only Britain is
pacifist . . . it is dangerous to preach Peace in England when Foreigners prepare for War . . ."

# JOHN SMITH'S CONCERN

# Chapter I

## WHAT THIS BOOK IS ABOUT

LOOKING at the world about him, noting the growing tension of the international situation, the failure after weary years of negotiation to secure the tiniest fraction of disarmament, the growth, even in nations of ancient culture and civilisation, of the spirit of violence and the crudest militarism, the teaching of little children to glorify war and bloodshed; the unchecked aggression of Japan, the impotence of the League in the presence of such aggression, its impotence in the presence of other wars—looking at all that, the plain man is apt to feel, not unnaturally, that the whole of the "idealistic" effort for peace of the last fifteen years has failed; that mankind is simply not ready for that kind of achievement; that we have no recourse but to stick to the old ways of each for himself, of "keeping our end up" in armaments, in order to make the catastrophe as little damaging as possible for ourselves when it does come. Or he is impelled to the belief that we must make a fresh start with some new plan, not yet tried.

This book attempts to face without evasion the situation created by the facts just outlined; to give full weight to the failures of the League, the consequences of American withdrawal, the failures of the Disarmament Conference, the implications of the Sino-Japanese crisis, and to consider the problem of peace from this standpoint: assuming the worst, assuming that certain nations are set upon war; that no peace assurance they give is worth the paper it is written on; that the League is a failure or a sham—what then? What are we to do?

[ 3 ]

What policy which will not increase the danger instead of lessening it, shall we follow?

No starting point could be much more "realist" in the sense of facing unwelcome facts, unless we take the view that nothing we can do can make any difference; that the will of man is impotent, that collective suicide is inevitable. But that view would condemn activities based on old policies quite as much as it condemns attempts to change the old ways; and is not realism at all.

Assuming then that past efforts have been no good, or very little good; that advocacy of plans that have been tried and failed serves no purpose; that a mere drift along the old way must produce in even worse degree the old results, we are still faced by the question: What are we to do?

On the assumption that we can do something better than surrender helplessly to the current which will carry us into the rapids and this time to annihilation, this book attempts to take stock of the whole peace argument in the light of post-war events, and to clarify it for the non-specialist. Those events show clearly enough why such stocktaking is necessary. Again and again, in one form or another, we have seen duplicated in the post-war years the experience of President Wilson: a whole nation seemingly assenting to a comprehensive peace policy, as when the American public during the later years of the War positively clamoured for a League to Enforce Peace (seldom has any policy had such widespread support) and then, the plan being actually drafted, the same public, on realising that it involves certain obligations, commitments, some fractional surrender of independence and sovereignty not at first perceived, turning violently against it; or rejecting it from motives of

[4]

party or political considerations of quite secondary importance. In either case it is clear that in its approval the public did not perceive the implications or the importance of the proposed change. But the story, repeated in America in the case of the World Court, and duplicated in Britain in the case of the Treaty of Mutual Assistance, the Peace Protocol, Disarmament Plans, and in some aspects of League commitments, shows also that the implications of rejection and of return to old methods are not understood either. The oscillations of policy in the last fifteen years, alike in Britain and America, reveal the difficulty which the public find in weighing the international alternatives in terms of the risks and advantages respectively of the possible courses.

There has been no dearth of plans or constitutional devices for ensuring peace in the post-war years. But any plan to be successful must demand on the part of the nations the shouldering of new burdens, the making of certain changes; and the nations decline to shoulder such burdens or make such changes because they simply do not see the necessity. The remedy does not lie in further plans, but in making clear the conditions necessary for the working of any plan. The trouble has not been in the absence of machinery, but in the absence of certain understandings necessary to the working of any machinery. To forestall an illustration used later in these pages, the better state of order obtaining in, say, Britain as compared with, say, certain Latin American Republics, is not due to the superiority of Britain's constitutional mechanism, but to a more general understanding on the part of the British electorate, the people as a whole, of what is necessary if any constitution is to be successful. Given that understanding a bad constitution will often give good results.

The wider realisation of that truth as applied to international relationships is one of the first understandings necessary. There is no general recognition of the fact that popular misunderstanding of what is a peace policy and what is not, is the greatest single obstacle to the establishment of peace.

If thirty years' experience in the rough-and-tumble of public debate has brought home to me one truth more than another, it is that the aspects of this problem, which are at once the most elementary and the most vital (they are principles indeed which underlie all organised society), are precisely the aspects least realised by the general public—which includes the "educated"—and are the aspects which still most need to be clarified.

Still is the conviction sincere, profound, unquestioned, that if we ourselves refrain from attacking other nations, we cannot possibly be charged with the responsibility for war, even though we demand as the condition of our defence national forces "second to none"; still do our public fail to see that such a demand is an obvious violation of elementary right, since it denies to some other the very means of self-preservation we demand for ourselves; still do we fail to see that such demands, however peaceful the intention behind them, must in the end provoke war; still do we fail to see that if arms are to be the instruments of peace, they must be the instruments of a law or a principle which affords to other nations a defence similar to that at which we strive; that peace cannot possibly, therefore, emerge from armed passivity.

The purpose of this book is therefore not to discuss

[6]

in detail the various plans before the world, but to clarify the principles by which, particularly in the light of actual experience, all plans must be judged; to furnish, at a time when all plans and policies are in flux, a guide to the general direction which policies, often necessarily modified from day to day, should take; the broad lines upon which plans should be re-shaped as changes of circumstance demand re-shaping.

Public opinion moves and develops by means of the everyday discussion of ordinary men and women. It may help to show how far this book bears on the commonly discussed aspects of this problem to list, as below, some of the questions with which the book deals.

Will the hurried reader note that in the last chapter he will find "short answers" to many of the points in the following list, short answers which constitute in fact a summary of the main discussion?

This book discusses the proposition that war
"Is inevitable" (pp. 31-32; 109-123; 306)
"Is ineradicable from unchangeable human nature"
(pp. 25-27; 118-123; 246-267; 306-307)
"Is a spiritual cleanser and healer, necessary to prevent slothful degeneration" (pp. 13-27; 246-254; 308)
"Must continue till men have ceased selfseeking"
(pp. 25-29; 35; 44-45; 60; 74-75; 250-254; 308)

\* \* \* \*

It attempts to answer the questions:
"What would you do if a brute attacked your sister?"
(pp. 20-23; 160-178; 308)

[7]

"Would you leave your house unlocked at nights?"
(pp. 160-178; 308-309)

"Would you take a poker to the burglar?" (pp. 160-178; 308-309)

"What would have happened in 1914 if we had listened to the Pacifists?" (pp. 34-44; 143-159; 313)

"Would not Japan pour her millions into Australia and the multitudes from Asia overflow once more into Europe if armaments were abolished?" (pp. 34-44; 274-301)

"What security have you that foreigners will keep their word?" (pp. 274-301; 320)

"Would not Greek culture have gone down at Marathon, British freedom been sunk by the Armada, American freedom at Fort Sumter and democracy in the last war if Greeks, Englishmen and Americans respectively had refused to fight?" (pp. 34-46; 313)

\*     \*     \*     \*

It discusses the proposition that war is caused by

"Struggles between conflicting ideals of nationality, religion, race" (pp. 116-123; 255-267; 313)

"The need of expanding populations for food and space" (pp. 181-202)

"The struggle for raw materials" (pp. 181-230)

"The struggle for markets" (pp. 181-230)

"Capitalist Imperialism" (pp. 181-245)

"International finance" (pp. 181-245)

"The need of disposing of the surplus goods the home market cannot take" (pp. 181-230)

"The profits accruing from conquests like that of the

Japanese in Manchuria, or of the British in India (pp. 181-230)

"The intrigues of armament makers" (pp. 74-94)

"The need for altering the *status quo*" (pp. 137-142; 169-178; 204-205; 289; 316)

\* \* \* \*

It discusses the proposition that

"We need armaments for the same reason that we need Police" (pp. 160-170; 317)

"Since the whole world knows Britain would never attack, her defensive armament threatens no one and must make for peace" (pp. 124-141; 146-159; 312)

"The strong man armed keepeth his house in peace" (pp. 160-170; 309)

"Armaments mean peace" (pp. 124-141; 157-158; 310)

"The British Navy must police the world or Britain starve" (pp. 134-137; 181-202)

"Peace is all very well for the 'saturated empires' like Britain that possess sufficient territory, but unacceptable to countries like Germany and Japan" (pp. 181-202; 226-230)

"There are some questions war alone can settle" (pp. 27-33; 204-205; 290; 315-316)

"War is the ultimate argument of sovereign states" (pp. 124-142; 313)

\* \* \* \*

Discusses the proposition that the way to ensure peace is

"To be stronger than any who might attack you" (pp. 124-142; 311)

[9]

"To remove the grievances which provoke war" (pp. 168-173; 317)

"To keep out of continental entanglements" (pp. 143-159; 175; 283-288; 312; 319)

"To consolidate the Empire" (pp. 125-159; 291-305)

"To make the Navy stronger" (pp. 125-159; 291-305)

"To create the biggest air force in the world" (pp. 143-159)

"To maintain the balance of power" (pp. 143-159)

"To abolish all armaments" (pp. 34-46)

"To make an alliance with France" (pp. 137-139; 274-278)

"To make an alliance with America" (pp. 138-139; 274-289)

"To create an international police force" (pp. 165-170; 295-297)

"To abolish the capitalist system" (pp. 203-254)

"To abolish the gold standard" (pp. 95-7; 109-123; 233-244)

"To introduce monetary reform" (pp. 95-7; 109-123; 250-254)

"To introduce the single tax" (pp. 95-7; 109-123)

"To refuse to fight" (pp. 34-46)

\*     \*     \*     \*

Discusses the proposition that any method of peace preservation by collective action

"Drags us into quarrels that don't concern us" (pp. 143-159; 175; 283-288; 312; 319)

"Means foreign entanglement, pledges which the country will not give because that policy failed in 1914" (pp. 143-159; 283; 288; 311)

"Is impossible without America" (pp. 280-281; 286-288; 293-294; 299)

"Asks strong and proud nations to submit to the judgment of foreigners" (pp. 23-31; 204-205; 277-281; 319; 321)

"Involves economic sanctions which would embroil Britain and America" (pp. 280-281; 286-288; 293-294; 299)

"Places British policy under foreign control" (pp. 143-159; 283-288; 311-319)

"Places British power at the disposal of foreigners" (pp. 28-30; 143-159; 295; 311; 319)

That the League of Nations

"Is impotent, a talking shop" (pp. 294; 297-301; 317-318)

"Failed to stop Japan" (pp. 294-301)

"Is a League of victors denying justice to the vanquished" (pp. 137-142; 170-178)

"Became impossible the moment America withdrew" (pp. 280-281; 297-301)

"Is dominated by foreign interests" (pp. 143-159; 283-288; 311-319)

"Is dominated by Capitalists" (pp. 74-88; 203-245)

"Is dominated by Socialists" (pp. 74-88; 203-245)

"Costs too much" (p. 319)

"That its court is partial and unjust" (pp. 28-30; 204-205)

"That its practical alternative is an Anglo-American alliance to preserve the peace of the world (pp. 138; 274-278; 293-294)

*    *    *    *

That

"You cannot trust foreigners to keep their promises"
(pp. 279; 283-288; 320-321)

"Only Britain is pacifist or peace loving" (pp.131-
142; 321)

"It is dangerous to preach peace in England when
foreigners prepare for war" (pp. 34-46; 143-178;
321)

"It is futile to talk internationalism while nationalism
gains in strength, as in Italy, Germany, Poland,
Hungary, the Balkans" (pp. 143-178; 275-285;
321)

"You can never tell who is the real aggressor" (pp.
162-170; 278-279; 315)

\* \* \* \*

"Short answers" to most of the above propositions or
questions are given in the final chapter of this book.
Such answers constitute a summary of the book's argument and the reader may find them useful in general
discussion of this subject (pp. 306-321)

## Chapter II

# AT WHAT PRICE DO WE WANT PEACE?

Some of us, including great dictators, and the authors of books on war and peace, haven't made up our minds whether we want peace or war. Do we want war without knowing it? The unconscious in us, mainly savage, may sometimes want war when the more civilised, conscious part of us compels us to recognise that peace is more desirable. In practical politics it resolves itself into the question of what we are prepared to pay for peace; of being able to choose knowingly between what we surrender in the way of certain emotional satisfactions, and what we get; of being conscious of our purpose; the purpose of organised society.

Do WE *want* to get rid of war? All men say they do. Even those heads of states who, like Signor Mussolini, tell us that "War alone brings up to its highest tension all human energy and puts the stamp of nobility upon the peoples who have the courage to meet it," or who, like Hitler, tell us that "By war alone can nations fulfil their destiny and secure justice." For they also tell us that their most profound desire is to avoid war; that the whole purpose of the policy which they follow is to ensure peace. This means that if the wars, which are so indispensable to the moral salvation of man, are to take place, they will have to be provoked by others. Indeed, these leaders, who so often praise and glorify war, are the heads of states that have formally and solemnly signed Pacts renouncing and outlawing war, declaring it to be a crime against humanity. Yet they have made it an offence punishable with imprisonment, and sometimes death, for any of their own people to say that exact thing. In the same way authors who write books in disparagement of peace and tell us that it leads to "stagnation, sterility and psychic suicide";

who tell us that the desire for it or the belief in its possibility is a denial of the Christian faith, tell us also with emphasis that the last thing they desire is another war, and that the purpose of what they urge in the way of increased armaments is to prolong as much as possible that state of warlessness which, if the effort were successful, would condemn us all to moral degeneration.

In Signor Mussolini's article in the Italian Encyclopedia on *The Political and Social Doctrine of Fascism* occurs this passage:

> Fascism believes neither in the possibility nor the utility of perpetual peace. . . . It repudiates Pacifism —born of a renunciation of struggle and an act of cowardice in the face of sacrifice. War alone brings up to its highest tension all human energy and puts the stamp of nobility upon the peoples who have the courage to meet it. . . . It opposes internationalism, repudiating any universal embrace, and in order to live worthily in the community of civilised peoples watches its contemporaries with vigilant eyes. For Fascism the growth of Empire, that is to say the expansion of the nation, is an essential manifestation of vitality, and its opposite a sign of decadence. Peoples which are rising, or rising again after a period of decadence, are always imperialist: any renunciation is a sign of decay and death.[1]

Yet, speaking in the Cathedral Square, Milan, on October 7th (reported in *The Times*, October 8th, 1934), and referring to Italy's war preparations, Mussolini said:

> Does this mean that Fascism aims at war? Not at all; for Italy wants only to be let alone in order to realise

[1] From a translation in the *Political Quarterly* (July 1933).

[14]

the beautiful and noble ideal principles which she has proclaimed. But will she be let alone? . . . If there is a true and fruitful peace, accompanied by justice, we will adorn our rifles with the olive branch, otherwise we will decorate the points of our bayonet with the laurel and oak of victory.

As in Italy, so in Germany—only more so. In *Mein Kampf,* the Bible of the national religion which has so largely replaced the older Jewish document as a moral guide in Germany, Hitler writes:

> Oppressed lands are not brought back into the pale of a united Reich by fiery protests, but by the thrusts of a mighty sword. To forge this sword is the task of a people's home policy; to safeguard the forging and seek allies in arms the task of its foreign policy. (Chapter XIII of Part II.)
>
> Lost territories are not recovered by "passionate appeals to Almighty God" or by "the fluent tongues of polished parliamentarians" but by "armed power, a polished sword and a bloody combat" (pp. 708 and 710). "An alliance that is not concluded with a view to war is meaningless and worthless" (p. 749).

If Mussolini ordains that henceforth children of eight shall begin the training for their real purpose in life, the battlefield, and acquire the military outlook by contact with soldiers, certain German school textbooks are even more definite.

The first and last purpose of education should, we are told therein, be the stiffening of the mind for war. Dr. Goebbels has declared that the highest purpose to which life can be put is death upon the battlefield; that women should bear children with that end in view, to which a good many German women seem to subscribe

since The Women's Order of the Red Swastika pro-
claims in its "Platform" or "Declaration" that "there
is no higher privilege for a woman than that of sending
her children to war." Yet, speaking at a reception
of the foreign Press in Berlin in the presence of almost
the entire diplomatic corps, Dr. Goebbels, Minister of
Propaganda, said:

> Germany has furnished abundant proofs of her love of
> peace. . . . It has been so often emphasized that it is
> hardly necessary to repeat that Germany desires peace;
> she desires to carry on the work of reconstruction in
> peace. . . . The peoples of Europe are longing for peace.
> Let us all do our share so that their appeal may not be
> in vain.

It would seem, therefore, that though it is right for
Germany to want peace, and though Germany believes
it to be a good thing, it is wrong and evil for Germans
(except Dr. Goebbels) to say peace is a good thing,
since the advocacy of peace as an ideal, "Pacifism," is
ranked with Communism as a grave offence against
the state, punishable with imprisonment, loss of civil
rights, flogging by Brown Shirts. Indeed, as we know,
well-known members of the Peace Movement have fled
from Germany to escape just those penalties. (And
"Pacifist" in Germany does not mean non-resister—
those who refuse to fight—but includes anyone active
in the advocacy of international institutions, like the
League.) Herr von Papen tells us that "On January
30, 1933, Germany struck the word 'Pacifism' from its
vocabulary." The use of violence against peace
advocates is, we are told, necessary for the health of
the state, and is urged by eminent legal lights.

This, too, has its English counterpart, "Not alone in war-time, but in peace time, is Pacifism a poisonous and anti-Christian doctrine," says Major Yeats-Brown, whose book, published in 1934, has been quite approvingly reviewed in a number of English papers. Its author tells us that "Pacifists, however sincere, would," if he had his way, "be deprived of their votes in national and local affairs. They would not be allowed to teach in schools supported by the State. They would not be eligible for any public office or employment. They would be marked men." [1] And note that in this case too the Pacifism he would thus treat is not merely that of the Quaker or non-resister type. He opposes all proposals for the international organisation of force as much as he does any proposal for its limitation or abolition; he is as much opposed to internationalism as to Disarmament. Without war we should decay; it would be "psychic suicide." Yet, "another war? Not that. The idea brings with it a feeling of horror and despair." [2] He wants peace, but "War represents the deep and honourable craving of man for the supernatural." [3]

The author continues:

Men want war for the same reason that they want the miraculous in their lives; and it is a legitimate need. Agnostics, as well as those who scoff at religions, are generally those who are most ready to pin their faith on the miraculous possibilities which they discern in internationalism. But Geneva is foreign to the ancient, widespread, half-secret hungers of the heart: it has no

[1] *Dogs of War*, F. Yeats-Brown (Davies), p. 183.
[2] Ibid., p. 150. [3] Ibid., p. 159.

bread to offer but the stone of safety, no wine but water coloured with the dye of modern culture. If danger were removed from the world, some spark of divinity—the spark we all see most readily—would go with it from our souls.[1]

There is in War, says this author, "a sense of belonging to a mystical body, a realisation (almost an incarnation) of truths otherwise beyond the grasp of the average man and woman." [2]

That is certainly a romantic view of processes which modern war quite indubitably includes, of which indeed in the future it is likely mainly to consist—the killing without quarter of those unable to defend themselves, of unarmed civilians, little children, helpless old women, the weak and sick; killing them in the most painful of all ways: by raining from the heavens poison gases which cause them to choke and gasp their lives out in slow agony; or, it may be, by disease germs disseminated through water reservoirs and other means of plague and pestilence—that poisoning of wells which is not a reversion to barbarism (because barbarians forbade it), but a new and completer barbarism.

If the civilian statesmen fail in the difficult problem of creating a world order which will avoid war (Major Yeats-Brown disparages even the attempt) our lads will face that job of killing the women and the children. But when Major Yeats-Brown tells us that men want such tasks, yearn for them with "deep and honourable craving," a craving supernatural in its roots, then indeed one may wonder whether men know what they want.

1 *Dogs of War*, F. Yeats-Brown (Davies), p. 160.
2 Ibid., p. 160.

One may ask: Would men face the indiscriminate killing of civilians, which modern war, *la guerre totale*, necessarily involves if the soldier saw on the spot the result of his work, had to use cruder weapons? The airman is aware that his bomb *does* disembowel women and children (as Mr. Baldwin reminds us) just as cruelly and obscenely as though he did it with a butcher's knife. But could he go through a household or a girls' school with a butcher's knife doing what he knows full well the bomb which he drops does? One may doubt it. But in view of that fact it is strange to read in the pages of the author just quoted this:

"Pacifists are ready to consent to any cruelty, provided it is hidden away so that they don't see it."[1]

and goes on to say that it may be more cruel to take away a man's living by commercial competition than to take away his life with a bullet. From which one would gather that the Major, using as he does at this point the Communist justification of class war, desires to replace the present competitive economic system with something less cruel. But not at all; he appears to dislike attempts, particularly peaceful attempts, to replace the present economic competition as much as he dislikes attempts to get rid of war. Asked to consider the spectacle of the shell-shocked man as one of the fruits of war, he retorts by asking us to consider the results of economic competition (which he wants to retain) and adds: "It is better to be killed quickly than die of starvation or through the heartbreak of continued unemployment." From which, again, one would not suppose that famine and starvation are ultimately made

[1] *Dogs of War*, F. Yeats-Brown (Davies), p. 199.

worse by war, that unemployment to the degree with which the post war years have made us familiar is its direct outcome; that but for war's dislocations this unemployment would almost certainly have been cut in half.

This military writer condemns pacifists because he says they are indifferent to the miseries of peace—unemployment and the rest—yet he criticises with bitterness a book which was written to show that war would increase unemployment. The desire to avoid economic miseries he says is a motive which should not weigh with honourable men as a reason for avoiding war.

But the contradictions go farther. The militarist puts forward defence and security as his main aim. But he does not really seem to have made up his mind whether it is defence and security that he really wants.

We are all familiar with such stock queries as: "What would you do if a German attacked your sister?" "Are you content to see foreigners lay waste our country? Destroy our trade? Starve us into submission?"

To that first question: "What would you do if a great hulking brute attacked your sister," an English Pacifist replied: "I would give him a sock on the jaw," and went on to explain, by implication, that if women are in danger of savage attacks, the men, unless they are indifferent brutes, won't be content to count upon brothers always being handy at the moment of attack, but will organise the community systematically for the suppression of brutal crimes of violence by means of police, magistrature, law and the rest. Women won't be safe, and property won't be safe, he added, until you have those institutions; and the truth applies particularly to international relationship, since it is precisely in war time that women—and men—are most exposed to outrage, to physical filth as a daily fare, to horrors of a nature which no peace time condition ever duplicates to a similar degree. And as regards the preservation of our trade from destruction and of our country from the devastations of unemployment following upon the dis-organisation of trade, avoidance of war is now the very first condition *sine qua non* of achieving that safety.

The internationalist says in effect to the militarist who asks the question about the attack on your sister, "You dislike violence, outrages upon the weak, the savage licence of the powerful? Good. Let us organise the community for the security of our women whose protection so much concerns you. By all means let us apply your analogy." Whereupon the militarist knight errant immediately turns round and begins to disparage even the desire for such security and to explain that the stories of what happens in war time to women are grossly exaggerated; that the poison gas won't really hurt them, or their children, in the next war.

Thus Major Yeats-Brown:

There are things more important than saving our skins: saving our souls is more important, and telling the truth. We have to do some hard thinking. You spoke of the shell-shocked just now. But what about the miseries of peace? Some of us are digging worse graves for ourselves with our teeth than would be our lot if we died fighting.[1]

[1] *Dogs of War*, p. 199.
Is truth telling commoner, then, in war than peace in these days of organised propaganda on both sides? Did not someone say that the

And he proceeds to tell us that war, after all, is rather a jolly business. He "enjoyed the war" (page 192) and as to the women and their slain lovers, sons, husbands, even so there are compensations.

> My thoughts go back to those war years, and they do not summon up a vision of unpleasant things, though I had a taste of terror and discomfort. I think rather of cocktails in the R.F.C. mess near Bethune, short leaves to Blighty, night clubs with knee-high skirted Wrafs and Waacs.

An accommodating memory.

And so the Major discovers that he does not want security, either for the women (they certainly won't get it in the next war) or for anyone else. He wants danger, like Spengler:

> The cowardly security of the end of the last century is ended. The dangerous life, the stuff of which history is made, comes into its own once more. The time is coming, nay it is already here, where there is no place for tender souls or primitive ideals. Primitive barbarism which for centuries has lain hidden beneath the strict forms of culture, is breaking out once more, and civilisa-

very first casualty in war time was truth? Professor Banse, a great protagonist of war, has the courage to write: "War is agitation and lies"; while on the British side Major General Fuller writes (*New Britain*, 4th July 1934): "Modern war is no longer like ancient war; it is no longer a contest of man with man. . . . It is a contest . . . in which men seek to demoralise men by attacking each other's women and children. . . . It has but one idea: devastation, destruction and death. Its whole forces are negative. War to-day destroys all morality, all sense of justice, even all sense of decency. . . . There is no chivalry in modern war, there is little heroism, there is no pity. More and more mechanical does war become, and as the destructive machine grows, so does the soul of man dwindle."

tion has turned into healthy warlike joy in one's own strength, which despises the past of rationalist thought.[1]

Note the same easy contradiction of purpose when our Major tells us that one reason why he won't have international organisation is that it means a degree of regulation and control fatal to individual freedom. Too much organization becomes hateful. We don't want our lives ordered for us by iron-clad regulations. . . . And one may think at this point that one has got at the root of his objection—dislike of a highly-organised society.

And then you discover that he wants conscription for his nation, the ironclad organisation of a highly militarised state. Indeed Major Yeats-Brown, manages to combine flaming protests against prohibitionary tendency and the subordination of the individual to the State, with more than a leaning towards Fascism, the Corporative State, which is hardly the apotheosis of individual freedom.

§

The reader may feel that a book which combines the theme that (a) war is glorious, a spiritual cleanser and healer, necessary to the well-being of a virile nation, with the theme that (b) war is too horrible to contemplate, so horrible that we should be prepared to make every man a soldier in order to avoid it, is hardly worth the space just devoted to it.

Yet it is important to examine these contradictions

[1] From Oswald Spengler's latest book, *The Decisive Years*, quoted by Robert Dell in *Germany Unmasked*, p. 41.

[23]

because they are characteristic of a widespread phenomenon (having a vital bearing on the whole of our
problem) namely the existence of an utterly chaotic
and unstable scale of values—the absence of any clear
decision as to what is important, what unimportant,
what good, what evil, any clear notion of what we
really want. In so many of these books we find that
the thing which is good on one page becomes evil
beyond measure on the next. What is declared to be the
highest purpose of life at one stage of the argument
becomes a trifle to be disparaged when that is con-
venient for another phase of the argument.

This would be no great matter if the intellectual
chaos were confined to the writers of silly or pretentious books, or their readers. But we see the same
instability of moral measure marking the actual policy
of nations when it is a question of war or refraining
from war. The purpose which at one moment we declare to be something for which we should be ready to
send our children to die in agony ("to make the world
safe for democracy," "to end militarism," "to vindicate
the rights of small states") becomes in only a few years
not worth a tinker's curse. The autocracies which our
sons gave their lives to destroy are replaced by far
more ruthless autocracies which we now praise and are
invited to imitate. Alsatians work for war in order to
re-unite with France; and then agitate against that
union. A Southern Slav murder, an assassination on
behalf of Slav unity helps to precipitate war, and
Southern Slavs then murder each other because they
don't want to be united.

What do we want?—want, that is, of our constitution-
making, our politics, our social efforts as a whole?

[24]

What is organised society for? Do we want peace? These authors have not made up their minds. Do we want security? They say that that is the purpose of their armaments—and that it is a mean and emasculate ideal. Is it prosperity these militarist writers want? They will fight and die, they tell us, to ensure it, to ensure the expansion of their nation, its place in the sun, economic advantage. But show that prosperity will be destroyed if we permit wars, and prosperity becomes "a huckster's creed," contemptible.

A million of our youth die with such slogans as "freedom and democracy" on their lips, and then, those who encouraged them thus to give their lives find afterwards that freedom and democracy are quite a mistake; that the autocracies which the war was waged to make impossible are after all the right method, even when expanded into Fascism with its castor oil, its secret executions, its anti-Semitism and its Nordic Christ.

We must know what we want; whether we want war or peace, what we want of war if we choose war, what we will pay for peace if we choose peace.

The ultimate decision depends in part, of course, upon our realisation of the real nature and results of war as distinct from romantic distortions of it; in part upon our scale of values, our notion of what is important and what unimportant; of what we want of organised society and our efforts towards a happier and more decent world; but most fundamentally of all, upon our capacity to make any choice which shall not be merely an unconscious or semi-conscious animal reaction to one impulse at one moment and a contrary one the next.

That capacity we don't seem to have developed much in the political field, even in peace time. We find a constituency racked with the miseries of unemployment voting for a candidate because he is a cricket or tennis champion; a Chicago, with a bankrupt city treasury, cheering itself hoarse over the Big Bill Thompson mainly responsible for it, because he has managed to excite the patriotic passions of the voters with fiery rhetoric about the tyrannies which their forefathers suffered under George III; or a Valera causing Irish farmers to forget their ruin in the joys of annoying the hated Saxon.

A young Nazi wrote the other day that rather than see one German under foreign rule he would prefer to see the whole of Europe perish in agonies of poison gas and bacteriological war: a statement almost paralleled by that of an Irishman, that "it is better that Irishmen should eat grass than that the wrongs inflicted on Ireland by Henry VIII should go unavenged."

It is the way, more or less, that *we* talked during the war about freedom and democracy. But did we really think that way about freedom and democracy? Because the same people, or some of them, who so talked, now tell us that democracy and freedom are contemptible things, and in any case most of us don't feel now about them as we did then. If the voters on the occasions just mentioned were "thinking with their blood" (which incidentally is the approved Nazi method) instead of their brains then they will think differently to-morrow from what they did yesterday, and the Nazis discover, a little late, that it was a mistake to drench Europe in bacteria or poison gas on behalf of one German. It is probable that if you were to take one of those English or Chicago voters above referred to away from what a Frenchman has called "the communicative warmth" of great mass meetings into the quiet of his secret chamber, and ask him, honest injun, whether he thought it better, better even morally, to use his vote to promote his children's or his family's economic security or to use it instead to testify his admiration for tennis, or as a means of satisfying an ancient historical grudge, as the case might be—if you were to put it to him quietly in those terms, there would be no doubt as to the result. He would, "on second thoughts," plump for well-being as the main purpose of organised society. It is not true, therefore, to say that the sort of passion and the scale of values revealed at times by nations is "inevitable" or "natural." They are only natural in certain circumstances or conditions, circumstances and conditions which we can alter. Semi-conscious, or even unconscious, motives may be rendered conscious by a process of analysis, by "stopping to think what we are doing." It is that fact which justifies some of the analysis of the praise of war which has preceded; and which follows.

§

Let it be said at once that there are many, especially when peace conditions are intolerable or burdensome, for whom war has a certain appeal. Mr. J. B. Priestley writes:

> I know scores of decent men who think of the war with something like regret, because they were competent soldiers then and remember the active life, the adventure, the comradeship, and contrast them bitterly with the

miserable competition, the ignoble struggle, the jungle tactics of the years they have known since. Most people delight in a feeling of solidarity, of fellowship with all their neighbours. The war gave them that; the peace took it away.[1]

So be it. We still have to choose between war and peace. Mr. Priestley makes his choice definitely for peace, and cites the attractiveness of war as a reason for so improving the conditions of peace as to deprive war of its appeal. Major Yeats-Brown shows no such clarity of decision, and holds out the attractiveness of war as a reason for disparaging the advocacy of peace. Mr. Priestley faces the attractiveness of war, such as it is, as one of the obstacles to be overcome; Major Yeats-Brown as one of the reasons why we should refuse to make any particular effort to overcome the obstacle, to pay any considerable price for war's abolition. It is just because the real question is not, "Are you in favour of peace?"—even the Hitlers and Mussolinis are in favour of peace—but, "How much are you in favour of peace? What are you prepared to pay for it in the way of modifying the old conditions of anarchy in order to get it?" that the praise of war for itself has a certain importance. For success in getting rid of it means a comparison of values. We must be able to strike a balance between war's advantages, such as they are, and its costs—social and moral as well as material. We must once for all decide whether we want the kind of world which war produces, or that which peace might produce, and which we cannot have if war goes on.

[1] *Challenge to Death*, J. B. Priestley (Constable), p. 307.

The militarist writer usually oscillates between the two purposes. He has not the clarity or courage to say: "I am for war, even if we could have peace, because I think war the better state." He declares that he recoils in horror from the very thought of another war. He is a pacifist in proclaiming his hatred of war and desire for peace, but abuses those who bend their conscious efforts towards attaining peace and face such sacrifices as the establishment may demand. The militarist, while refusing to accept the odium of declaring that he would precipitate war, uses its attraction to rally opposition to policies designed to prevent it. The praise of war, the constant suggestion that it has so many compensations that, after all, it may not be very bad, has the effect of creating disastrous indecision in policy, and may explain largely the oscillations of the last fifteen years. We are all familiar with the way in which all too frequently discussion on this subject develops. A man assures you that his desire for peace is passionate, that he yields to no one in the sincerity of his intention to obtain it. The discussion moves to methods. Arbitration (say) would seem to be a necessary element. "But suppose the verdict were unjust; we could never take that risk!" You find that he regards it as incompatible with national dignity to submit *any* important question to arbitration, or to "courts composed of foreigners." His assurances that he wants peace "passionately," mean that he wants it provided it will not involve the smallest sacrifice of national advantage, even in a world where complete justice is a moral impossibility and even though the old condition involves inevitably injustices immensely greater. In arriving at that decision, his feelings of just *how* bad a thing war really is (not in its suffering but in the inherent injustice of its results), is all important. The man who feels that it is supremely bad almost above everything else would not allow some microscopic material disadvantage resulting from a defective arbitral award to weigh in the balance against getting rid of war.

It would be true to say of peace, as of so many things, that we shall get it when we are ready to pay the price for it, and realise what the price is; are able to weigh what we give against what we get. Civilisation rests upon our being able, amongst other things, to make a choice between wants: to pay for to-morrows security by to-day's restraint, upon a capacity to balance values. Smith does not like having to catch the 8:20 to town every morning, but he likes poverty still less. He gives up the luxury of lying in bed for the luxury of giving his children a decent education. He cannot have both, and his capacity to weigh the two values is the mark of the civilised man. The savage, like the animal, refuses to forego the momentary satisfaction. He gorges so long as food lasts, and then starves.

The things which we surrender for the purposes of civilisation may well contain elements of attraction. It is delightful "to stand and stare," to saunter on the roadway, but if we insisted on retaining that right, the motor-car would have to go. We purchase safety on the road by the observance of rules and regulations which are often extremely irksome; freedom from pestilence by a sanitary care which much of the easy-going East simply refuses to take. The West has decided that freedom from Black Death is worth the cost in sanitary regulation. Men want peace. But they want certain other things which are incompatible with it, usually without realising that they *are* incompatible. Until that incompatibility is realised they cannot even weigh one want against another. They are unable to make a choice, the will struggles against itself, and the outcome may well be that neither desired end is attained. 49582

War is a world-wide, very ancient, very persistent scourge; so ancient, so persistent that its roots are likely to be very deep. For man to shake off that scourge will be difficult in any case. But it will be quite impossible if he does not know even whether he wants to shake it off or not, is in two minds about it, at one moment declaring it to be the greatest of all crimes and the next that we cannot do without it and that it is time we had a dose.

§

And it will be equally impossible if he has decided that "war is inevitable." What precisely does the common militarist assertion that "War is inevitable" mean? Does it mean that any war proposed at any time by any interested party—silly and irresponsible newspapers, demagogic politicians, armament firms—is inevitable? Of course not. Then which war is inevitable and which avoidable? Not a few historians and statesmen have declared that the existence of a League of Nations in 1914 would have prevented the Great War. If we cannot be sure of that, neither can we be sure of the contrary.

Though we do not know whether "war" is inevitable,

we do know that disease is inevitable. Yet, in the West, plague, cholera and leprosy have been wiped away. Is that no gain? It is a gain which we could not possibly have made if men had said: "Pestilence is inevitable. It is fate. What can our poor human wills do against fate—and perhaps Providence? These scourges must be accepted as one of the conditions under which we live on the planet. And who knows? They may be a cleansing tide." I say that we could never have fought pestilence if that fatalism had dominated us, because where that philosophy does dominate, as in certain areas of the east, these pestilences still rage. They rage because many Orientals look upon sanitary precaution exactly as the militarist in the West looks upon the efforts of Pacifists and internationalists; the tiresome interference of fussy busybodies, professing with their chatter to hold back tides that have poured over the world since the world began. In the face of that fatalism Western sanitation is impotent to do what, with another philosophy, can be done; as the facts of the West prove.

A similar fatalism in the presence of the ancient pestilence of war will produce a similar impotence. But it will not be an inevitable impotence, as in the presence of storm or earthquake. Men do not make the earthquake and have no responsibility for it. They do make war. Army budgets do not get voted and battleships built by "Nature" nor by "fate." Men do the voting and the building and the firing, and must not shunt off the responsibility to "fate" or "destiny."

No one pretends that it will be easy to conquer war. It will be impossible if we have not even made up our minds whether we *want* to win; if every effort to that end is disparaged, treated with contempt and sneers. If such is our attitude, we shall fail, fail because we so willed it. But the responsibility will be man's, not nature's.

## Chapter III

# THE PRICE NATIONS WILL NOT PAY

There is one price all great nations make plain that they will refuse to pay for peace: they will not surrender armed defence. The question, therefore, is reduced to which method of armed defence will involve the least risk of war: the collective or the individual method? The pacifist who does not believe in either has still an obligation to answer the question put by the public to him: Which of the two does he regard as less dangerous? If the pacifist does not answer that question, he will in fact be siding with those who prefer the more dangerous.

WHEN all the qualifications considered in the last chapter are taken into account, it nevertheless remains true that most men sincerely want peace. Yet they may want certain things which are incompatible with peace, without realising that they are incompatible. They pursue policies the honest intention of which is peace, but the inevitable result of which is war. War is usually the outcome, not of conscious evil intention, but of good intention which miscarries.

Note first this: There is one aim which, without quite realising it, men everywhere set above peace, that aim being national self-preservation, defence. That this purpose in fact comes even before peace is revealed not merely by what statesmen and their peoples say (though they say it clearly enough) but particularly by what they do, not spasmodically or in moments of passion or anger, but coldly, steadily, year after year, with ample opportunity of reversing their policy if so be they desire. All the great states retain their armed forces; will not surrender them even after weary years of Disarmament Conferences. Ten years of prolonged discussion has not induced them to surrender one fraction.

Which means, of course, that in one contingency at least they would use them; in one circumstance fight. If we had really decided to put peace above all else, decided that nothing would induce us to fight—neither invasion by Asiatic hordes, nor the seizure of our government by Hitler or Stalin, nor any other similar imaginable circumstances—then we should not have an army or navy at all. If we literally put peace first, the maintenance of army and navy would be meaningless. Their maintenance means that we will fight for national self-defence, accept war if we are attacked.

If this were not the general decision governments could not, year after year, secure the voting of burdensome military and naval budgets, the increase of taxes involved, the continuance (in the case of Continental countries) of conscription, and all the other sacrifices of war preparation. People do not like these things. They are sincere when they speak of their hatred of war, its miseries, waste and horror, and the burden and cost of its preparation. But they accept those sacrifices rather than surrender the armed defence of the nation; rather than suffer invasion, the dictation of foreign states, or the placing of national rights at the mercy of stronger Powers.

This decision to stand by the armed defence of the nation is common to all great states—to ourselves, to America, to Russia, to Italy, to France, to Germany. For national defence, in every country, at all times, the ordinary man—not, it may be, usually self-sacrificing or heroic in the normal grind of daily life—can be

[35]

induced to spend his money like water, to suffer unimaginable miseries and agonies; to give life itself. This is not speculation, or wild statement. The proof of the amazing fact is in the actual behaviour of millions of ordinary folk in this generation as in the last. Tell the millions of any nation that arms are needed to prevent their country being placed under the government and oppression of foreigners, to prevent humiliation and gross injustice, and the arms will be paid for—however big the fortunes of the armament makers. Where, in the absence of those motives, John Smith would not vote sixpence, nor give an hour's labour, he will, under their influence, pour out uncounted treasure, submit to years of military servitude, give his life. And, incidentally, it is that motive in the millions which enables the armament makers, the vested interests of war, the intriguing diplomat, to wield their power.

The reader must not run ahead of the argument here developed. It is not the decision to retain armed defence which is necessarily incompatible with peace. It will be part of the purpose of these pages to show that armed defence in the international field is no more incompatible with peace and a steady development towards juster conditions than the existence of armed power within the nation—police, or the *posse comitatus,* or the militia—is incompatible with internal peace. But these pages will also attempt to show that the method of armed defence heretofore adopted by the nations, and still in fact followed—that of each being his own, and sole, defender—must inevitably end in war. The cause of war is, beyond doubt, not armed defence, but the particular form of armed defence, the armed anarchy, to which we still cling.

Let us be clear as to the issues. It is quite true, indeed obviously true, that if all nations would surrender all their arms the problem of war would be solved: without artillery the artillery duels of the future would not be very murderous; without gas, the gas attacks fairly innocuous; without bombs, the bombing not very destructive. It is also true that non-resistance by an unarmed power to an armed one would prevent war, would probably be an effective form of defence. The Ruhr and its inhabitants suffered less by not fighting than they would have suffered had they been able to resist.

It is also true that unilateral disarmament, the definite acceptance of a power-position inferior to that of others would not involve the danger we usually suppose. It is the position of the most highly civilised and probably the most secure states in the world—Norway, Sweden, Denmark, Finland, Switzerland. They are compelled to be definitely and unquestionably less powerful than their neighbours. It is doubtful whether they are less secure.

All these things are true, and it is useful to point out their truth, to go on pointing it out. This present writer has attempted in previous works [1] to clarify some of the facts which explain those things; to show that the notion that modern wealth can be "seized and carried off" by a foreign army as a burglar might take jewellery, is nonsense; that trade cannot be "captured" by military victory, and that most of the notions underlying such assumptions are fallacious,

[1] *The Great Illusion* and *The Unseen Assassins.*

[ 37 ]

and that non-resistance by a nation is not in the same category as non-resistance by an individual.[1]

Of non-resistance or non-military defence one can safely say two things: (a) there is an immensely strong logical case for the adoption of the policy, a case supported by abundant actual experience; (b) there is not the slightest chance of any potentially powerful nation adopting the policy. So long as a nation has potentially the power to enter this power contest, it will do so. The case of Germany is the latest illustration. The welfare, lives, property of the German people were far more secure when Germany was all but completely disarmed than they are likely to be when she becomes once more a great power competing with others. Yet the appeal which, this last year or two has, more powerfully than any other whatsoever, attracted the German people, has been the appeal for greater national military power. So with other cases of armament inferiority. No American could suppose that the material inferi-

---

[1] "If an angry man lunges at me with an axe and I do not manage to disarm him, that is the end of me. I cannot very well go on with the argument, and try to show him the error of his ways. And if, afterwards, my assailant does repent, that does not really help me very much. But in the case of a nation it is otherwise. If, owing to some disagreement about the construction of the Baghdad railway or the exploitation of the mines of Morocco, we are in danger of fighting (say) Germany, and we say: 'Rather than sacrifice a million lives and ruin our whole commerce, we will concede your point about the Morocco mines and hope that later you will see that it is to your interest to adopt our policy'—in that case we can still go on with the discussion. And when Germany, short of money, needs our capital, or is anxious to build up certain trades in some of our markets, we could probably come to a bargain, and in the end find we had really lost nothing at all by conceding a point that looked at the moment important. Most of the things about which we quarrel internationally are completely unimportant, and plainly do not need defending by power at all."

ority of the American Navy exposed him to the danger of aggression from Britain, yet the popular appeal for an American Navy equal to that of Britain was irresistible. We may take it as certain that no nation will willingly and consciously adopt the policy of non-resistance, accept a position of inferiority, place itself, that is, within the power of a foreign state.

Those who believe in non-resistance should yield no fraction of conviction concerning it. But if they are not to make the perception of their truth the enemy of other truth, and the enemy of peace, then neither must they dodge certain questions which this generation puts to them.

The most vital of those questions is implicit in the fact noted at the beginning of this chapter, the fact that all the great nations have decided to defend themselves by arms, a decision reached, not suddenly or sporadically, but with a deliberation renewed again and again, with a judgment constantly reviewed. They reject the total abolition of arms, they reject unilateral reduction, they reject non-resistance, they reject passive resistance. There is no doubt at all as to one "want" which they express: they want, at least for the time being, armed defence.

But they hesitate between two possible methods of armed defence. They have so far suspected the effectiveness of the armed anarchy, of each being his own and sole defender, as to turn tentatively to the collective method of defence, operating either through the League machinery or by regional arrangements within it (e.g. the Locarno type of Treaty) or by enlarging the scope of the Kellogg Pacts, or by some means rallying the potential common power of civilisa-

tion in resistance to the war-maker so that a single
state has something other than its own force to look to
as a means of defence. The mood is sceptical, the
understanding of the method's implications confused,
but the experiment has been begun. The note of
interrogation about the old method is in the public
mind. It may well be the beginning of a very fundamental change in the way in which nations are to use
force.

What is to be the attitude of the Pacifist "absolutist"
to that change? How will he, as one who by his
counsel assumes a responsibility for the right guidance
of his nation in the way of peace, answer Mr. John
Smith, who puts to him this question:

> I cannot follow you in your non-resister position. I
> believe in armed defence—please accept that as final.
> But there are two methods of armed defence available;
> the old, each for himself method, and the method of
> collective defence, indicated in the Covenant of the
> League. Which of these two methods do you regard as the
> lesser evil? *I am not asking what you, who do not believe
> in military force, would do, but what I, who do believe
> in it and am determined to use it in one way or another,
> should do.* Which of two possible methods of force
> should I choose in order to make the use of force least
> likely? Which of two methods, both of which you regard
> as evil, is the less evil, the less dangerous?

Please note that the Absolutist is not there asked
any question about the ultimate morality of force, so
any answer on that point would evade the question.
He is not asked anything about his own conscience.
He is asked an entirely different but an entirely plain
question to which, as one who professes to have

[40]

considered this problem, he has certainly an obligation
to give a plain answer.

I suggest that if the non-resister is to answer truly the
question outlined above, and not to evade it by answering an entirely different question, he must reply in
some such way as this:

> It would be infinitely better that you should not seek
> defence by arms at all; but as it is not on that point that
> you seek counsel, I reply that if you must use arms for
> defence, they are less likely to provoke war if linked
> clearly and visibly to the collective system instead of to
> the old method of each his own defender. If you are
> determined either to retain the armed anarchy or make
> an armed society, far better to make an armed society.
> If arms there must be, far better that they should be put
> behind the law than left in the hands of the rival
> litigants.

Does that answer involve any surrender whatever of
any pacifist conviction?

But it is not usually the answer that "the convinced
Pacifist" gives (though there are notable and splendid
exceptions). In so far as the "absolutists" answer my
imaginary questioner at all, they tell him, by implication, that since he must come to some military arrangements with foreign nations, the "military understandings," like those made with France before 1914,
are to be preferred to those of Article XVI of the
Covenant; that if he has to choose as between armed
anarchy and an armed society (*not* as between an unarmed anarchy and an armed society) it is better to
choose the armed anarchy.

He is, of course, right in giving that answer if it is
his sincere conviction that alliances designed to create

overwhelming preponderance against the disturber of the peace, the nation which refuses peaceful settlement, are more likely to provoke war than the older type of competitive alliances like those which preceded the Great War.

But his ground of objection is not usually that at all. It is that the collective method "sanctions the use of force"; that it is an attempt to cure war by going to war; that war is not less war because you call it "police action"; that international combinations of power would not operate at all as do our Men in Blue; that bombs dropped by armies acting as the result of international sanction would maim and kill as painfully as in the old kind of war. All of which is true, and all of which evades the question put by Mr. John Smith, and refuses the help he seeks. If Mr. John Smith had asked, "Shall I use military force at all for defence?" it would all have been relevant and useful. But Smith had asked an entirely different question. Determined in any case to retain armed defence, he desired to know which form of it would be least likely to lead to war, and the reply about the bombs and the rest does not answer the question at all. *For all those things would be involved under the only alternative method with which Smith will agree.* The question is not whether an international collective system would operate if it came to the extreme of coercion, as the Metropolitan Police operates, but whether its action would be worse than that of the older type of pre-war alliance; and whether the collective system would be more effective in avoiding war altogether. When we are asked to counsel others as to the choice between two courses, both of which we regard as evil, is it more moral to urge the course which will produce the greater evil than to urge the course which will produce the less?

Somehow it is extremely difficult to get a certain type of peace advocate—sincere and single-minded as he usually is—to face Smith's question and not to dodge it by answering another. The effect of pronouncing against the collective system is, of course, in the actual circumstances of the world to support the nationalist and militarist system. The best—no force at all—is made the enemy of the better, some international pooling of force behind law (the law that there shall be no more war) which is assuredly a step in the process of abolition if it is to be accomplished at all.

The internationalisation of defence, of power, would not put us in a worse position than at present to go forward to getting rid of military force altogether. It would put us in a better position. In no sense is it true to say that agreement to a pooling of power, to the provisions of Article XVI of the Covenant, is incompatible with efforts to secure complete abolition.

This book not only accepts that motive of defence as the main operative force in international politics, but suggests further that it is precisely upon this desire of the common man to defend his country that the peacemaker may most usefully build, since the cause of war is, beyond doubt, the particular system of national defence to which we still cling. War is inherent in that system, is an inevitable though unintended and undesired outcome. Yet it is a system which, regarded purely from the point of view of national defence, is utterly ineffective. It betrays

[43]

defence is disastrously as it betrays peace. If the present system of competitive arming really did defend the things which we desire to protect—our political freedom, our national culture, our chosen way of life, the lives of our people, means of livelihood, prosperity, wealth, welfare, property, trade, the processes of civilisation—we should be faced by the tragic dilemma of surrendering defence or surrendering peace.

And that, indeed, is usually the underlying assumption in this debate of war and peace, and the cause of much of the heat which so often vitiates it, the assumption that the two wants of peace and defence are incompatible. The Nationalist, or Militarist, concerned mainly with defence, by implication accuses the Pacifist of being indifferent to it; the Pacifist, concerned mainly with peace, sometimes by implication accuses the militarist-nationalist of being indifferent to that end. There is a false antithesis at the start.

Closely related to the confusion just mentioned is another, into which at times the peace advocate is apt to fall, namely that war is the result of evil intention, selfishness, avarice. This evades one of the strangest but most significant facts about war, namely that it endures, not because the motives behind it are evil, but because so many of them are good. If all its motives and all its results were obviously and unmistakably evil it would have disappeared long since. Men in the mass are only trapped by evil when it can masquerade as good or be mixed with good.

The force which makes for war derives its strength, not from the interested motives of evil men but from the disinterested motives of good men; is not made by wicked men knowing themselves to be wrong but by good men passionately convinced on both sides that they are right. (The more passionate the conviction of each side that it is right, the more difficult does the avoidance of war become, and the more bitter it is when it does come.) War always involves great sacrifices on the part of the mass of men, and men do not make such sacrifices for a cause which they believe to be wrong and evil. Young men do not go to their deaths as to a feast, from selfishness and avarice—unless they are quite unusually certain of their mansions in the skies. War can secure from the ordinary man and woman a degree of self-sacrifice which no other purpose whatsoever can usually secure.

Pacifists, as a rule, evade that truth as making too great a concession to Mars; as seeming to imply (which it does not in fact) that, in order to abolish war, men must cease to be noble.

Base motives are, of course, among those which make up the forces that produce war. Base motives are among those which get great cathedrals built and hospitals constructed—contractors seeking profits, the vested interests of doctors or of clergy. But Europe has not been covered by cathedrals because contractors wanted to make money, or priests wanted jobs. How did the contractors, or if you will the priests, induce the public to part with the money and maintain the Church? No one can be ignorant of the fact that armament firms grow rich on armament competition. But John Smith does not face a five shilling income tax, expose himself to death and mutilation for the *beaux yeux* of armament makers. What is it that in-

duces him thus to hand over his money *and* his life, or
that of his son, as sacrifices to the God of War?

To say that they are "forced" to fight by, say,
dictators or armament makers, or small interested
groups, does not, as we shall see in a subsequent chapter, really explain anything. Two dozen munition
makers cannot "force" a hundred million people to do
things. The physical preponderance is hardly on the
side of the two dozen, even less on the side of a single
dictator, a Hitler or a Mussolini. He can only achieve
his purpose by getting at the will of millions, persuading them to follow his policy by promising something
that those millions want—if not peace, then vengeance,
or a corrected frontier, redemption of some terra irre-
denta, or national advantage or honour in return for
the sacrifices demanded. This desire on the part of
the multitude to see achieved some promised end forms
the basis of the autocrat's power. He becomes autocratic indeed by undertaking to give the millions what
they want, by persuading them that if they obey him
the desired results will ensue.

## Chapter IV

# ALL OTHER PUBLIC PROBLEMS DEPEND ON THIS ONE

The prevention of war has suddenly become supremely important not so much because of what happens in war, but because of what happens in peace as the result of preparation for war. Under the system of competitive arming the purpose of society is turned from the ends of welfare to the ends of military victory. In the stress of that competition we forget the purpose for which society was created. The kind of nation that can best win wars is the kind of nation that has sacrificed both freedom and welfare. What we do about the war problem will determine the kind of world in which men are to live and the kind of men that are to live in it.

WHY has the prevention of war become suddenly the most important of all questions of public policy?

Not primarily because war involves bloodshed, the taking of human life, miseries, cruelties, waste (many peace activities do that), but because all other major questions of public policy, the very form that human society is to take, depend upon what we do about this question. War is important, not merely because of what it does in time of war (though that is evil enough), but much more because of what it does in times of peace. What we do about war will determine the kind of world in which men are to live; and the kind of men that are to live in it.

"We use the same word as our forefathers when we talk of war," said Edward Grey on one occasion, "but we don't mean the same thing." For our forefathers war was a contest between rival armies which might at times be very costly and destructive (as in the Thirty Years War, which by its actual material destruction nearly engulfed civilisation over large areas of Europe). But it could come and go and leave the form of society,

the way men lived and thought and felt, relatively unchanged. Wars might be going on, and those lucky
enough to escape the attention of the armies engaged
remained almost unaware of the fact.

But modern war is not of that nature at all. It is no
longer a contest between armies, but one between
nations; no longer a matter of organising and training
an army within a nation, but of organising and training
the nation itself, by a long peacetime preparation in
which the whole national life, every political, economic,
educational, domestic, religious function is directed
towards the one end of "winning in the coming war."
Not only is the purpose of organised society deflected
from ends of welfare to those of military victory as an
end, but the human mind itself, the human character
and all human values are profoundly modified.

Professor Arnold Toynbee has pointed out that "War
and Diplomacy have ceased to be the exclusive business
of a tiny class of professionals, and have become everybody's business. The sum total of the social forces of
the modern world has now 'got into' both Diplomacy
and War, and has thereby changed their character and
their effect upon the rest of human life and fortunes."
It demands, as he says, a profound revision of our attitude and action in regard to both War and Diplomacy.

"A thing which, in the eighteenth century had been
practically reduced to a game played by teams of professionals, has, since then, progressively extended its range
until now everybody, in each belligerent country, is involved in every way. . . . Modern war engulfs the whole
of social life, which has followed from certain political
and economic changes."

[48]

One gets a hint of how far the transformation may go by recalling what actually happened in our own country in the last war, by what has been taking place in Germany, first under the impulse of Prussian military organisation before the war, and then under the impulse of the Hitlerian, totalitarian conception of government and society which followed defeat.

To get some inkling of what has really happened, let the reader throw his mind back and compare the values, the political and social purposes with which we entered the war, and those values which we proclaim less than two decades later.

The war was primarily, of course, on our side a defensive war against the threatened preponderance of a rival combination, a preponderance which, realised, would have deprived us of the means of defending ourselves in an anarchic world. But, associated with that purpose were certain moral aims: the defence of democracy as a principle in the world's life; the destruction of militarism and of militarised autocracy, "the ending of this tramping and marching," "the rule of the drill sergeant"; the vindication of the rights of small nations as against imperialism, of individual freedom threatened with submergence in the ever encroaching autocratic state; of the truth that the state was made for man, not man for the state. Let the reader recall those aims and then look about him over the European scene, and look also at what has been happening within his own state and within the minds of his own people.

The war to make the world safe for democracy has been followed by a very epidemic of dictatorships throughout the world; autocracies so amazing and so "totalitarian" that the government of the Kaiser which we held up as the ruthless enemy of all freedom and right seems now in comparison the very acme of liberalism. But that fact is not the strangest part. The strangest part is that many of us in Britain rejoice in this outcome; that the self-same popular newspapers which were the fiercest critics of the Kaiser for the illiberalism of his *régime* now declare the Hitlerite type of rule to be quite the best way of government and of life, and give encouragement to British politicians and organisations whose purpose it is to introduce those ideas and that way of life into Britain.

The selfsame men and women who in 1914 were ready to encourage hundreds of thousands of our young men to go to their deaths "in defence of freedom," who told those young men then with such eloquence that to save the world from autocracy and militarism was worth dying for, proclaim in 1934 that freedom, democratic and parliamentary government are false ideals; that some form of autocracy is the inevitable and right form; and echo Mussolini's disparagements of liberty and liberalism. They seem to find it quite natural that the popular newspapers which they read and which in the years before the war screamed at the Kaiser for his autocracy and held the German people up to scorn for tolerating the invasions of freedom which marked pre-war Germany, should in the years after the war commend the government of Hitler, and openly urge Fascism for this country.

Before the war, in the time of that *Kaiserlich* Germany, which we had to destroy in the interests of freedom and democracy, the greater part of the German nation was shocked and rose in claimant protest when a becollared Prussian officer clouted a not very polite shoemaker over the head, as the Zabern incident revealed. What should we then have said, in that distant pre-war world, if the Kaiser, desirous of making changes in the cabinet or general staff had gone into private houses at the dead of night, into the bedrooms, had had ministers shot down then and there, had directed the executions to the extent of "bumping off" dozens of men who had been in his service, the executions running in some cases to the wives of his army officers. Even the stately London *Times* heads its leading article "Government by Murder" and bears witness to the fact that we have put the clock back in Central Europe some six or seven centuries. But other papers which could never before the war refer to Germans except as "Huns" now excuse or praise a *régime* marked by the sudden assassination of scores of those in high places, by others in high places; by torture for the purpose of exacting confessions; by imprisonment without trial; by the taking of hostages; by all those features which marked the Inquisition, by the fears which go with the spy and the agent-provocateur; by terrorism as a feature of daily life. The Germany of to-day is nearly everything that the older pre-Bismarckian Germany was not. If, as someone said, the war of 1870 was "the war which made Germany great and Germans small," the war of 1914 may be described as having turned small Germans into dangerous gangsters. Yet the Press which could not tolerate the Kaiser finds Hitler good.

Remember, furthermore, that defeat was to "larn" the Germans, to cure them of their arrogance, of the qualities which constitute Prussianism. The cure does not seem to have been notably successful. And we have simply forgotten what the war's purposes were.

[51]

That is the tragedy of the war. We enter the greatest
war of history, the ultimate purposes of which, apart
from national defence, we declare to be to vindicate the
principle of democracy, to save democracy from the
ruthlessness of great military states; to end the Prussian
conception of a highly centralised, autocratic, regi-
mented society; to preserve individual freedom, parliamentary government. A million of our youth give
their lives for those ends. We win the war. And then
we find that after all democracy is a mistake; that autocratic government is the right kind of government; that
liberty is an illusion; liberalism an outmoded creed;
that Freedom, in Mussolini's phrase, is "a stinking
corpse that should be buried"; that autocracy, far from
being a thing to fight, is a thing to imitate. The thing
on behalf of which a million of our youths are slain we
now declare to be something we don't want at all. Our
deepest values and ideals have by an unnoticed, almost
unconscious process, been gradually abandoned and
turned upside down; what before the war we thought
good, has become evil; what we then thought evil has
become good; what we hated before the war we now
admire.

Now, it may be that our new view is right and our
pre-war view wrong. But the point is that the change,
good or bad, has not been made consciously with a view
to human welfare but has been a largely unconscious
adaptation to the ends of war, to the need of avoiding
defeat.

We did not abandon the relative freedom and toleration, the democracy, the respect for life, for order which
we possessed in the pre-war years, because we de-

liberately decided that they were poor things. We abandoned those things because they got in the way of our "winning the war," which demanded autocracy, "action," violence, ruthlessness; and we acquired a taste for those methods, preparing the way for acceptance of Fascism and its cousin Dictatorship of the Left. These vast changes in moral and social values are a by-product, an unanticipated and unintended by-product, of military needs.

With these moral changes have gone changes in the economic structure, useful as indicating the process at work because they are more measurable and ponderable, though not less important than the moral changes.

It may well be true that behind the economic changes, as behind the coming of dictatorship and the totalitarian state, lie many causes and motives not directly related to the war. But the fact remains that the type of national organisation most fitted to wage war, which must inevitably be brought into being if the competition in war-waging capacity is to continue, is the totalitarian type, alike on its economic and moral side. "To wage war, or prepare for war on a modern scale," writes Dr. Conze, the young non-Nazi German writer, "all power must be in the hands of the state." It must plan on a national scale. But the planning, please note, is not concerned with the welfare of the people, the standard of living of the workers or any such object. "It is only concerned with massing all the powers of production into one mailed fist; at turning a whole country into one big war factory." But as we shall see in a moment, that factory must turn out more than purely economic things; the means which we employ for a given end, become themselves ends, and (which is the most important point perhaps) the process of change is unconscious.

Let us note certain features of the process.

In 1914 you had in Britain and America a bourgeois and capitalist society in which the most influential elements—"big business" and the average middle-class business man—were resisting tooth and nail the tendency towards what they called Socialism, "government interference in business," bureaucratic control and the burdens of increasing taxes which the tendency involved. The kind of world which the English bourgeois wanted was one of "rugged individualism," with private property as its economic basis, and as much personal freedom as possible. The feature of German life which he pitched upon as the most menacing to "democratic freedom" was the regimentation, the bureaucracy. The English bourgeois ideal (which was also, be it said, the ideal of large sections of the working class as well) had both an economic and a political side, though the two were interrelated.[1]

It is not a question for the moment whether the pre-war ideal was good or bad, workable or unworkable: it is what the great American and British bourgeoisie obviously desired—this way of life based upon

[1] The Socialist may not object to the frustration of the bourgeois ideal; but unfortunately the war has meant frustration of the Socialist ideal as well. Nowhere in Western Europe has Socialism emerged from the war chaos. There have been revolutions, but ending always in counter revolutions, in which Capitalism loses such liberal features as it may have acquired. The establishment of Democratic Socialism and Capitalist Liberalism have a common interest in the preservation of political order and the prevention of a chaos from which emerges a Fascism fatal alike to either purpose. Russia's membership of the League is testimony to her belief that Socialist and Capitalist societies have a common interest in the prevention of war.

[ 54 ]

private property, a minimum of government control, a minimum of taxation, a maximum of personal freedom, a hatred of bureaucracy and regimentation, a resistance to Socialism.

Comes the war. And over-night we find the individualist opponent of government interference in business claimantly demanding that all business be taken over by government. In a nation where the rights of private property had been sacrosanct private property and private rights ceased to have much meaning.

Banking and monetary policies were controlled with a view to one end: financing the war. War finance involved methods which it would have been utterly impossible to have applied for any peace purpose whatsoever. Private investments (e.g. foreign securities) were impounded (for exchange purposes). Britain lost her creditor position and became for the first time in modern economic history a debtor. Monetary policies which had guided the nation for generation and had always been regarded as the very first condition of sound finance were abandoned from one day to another. The gold standard itself was sacrificed. Every industry was controlled, very many were directly managed. Prices were fixed. Commodities were commandered and rationed. The railroads took their orders from the government. Farmers grew only such things as the government permitted. If the appropriate committee ordered tennis lawns to be dug up for planting potatoes, the lawns were dug up. (Imagine this being done for a peace purpose, say to find work for unemployed.) Manufacturers got only such raw material as the government saw fit to let them have. Food control was extremely strict. There were cards and permits for bread and butter and sugar and milk. Existing industries in many cases were practically destroyed and new industries took their place; some were shifted from one side of the world to the other. In short, the whole economic life of the nation was re-directed from top to bottom.

Had the purpose of those changes been a peace purpose, some end of welfare, they would have been resisted tooth and claw at that time by bourgeois society. Men of business would have proved to you that society could not survive the shock of such methods, that even if they worked more or less as an economic method they would involve a degree of bureaucratic control which would turn the nation into a barracks.

Once they became necessary for war they were accepted from one day to another. The idea may have been that after the war the omelette could be unscrambled. We now know better.

As with things economic, so with things of the mind and spirit.

In war time we discovered that neither a man's life nor his conscience are his own. That they too belong to the state. If the state commands a man to walk to certain death, to death he walks. More. If it commands him to kill, disembowel, dismember and torture women and children, he does these things or is himself killed by the order of the state. It all actually happened in the last war. This writer has himself heard young, fresh-faced boys, only a year or two from school, relate with laughter and jest (laughter and jest due to the realisation that they themselves were still alive after their adventure) how they had just dropped bombs on border cities of the enemy, destroying railway stations and "other big buildings." The "other big buildings"

turned out to be schools with children in them.[1]  And
that sort of task will not be less frequent or more avoidable in future wars.  It will be characteristic of the main
operations, normal, quite unavoidable.  War in the future will, if experts can be trusted at all, be mainly war
from the air, in which the distinction between civilian

[1] The following—which appeared in *The Times* of April 17th, 1915—
is merely a type of at least thirty or forty similar reports published by
the German army headquarters: "In yesterday's clear weather the airmen were very active.  Enemy airmen bombarded places behind our
positions.  Freiburg was again visited, and several civilians, the majority being children, were killed and wounded."  A few days later the
Paris *Temps* (April 22nd, 1915) reproduced the German accounts of
French air-raids where bombs were dropped on Kandern, Loerrach,
Mulheim, Habsheim, Wiesenthal, Tüblingen, Mannheim.  These raids
were carried out by squads of airmen, and the bombs were thrown
particularly at railway stations and factories.  Previous to this, British
and French airmen had been particularly active in Belgium, dropping
bombs on Zeebrugge, Bruges, Middlekirke, and other towns.  One
German official report tells how a bomb fell on to a loaded street car,
killing many women and children.  Another (dated September 7th,
1915) contains the following: "In the course of an enemy aeroplane
attack on Lichtervelde, north of Roulers in Flanders, seven Belgian
inhabitants were killed and two injured."  A despatch from Zurich,
dated September 24th, 1915, says: "At yesterday's meeting of the Stutt-
gart city council the mayor and councillors protested vigorously against
the recent French raid upon an undefended city.  Burgomaster Lau-
tenschlager asserted that an enemy that attacked harmless civilians
was fighting a lost cause."

In 1934 there appeared among British films one in which were given
pictures of *Allied* planes, dropping bombs on nurses, women, priests,
civilians and neutrals during a religious ceremony.  The actors in this
film included Sir Gerald du Maurier.  It was given all over the country, and I am not aware in a single case that it was urged that this
picture libelled the British forces when it showed them dropping
bombs in the midst of a religious ceremony.  During the war we
should have denied heatedly that our airmen ever did such things.
Twenty years after the beginning of the war these things are now
accepted so much as matter of course, that even in a patriotic film the
British public can be shown British planes doing that precise thing.

[ 57 ]

and military will completely disappear; in which the effort will be made first and last to destroy "nerve centres," like railway stations, water reservoirs, big industrial towns, where factories are located; and they will be destroyed, not only by high explosive bombs, but by the incendiary bomb, the poison gas bomb, the disease germ bomb. In savage times the poisoning of the wells was regarded as an act beyond the pale of humanity. In war, as we now face it, the poisoning of the wells will be regarded as a normal and effective military operation.

Now, again, the moral effect of that is not something which we can shut off by watertight compartments, confining it to war time. It indicates an attitude which shapes life in peace time permanently, as the events of 1934 in Germany and Austria and elsewhere demonstrated.

The process of change in this respect is more visible in Italy and Germany than in Britain. But even if we were not urged by increasing numbers of leaders and newspapers to imitate the German and the Italian models we should inevitably be pushed by the process of competition to the employment of a "totalitarian" technique in which the state becomes omnipotent in the moral as well as the material sphere. The beginnings we made during the last war were a mere foretaste of what we may expect in the next, particularly in the shaping of the mind and spirit during peace time into the instrument best fitted for the purposes of military victory. For nothing, all the experts are agreed, is so important in war as "morale."

"The greatest evil of modern war," said Mr. Walter Lippmann once, "is not poison gas. It is the kind of public opinion it produces." So complete now is the control of the mechanical means of communication—Press, books, wireless, cinema, church, school, university—that a government has the means of making of the public mind anything that it chooses.

But governments become prisoners of their own propaganda. They produce a certain type of mind or flow of emotions for the purposes of war. But that flow cannot be turned off like a tap when the war is over, as we shall see. The peace comes, and then governments are compelled to make a peace they don't want to make, because the state of mind produced during the war clamours for that kind of peace. And then that kind of peace makes more war. Or governments and rulers and leaders become prisoners of their own Frankenstein monsters in another sense: they end by believing their own propaganda. A state of mind created for one purpose comes to dominate all purposes. A country may possess a great culture, a great tradition of learning, of philosophy and then, almost over night as in the case of the economic changes, the term "intellectual" becomes a term of contempt, and the very guardians of the things of the mind and the spirit, the universities and seats of learning, become instruments for the destruction of the culture that generations have so painfully built up.[1]

[1] Mr. Robert Dell, the well-known journalist, quotes a Nazi leader thus: "The very word culture gives me a pain and I look for my revolver." One of the first acts of the Nazi government was to decree that Nazi students who had failed in their examinations should be given degrees nevertheless.

Mussolini has now decreed that military education in Italy shall begin at the age of eight, and an Italian newspaper in approval remarks that Italy will win her due place in the world not with scholars but with soldiers.

It is an inevitable part of the competitive preparation for war in which "morale" is all important. What one side does the other must do sooner or later. If material production is to be controlled and centralised so also, and more importantly, must thought be controlled and centralised. In his book Hitler laments that "Germany might have become mistress of the world if the German people in their historical development had possessed a unity like that of a herd of cattle."[1] It is the plain purpose of his *régime* to make them as much like a herd of cattle as possible, because only by so doing can their strength as a national unit be brought to its highest possible effectiveness for war purposes. A demagogue can achieve that unity best, Hitler tells us (and he ought to know), by causing a people to forget welfare, "daily bread." In *Mein Kampf* he writes that:

"As long as the German people continued to think in 1914 that they were fighting for ideals they stood their ground. But the moment it became evident that they were merely fighting for their daily bread, they were glad to throw up the sponge." In other words, the purposes of society must be diverted from conscious ends of well-being to ends which cannot be put to any ponderable or measurable test. Men must be induced to forget "what society is for" if they are to be induced to fight. Mr. J. B. Priestly says:

> There has to be a romantic appeal. Men fight for the glory and honour of the fatherland, the motherland, for right against might, for the king and flag, for the women and children. Not for the most iron discipline, not the most urgent necessity for new markets and old coalfields

[1] In a passage on p. 437 omitted from the English edition.

can keep armies from crumbling away once the romantic appeal is discovered to be a tricky lie, once the last glimmer of chivalry has vanished.[1]

The first purpose of all training of the youth in schools is, Hitler says, in a physical fitness and a spiritual attitude which will best fit them for war. "The chief aim of education is physical fitness and preparation for national defence . . . by means of obedience and absolute subjugation to the will of the leader which must be expressed by the teacher. . . . Only after that the acquisition of knowledge."

In the manual for schools prepared by Professor Banse we see the fact faced very plainly. The author of this school manual tells his young readers:

> Nobody capable of thought can doubt that war stands between us and happiness . . . nowadays war is no longer the fresh and merry war of old, with music and banners, triumph and honours. War to-day is a bloody fight for annihilation; it is destruction. It is gas, tanks, the horrors of attack by air, penury and famine, agitation and lies, renunciation and sacrifice.
>
> A people can pass through these trials and win the war if every individual member of it is deeply convinced that his life belongs not to him but to the state and to the state alone.

One notable feature of the post-war counter revolution of social and moral ideas is in the position of women. In all the Fascist states we have returned to the Nitschean conception of the position of women as the warrior's relaxation and the producers of warriors who in their turn shall be the producers of warriors.

[1] *Challenge to Death.* (Constable). p. 315.

How far the process of spiritual and intellectual preparation for war must be carried, a Nazi German, Herr Friedrich Sieburg, in his book *Es werde Deutschland* makes clear. It is to go on, in the case of Germans, until they have ceased to have any private rights, ceased indeed, he tells us with pride, to be human beings.

> There are to be no more private Germans. Each is to attain significance only by his service to the state and to find complete self-fulfilment in its service. Thus to express it in more emphatic terms, there are to be no more human beings in Germany, but only Germans.[1]

All this has a certain consistent logic in it. Modern war cannot be waged by normally civilised men: men must therefore be de-civilised. And modern propaganda, using school and church and press and cinema, is quite capable of doing it.

The appropriate morality for the effective use of propaganda is to be created. "Objective truth" is to be replaced by "German truth." Dr. Goebbels and the Nazi leaders are particularly hostile to "objective" history (i.e. an attempt to state what really happened). Objective history, they say, is a "liberal aberration." The duty of all Germans is, in Hitler's own words, "not to seek out objective truth in so far as it may be favourable to others, but uninterruptedly to serve one's own truth." Things like the Versailles Treaty should be used to work up "blazing fury and passionate hate."

> All printed matter from the child's primer to the last newspaper, every theatre, every cinema, every advertise-

[1] Herr Herman Gauch, in his book, *Neue Grundlagen der Rassenforschung,* published in 1933, declares that the real distinction is not between the human race and other animals, but between the Aryan race and other animals, including all the other human races.

[62]

ment pillar, every hoarding, must be pressed into the service of this single great mission until the anguished prayer of our confederated patriots "Lord set us free" is transformed in the brain of the tiniest child into the fervent prayer "Almighty God, bless our arms in the future: be just as Thou hast ever been, decide now whether we yet deserve our freedom; Lord bless our battles."

Given such methods, there is no reason at all why the whole German nation should not become imbued with the blood lust of dervishes, ready, like dervishes, to throw away their lives if Mahomet in the shape of Hitler so wills; but, unlike dervishes, possessed of technology and its instruments by which non-German (i.e. inferior and savage) Europe can be wiped out.

If a tradition like that of Christianity should prove inconvenient for the proper conditioning of a people for war, the experience of Germany, the land of Luther, shows how readily that tradition too can be wiped away in the interests of war preparation, and how easily masses of educated folk can be turned back to a more warlike ethic. Almost from one day to another ancient gods may be made to bow to the all-embracing God-state.

When these "German Christian" absurdities, the "Nordic" Christ, and the rest, first began, Christendom laughed, declining to believe that a tradition of twenty centuries could thus be "uprooted in a Nazi week end" as one critic put it. But the day's *Times* on my desk has from its Berlin correspondent this passage:

Despite periodical ambiguous denials, orthodox churchmen and churchgoers have been forced to the firm conviction that certain "Nordic" conceptions in the philosophy of Herr Alfred Rosenberg, the author of

[6₃]

*Mythology of the Twentieth Century* (which, incidentally, the Pope has placed on the *Index*) , are being and will continue to be subtly, but steadily and relentlessly, imposed. . . .

The resisters now feel themselves confronted, not merely by clumsy "German Christian" attempts to enliven the Church by the introduction of a few heresies, but by the slow-moving, relentless will of a movement which is determined to impose the National-Socialist *Weltanschauung,* or outlook on life, on the religious communities.

The right of persons or groups in National-Socialist Germany to promote a return to Nordic or Germanic customs or beliefs, or even to endeavour to build up a new German religion distinct from Christianity, and win the people over to it, has never been challenged. The "German Faith Movement" of Professor Hauer and Count Reventlow is frankly pursuing such aims.

It has the state on its side. And while the state is repressing ruthlessly anything in the nature of "Pacifist" interpretations of the Christian doctrine, it encourages the dissemination, not only of the books of the German Faith Movement, but of works like that of Professor Ernst Bergmann, who, while adhering to the German Faith Movement, would quicken it. His section may be regarded as a sort of "Oxford Group" of the German Faith Movement. Here are some of their "theses" and Professor Bergmann's comments:

*Thesis* [8]. The German of to-day needs a healthy and natural religion, which will make him courageous, faithful and strong in the struggle for People and Fatherland. The German Religion is such a religion.
"Christianity is an alien religion."

"In almost all points it is contrary to the German conception of decency and morals."

"Christianity is the example of an unhealthy and unnatural, decaying religion."

*Thesis* [8]. God is a moral idea, which we recognise in the eternal creative power of natural working in the world and in man. The belief in a God outside this world, or in heaven, is not of Indo-Germanic, but of Semitic origin.

"Christianity and Religion are to-day a contradiction in terms" (p. 19).

"Our religion no longer recognises the international Christian God who was unable to prevent Versailles" (p. 21).

"Those who are in favour of weeding out the inferior and selecting the superior, those who want a Social Aristocracy, can no longer remain Christians, for Christianity is the religious mode of Social Democracy. Both are international, democratic, and stand for the equality of man" (p. 41).

"If Germany, the leading country of Nordic Humanity, had been spared the Jewish-Christian ethics of sin, the moral face of the world would wear a different aspect to-day" (p. 56).

"Christianity has meant for Germany 1,000 years of religious Versailles" (p. 70).

*Thesis* [21]. We believers in German Religion demand the introduction of religious lessons in school. The Christian lessons can no longer be looked upon as a sufficient substitute for religious lessons just as Christianity can no longer be regarded as a religion such as we understand it (Thesis 1, 2 and 3).

"A people which comes home to blood and soil, and which has fully realised the world danger of international Jewry, can no longer permit a religion which claims the sacramental scripture of the Jews as its own Gospel, to remain in the Church" (p. 74).

I have given those quotations at some length mainly to illustrate the relative ease with which the most ancient of traditions or culture can go down in the currents which preparation for war sets up. For what we see going on in Germany is only special to Germany in its degree. Its roots are common to the post-war world; on some soil it flourishes better than on others, but its seeds are inevitably planted in all war preparations.

Throughout, one sees this adaptation of the human spirit to the needs of war, an adaptation sometimes conscious, sometimes unconscious. Because war is rapidly becoming something that civilised and thinking men could not wage, a nation, if it is to "keep its end up" in competition with others, must face that fact and de-civilise and de-rationalise. The habit of asking what war is for, how it will profit men, and, still more importantly, how nationalism and its aims may profit man, the habit of consciously weighing values, must be discouraged. Thus arises the close association of mysticism, anti-rationalism, the disparagement of reason, and the disparagement of tangible economic values as the criterion of political effort which one sees, not only in German, but in all nationalism in lesser or greater degree. Most impartial observers are struck with this disparagement of rationalism, a disparagement almost as common in Italian as in German Fascism.

A German-American observer writes:

The Nazi movement from the beginning has been a revolt against reason and a constant crescendo of ultra-patriotic frenzy. "We think with our blood!" is a proud

Hitlerite boast. The forty million or more Germans who vote "Yes" on November 12 will vote with their blood —in fever or in fear. They speak with the voice of fierce hatreds and primal hungers which have been deliberately evoked and skillfully mobilized around the symbols of Fascist fanaticism. They act toward the world in a spirit of proud desperation shot through with dementia. Here is Germany's tragedy. It is this new *Furor Teutonica,* turned against itself, which is destroying all that was liberal, and hopeful in German culture. It is this same madness, directed outward, which makes any increase in armament by the Third Reich a deadly menace to all prospects of peace and order among nations.[1]

Aldous Huxley notes the same phenomena:

The Nazi movement is a rebellion against Western civilisation. In order to consolidate this rebellion, its leaders are doing their best to transform modern German society into the likeness of a primitive tribe. Homogeniety is being forced on a people that was enjoying the blessings of variety. Proximity in space cannot unfortunately be abolished; but psychological gulfs can be and are being deliberately opened on every side. Mentally and emotionally, Germany is to be made as remote from Europe as New Guinea. The last and perhaps the most formidable obstacle to the strict conditioning process in primitive societies is, as we have seen, the scientific attitude. Nazi philosophy has a short way with scientific attitude. The duty of all Germans is, in Hitler's own words, "not to seek out objective truth in so far as it may be favourable to others, but uninterruptedly to serve one's own truth." An ethic of head hunters is to be justified by a philosophy of paranoiacs. The result promises to be extremely *gemütlich.*

[1] Frederick L. Schuman in *The New Republic,* November 22nd, 1933.

The French are the people most immediately menaced by Nazi fanaticism; and there is in this an element of poetic justice. For the two cardinal points in the philosophy, by which the Nazis justify their violences, were both invented by Frenchmen. Gobineau was responsible for that doctrine of race superiority used by the Nazis as an aphrodisiac to arouse hatred for Gobineau's own countrymen. And it was Bergson who led the intellectuals' disastrous attack on the intellect, and so prepared the way for the systemized paranoia of Hitler. The sins and errors of the Brahmins are visited in a most disquieting way upon the low-caste masses of their fellow-men.[1]

One gets back to the original indictment, and the original question. War and its preparation render men less able to manage a free and peaceful society, cause them indeed to forget what human society is for. We want of organised society, obviously, certain agreed goods, material and moral, economic and social. We desire to avoid the absurdity which compels us to starve in the midst of plenty: so to manage the amazing tools which our conquest of matter has put into our hands as to banish, for the mass of men and women, scarcity, hunger, toil, pestilence, insecurity and anxiety, cruelties and oppressions. That the thing is possible and the obstacles are not in inanimate nature has now become clear. The obstacles are in defects of social co-operation. We fail at that point. The last twenty years has revealed how precarious and vulnerable is the mechanism of our complicated society. Our social co-operations are always being wrecked upon the rock of our pugnacities, misunderstandings, prejudices. If we cannot somehow manage to overcome these difficulties, our

---

[1] *Beyond the Mexique Bay*, by Aldous Huxley, pp. 179-181.

civilisation will go the way of a dozen previous civilisations. But our going will be marked by even worse cruelties, worse abominations than those which marked those earlier failures.

To solve our difficulties, to use physical science to create a world which shall be full of welfare, freedom, happiness is not impossible, but it is difficult. We shall not do it unless we direct our minds and energies to that purpose. We are not turning our minds to it. The main objective of the efforts which we make has been unconsciously diverted from ends of welfare to ends of rivalry for itself. The rivalry would not greatly matter if it were an innocuous rivalry; but it is one which, by its processes, transforms the human spirit and human society.

Elsewhere I have put the final indictment thus:

"For the purposes of avoiding defeat in war we will accept anything that the strength of the enemy imposes: we will be Socialist, autocratic, democratic or Communist; we will conscribe the bodies, souls, wealth of our people; we will proscribe, as we do, the Christian doctrine, and all mercy and humanity; we will organise falsehood and deceit, and call it statecraft and strategy; lie for the purpose of inflaming hate, and rejoice at the effectiveness of our propaganda; we will torture helpless millions by pestilence and famine—as we British with our blockades, even our post war blockades, have done—and look on unmoved; our priests, in the name of Christ, will reprove misplaced pity, and call for further punishment of the wicked, still greater efforts in the Fight for Right. We shall not care what transformations take place in our society or our natures; or what happens to the human spirit."

"If some of us have felt that, beyond all other evils which translate themselves into public policy, those with which these pages deal constitute the greatest, it is not because war means the loss of life, the killing of men. Many of our noblest activities do that. There are so many of us that it is no great disaster that a few should die. It is not because war means suffering. Suffering endured for a conscious and clearly conceived human purpose is redeemed by hope of real achievement; it may be a glad sacrifice for some worthy end. But if we have floundered hopelessly into a bog because we have forgotten our end and purpose in the heat of futile passion, the consolation which we may gather from the willingness with which men die in the bog should not stand in the way of our determination to rediscover our destination and create afresh our purpose. War has left us a less workable society; has been marked by an increase in the forces of chaos and disintegration. That is the ultimate indictment of the last war, as of all wars: the attitude towards life, the ideas and motive forces out of which it grows, and which it fosters, makes men less able to live together, their society less workable, and must end by making free society impossible. War not only arises out of the failure of human wisdom, from the defeats of that intelligence by which alone we can successfully fight the forces of nature; it perpetuates that failure and worsens it. For only by a passion which keeps thought at bay can the "morale" of war be maintained. The very justification which we advance for our war-time censorships and propaganda, our suspension of free speech and discussion, is that if we gave full value to the enemy's case, saw him as he really is, blundering, foolish, largely help-less like ourselves; saw the defects of our own and our Allies' policy, saw what our own acts in war really involved and how nearly they resembled those which aroused our anger when done by the enemy, if we saw all this and kept our heads, we might stop the war. A thousand times it has been explained that in an impartial mood we cannot carry on war; that un-less the people come to feel that all the right is on our side and all the wrong on the enemy's, our morale will fail. The most righteous war can only be kept going by falsehood. The end of that falsehood is that our mind collapses. And although the mind, thought, judgment, are not all-sufficient for man's salvation, it is impossible without them. Behind all other ex-planations of Europe's creeping paralysis is the blind-ness of the millions, their inability to see the effects of their demands and policy, to see where they are going."

## Chapter V

# JOHN SMITH SETTLES IT

Wars are not made by governments, capitalists, financiers or armament makers, but by the ordinary man acquiescing for a variety of reasons in policies that often suit the ends of predatory governments, capitalists, financiers, armament makers. A few obese financiers cannot force, they can only persuade, untold millions to do their bidding. It is John Smith's ideas on such things as the proper method of national defence, internationalism, patriotism, religion, empire, which made the last war and will make the next, unless those ideas are changed. War is usually the last thing that Smith desires but is often inherent in the policies which he imposes upon his governments.

WHEN, in the discussions which take place between acquaintances who meet on the morning train to town, at the club, at the luncheon hour in the restaurant, at the dinner table in the evening, or over the evening glass of beer at the public-house, talk turns to such things as war and peace, views, much like those expressed in the snatches of actual conversation reported below as accurately as memory can serve, are pretty certain to be expressed. The conversation went something like this:

SMITH: I never said I wanted war; I said we should get war if we went on reducing our armaments while the foreigners increased theirs. Of course, I don't want war. What sane or civilised man does? But we've got a good deal that foreigners would certainly like to have and we've got to protect it. As to making war more likely by increasing our defences, you might as well say you encourage burglary by bolting your doors at night. "The strong man armed," you know. I agree with Beatty that a strong British navy is the best guarantee of the peace of the world.[1]  What should we have done in 1914 without a navy?  If we had had one twice the size there would have been no war.

BROWN: It is not as though we were an aggressive nation. Is A suggesting that we want to go to war with anybody?  What for?  What do we want?  Foreigners must be perfectly aware that we should never start a war, that our power threatens no one.  The more power, the more peace.  When Reggie's headmaster asked me if I'd like the boy to join the O.T.C., I said the boy ought to get a good licking if he didn't.  I'm all for peace—I had my fill in the last war.  Eleven wounds are quite enough, thank you.  But the days of war aren't over yet, despite what our Pacifist friend says, and we must keep our powder dry.  This business of solemnly promising to be a coward, "never to fight for king and country," smells rather bad to me.  I don't see a very fine race of men coming out of it. . . . I'm on the board of governors of our town grammar school, and when it was suggested that X., that Pacifist fellow, be invited to lecture to the boys, I put my foot down, and the rector supported me and the Board decided not to allow it.

SMITH: I put my foot down too when our party headquarters in London suggested that we accept Alderton, that League of Nation's fellow, as our Parliamentary candidate.  The League's all right, of course, but on a narrow majority his ultra peace line might be a handicap.  It might be different if you could afford to lose a couple of thousand votes.  I got the editor of the party's paper to back us up.

JONES: Well, I'm a member of the League of Nations Union.  I believe in doing what you can for peace.

[1] "The best method of preventing war was to have a navy strong enough to preserve peace, as it had done in the past." Lord Beatty at Portsmouth, reported in *The Times*, August 6th, 1934.

But I confess I'm uneasy at all these new commitments. I don't see how you're going to get peace by increasing the number of occasions on which you promise to go to war. It seems to me the best chance of peace is to mind your own business and to intimate to foreigners that we want them to mind theirs. We induced our branch of the League of Nations Union to pass a resolution to that effect. I swallowed Locarno and would stand by it, but I don't think. . . .

ROBINSON: But is it going to make the faintest difference what you and I think—or do? Do you really suppose that your Union or the Peace societies are ever going to stop war? Have they ever done so? We don't want war, but we shall get it if it's got to come. We shall be in before we know it has begun. Our opinion won't be asked and won't make any difference to the big bugs, big business and the brass hats, who will just tell us it has begun and that it is up to us to get on with it.

Robinson's point secured the greatest measure of agreement. What the ordinary man thought about war would make not the slightest difference as to whether we should get another or not. There followed much talk of armament makers and international financiers, of capitalist interests of various sorts, but finally it was unanimously agreed that, whoever brought about wars, certainly the ordinary citizen did not; that he had nearly nothing to do with them except to fight them, die in them, suffer from them, pay for them and be ruined by them.

It is entirely characteristic of this subject, that the most obvious truths which bear upon it are often those most obstinately denied.

§

In the last analysis war is caused, not by governments, nor capitalists; nor armament manufacturers, nor by nature, nor by fate, nor by accident, but by men: the average human being, the man in the street. It takes place, not because the average man wants it, he does not; nor from any particularly evil motive on his part, his motives are usually of the best; but because men in the mass—the mass who in parliamentary countries make or unmake governments—insist on policies (particularly policies of defence and those inherent in unqualified nationalism) the intention behind which may be peaceful enough, but the result, the inevitable result of which, is war.

This does not mean that armament manufacturers or other capitalist groups have no interest in war and may not intrigue actively to promote it, nor that it is not useful to expose their intrigues, but that they would be impotent for mischief were it not for the willing acquiescence of the average man in policies and ideas which serve their evil purpose. The "arms racket" is an evil thing, and needs exposure,[1] but it would be powerless if it were not for the ease with which John Smith can be persuaded to vote for policies which necessarily mean ever-increasing armaments.

When we are told that fifty munition makers "force" fifty millions or five hundred millions to go to war, the words are meaningless. Fifty cannot "force" fifty millions; the force, the overwhelming force, is on the

[1] And this present writer, for one, trusts that what the Senate inquiry into the arms traffic has been doing for America will be duplicated in some form for Great Britain.

[75]

side of the millions. Four dozen men want the fifty millions to go to war. Why do the fifty millions obey? The four dozen can only persuade, bamboozle. By appealing to what motives? By what means are the vast majority of men persuaded to do the will of a tiny minority; to follow a course fatal to the best interests, the wealth, welfare and inclinations of the majority? It cannot be by force. The minority must somehow get at the will and mind of the majority.

To keep on repeating parrot-like that "it is the influence of the armament interests" explains nothing. As truly might one say that fifty million Americans drank bootleg liquor during fifteen years because Al Capone and other gangsters wanted to make a lot of money. Al Capone made a lot of money because Americans wanted to drink hooch. To "explain" the phenomenon of German Nazidom by the statement that Thyssen preferred Hitler to the Kaiser explains nothing. If it were reported that Al Capone had become President of the United States it would not explain the phenomenon to say that Capone preferred the White House to Leavenworth prison.

The important thing in that situation would be, not the wickedness of Al Capone, but the impotence of the American people, the breakdown of organised society in the United States in its fight with crime.

Before war can be fought a long series of necessary steps, which quite obviously are not and cannot be enforced steps, must be taken by the mass of men. Naval and military budgets must be voted in parliaments and congresses, not just once or twice in a generation, but year after year; not secretly, but accompanied by long and public discussion; the budgets being supported by members of parliament or deputies or congressmen who are still in many states continuously re-elected in free and secret franchises, often by great majorities. The voters who thus elect parliaments that vote the money that the armament makers receive are not driven to the polls at the point of a bayonet; they are not even bribed. If those votes really are explained by the power of vested interests it is clearly not the power of direct physical force. Somehow, by some means, the minority must secure the free acquiescence of the majority in policies that defeat the majority's purpose. How is that acquiescence achieved? To what motives do the minority appeal? By what confusions do they profit?

Persuaded by a "bought" press? Face this fact: In the capital cities of Britain and America you may usually find two types of daily newspaper, one which tries to tell the truth about international affairs, to enable its readers to understand the foreigner's point of view, to avoid sensations which embitter the nation's foreign relations. The *Manchester Guardian* may serve as illustrating that kind of paper. In competition with it is another type; the type that looks first, not for news but for "stories"; which far from minimising international differences, develops them as "features"; which is usually running some "stunt," the net effect of which is to create suspicion of foreign nations, to embitter relations with them, to set up a clamour for increased armaments. Jingoism, exploitation of international differences are its standing dish. One has only to recall the Anglophobia and Jingoism of the Hearst Press in America and the pre-war campaigns of the Northcliffe Press in Britain, the post-war rampage of the Beaverbrook Press against the League to appreciate the point.

Which of these two types makes the readiest appeal to the public? The type which, as at this moment of writing, is carrying on a violent campaign against the Disarmament Conference and for increase of air and naval forces, or the type exemplified in the *Manchester Guardian,* which is trying to save the Disarmament Conference and oppose increase of air armaments? Both are capitalist enterprises. Great fortunes have been lost in attempting to establish firmly in public favour organs like the *Manchester Guardian.* To establish such a paper is known to be a costly, difficult and most hazardous undertaking. But vast fortunes have been made again and again by papers of the Jingo, pro-armament, Hearst-Rothermere-Beaverbrook type. Why do the public so readily buy the latter type and so studiously avoid the former? Are they "forced" every morning to fish pennies out of their pockets to make vast fortunes for the Hearsts, the Rothermeres, the Beaverbrooks? Does a policeman stand over Smith at the station bookstall to see that he buys a Jingo instead of a peace-promoting paper?

The word "force," as implying physical compulsion, has no meaning in this connection. When John Smith of Surbiton gives his penny in the morning for a paper that daily derides peace and attacks the League[1] instead

[1] The estimate which this type of paper makes of the intelligence of its readers is illustrated by one point in the campaign against the League which the Beaverbrook Press has been running for some years. It "featured" in that campaign the cost of the League, creating the impression that it constituted a severe drain on the country's resources. In fact it bears the same relation to our national income that the contribution of half-a-crown a year would to a man having an income of three thousand pounds. Our contribution to war costs, including

of for one that defends those things, he can hardly plead that newspaper capitalists or armament firms "forced" him. It is by an entirely voluntary act that he adds enormously to the forces making for war.

To shut our eyes to the part that John Smith plays in the perpetuation of unworkable policies, in building up the forces of which he becomes the victim is to perpetuate his victimisation. Probably the most powerful of any single political force in the modern world is the appeal of Nationalism. If the political structure of Europe is on a basis of separate independent sovereignties instead of being, as it once was and as most of North America now is, on a basis of Federalism, it is because the Nationalist appeal finds response in deep human impulses, instincts, in psychological facts which we must face, just as much as we must face economic facts. To pretend that our nature does not include pugnacities and tempers, desires for domination and retaliation, sadisms and lusts, often hostile to material interest, often frustrating conscious intention, is to fly in the face of daily experience as well as the experience of all recorded history, with its long story of tribal feuds, racial bitterness, religious wars, Bartholomew massacres, revolutionary ferocities. Without certain moral disciplines, by which the first thought of instinct is made subject to the second thought of experience, these impulses will destroy us as surely as the impulse to rush for the boats in a shipwreck will destroy those who yield to their panic. To pretend that we shall not need these disciplines if only we eliminate the

debts, is at least two-thirds of all the taxes we pay. The League costs us a penny-farthing per head per year. War expenses (debt interest, pensions, estimates) £10 per head per year.

capitalist or financier, that the tempers, pugnacities, jealousies, will all disappear or become innocuous with the right economic system, is to invert a vital social truth. A better economic system will need at least in some respects more moral discipline, not less. Failure to grasp this truth will make Socialism as unworkable as current misunderstandings make Capitalism.

For some years before the war, during the war, and for some years after, all realist discussion of the causes of war was rendered impossible by "the guilty nation" theory. The cause of war was the wickedness of Germans. To establish peace you had to do little more than destroy German militarism. It was easy, simple, provided a scapegoat; kept agreeable passions awake and sent the public mind completely to sleep. There was no problem—nothing for the virtuous non-Germans to do about war except suppress Teutonic wickedness. We are now in danger of substituting for the guilty nation the guilty class—the Virtuous People v. the Wicked Capitalist. With a very great many among the political Left it is impossible to get any serious attention paid to problems of nationalism or the political anarchy which arise therefrom: there is an implied flat denial that in grappling with this ancient evil, which antedates, not only Capitalism, but history itself, "the people" need do anything at all in the way of revising old ideas or disciplining old passions.

War, more ancient than history, is the outcome of defective institutions and of follies, fallacies, misconceptions, common to the great mass of men. They are not incurable misconceptions, not incurable follies. But they may well become so if we persist in assuming

that they don't exist; that we need not trouble ourselves about them because war is due to a little clique
of evil "interests." So long as we take the line that
"the People" (i.e. we ourselves) are innocent of error,
then we might hang every war-profiteer in existence,
and find, on the morrow, human society as helplessly
as ever in the grip of some new folly, stimulated by a
new group interested in exploiting it.[1]

[1] The above had been written before seeing a review by Mr. Frank
H. Simonds (*The Saturday Review of Literature*, 28th April, 1934),
the eminent American journalist, who writes:

"When Mr. Seldes says that 'No reason for war remains except
sudden profits for the fifty men who run the munitions racket,' he
says what is demonstrably inexact. The reasons for war are well
nigh innumerable, and most of them reside in our 'accepted
ideology,' which is Nationalism. It may be true that the Krupps
and Thyssens have welcomed Hitler, but you have only to read the
Führer's book to discover that his is a vision of Germany as far
removed from the influence of Zaharoff as was Jeanne d'Arc's vision
of France from the inspiration of the armour makers of her
time. . . .

"Having attended all the disarmament conferences of the post-war
period, and having also been at Paris when the Peace Treaties were
made, I find it difficult to believe that the 'Merchants of Death' have
ever had much to do with the failure of these conferences to provide
peace or disarmament. If you could somehow prove that Basil
Zaharoff, for example, was the true author of the Polish Corridor,
the case against at least one of the 'Merchants of Death' would be
established. But it was Wilson who was the architect of the Corridor.

"In the same fashion, if you could saddle the arms makers with
the responsibility for conditions in Central Europe to-day, then it
would be simple to prove that the cause of peace would be advan-
taged by the removal of the guilty persons. But, again, however
guilty otherwise, the munitions makers were not to blame for applying the principle of self-determination to the Danubian area. . . .

"But it is what the people *en masse* accept as their rights, as the
rights of their countries, sovereign and imprescriptible, and call
upon their leaders to maintain uncompromisingly, that make wars.

"When, therefore, as in the present books, you start muckraking

§

If the reader will turn back to the report of that conversation with which this chapter opens, he will appreciate the way in which the opinion of the ordinary man gets itself translated into public policy, imposes itself upon public authorities.

That conversation tells us how a member of a city council—just the ordinary tradesman or professional man who gets elected to that kind of body—"puts his foot down" to prevent the "teaching of pacifism" to boys, influencing thus, it may be, the outlook of some hundreds of future citizens and voters; it reveals him as influencing the attitude of the headmaster of a public school in the same sense, and thus extending that influence to some hundreds of other boys; as having an influence upon a rector of the Church of England, who thus passes on the influence to a whole congregation. That talk reveals also how another ordinary citizen managed to exclude a man of internationalist opinion from a parliamentary candidature; influencing thus,

the arms trade, whatever useful reform you may accomplish in that direction, nevertheless you inevitably draw a red herring across the main trail. You help to sustain the individual in his comfortable belief that wars are made by wicked foreigners or dishonest natives, by the Hitlers abroad or the Zaharoffs at home. You start him full tilt after some-one who is, in effect, only his own accomplice. For it is the man in the street, he, you and I, who are actually responsible, and such a crusade can only strike at the effect and not the cause of existing conditions.

"The trouble is that they leave the reader with the idea that he can keep the ideology and escape the consequent conflict. But he can't. Thus, while the effect of this muckraking of munitions-racketeers may make mass murder cleaner, it will not affect those motives which make such murder frequent."

not only the character of the membership of the House of Commons, but the attitude of party leaders to this question, for it is pretty certain that the attitude of party leaders on this matter would influence greatly the minds of cabinet ministers, confirming in them the notion that it is better to avoid going very far in an internationalist direction. The same talk shows us still another ordinary citizen adding his little rivulet to this already big current of opinion and feeling by checking the tendency of a large society (organized for the purpose of promoting League policy) to support the collective system.

Let the reader take stock of certain policies pursued on the morrow of the war, policies which to-day by universal admission endanger peace, and then recall the public attitude to those policies at the time they were enforced. Take, for instance, the Treaty of Versailles. Very few to-day defend it. Very many agree that, unaltered, it will help to provoke a new war. Its terms have contributed enormously to that new sense of bitter resentment which so largely explains Hitler's success in Germany, and the dangerous situation resulting therefrom.

When the peace terms were under discussion, did popular feeling as a whole demand moderation—as for instance, in the Reparation conditions? The very question will be grimly humorous for those who, trying to do their bit to secure a workable peace, one that might make the appeasement of Europe a possibility, can recall what the effect of such advocacy was upon popular opinion at that time. The public were out for blood, not only that of Germans, but more particularly that of any misguided Englishman who seemed at all

[83]

tainted with "pro-Germanism."[1]   A score of statesmen
who have participated in the settlement have testified
to the fact that the terms would have been more workable and sane, particularly in the matter of Reparations,
but for the intensity of public passion.   (Recall the
1918 election, the deafening clamour for "punishment,"
"punitive terms," to "squeeze 'em till the pips
squeaked.")

The story has been told that when Mr. Maynard
Keynes protested that it was dangerous nonsense to
talk of Germany paying sums which capitalised represented about twenty thousand million sterling gold, Mr.
Lloyd George replied: "Twenty thousand million!
My dear fellow, if the election (that of 1918) had gone
on a fortnight longer it would have been fifty thousand
million."[2]

[1] One of the present writer's interesting recollections of that time
is the attempt of some five hundred undergraduates to chuck him in
the river; of being rescued in the nick of time by a police squad; of
being for an hour or so the shuttlecock of a game—Police v. Undergraduates; spending most of the night in a fire station and going home
early in the morning to the house of a don with whom he was staying,
to find a considerable part of it razed to the ground.  Just youthful
high spirits, of course, but still indicative of the temper of that time,
and he, like others of similar opinions, have had not dissimilar experiences in wartime with audiences made up of working class folk.

[2] Mr. Lloyd George in the House of Commons referred to his part in
the Reparations thus:

"There was no Ministry in France at that moment which could
have accepted any figure such as has been suggested.  It is no use,
if you are dealing with realities, not to take political realities into
account.  M. Clemenceau was one of the most courageous statesmen
who ever presided over the destinies of France.  He was not afraid
of facing opposition in the Chamber; but even he would have
shrunk from going to the Chamber at the time and urging them to
accept a figure which at present might be regarded as quite accept-
able even by French statesmen.  It was essential that you should

Almost from the beginning the experts, the bankers, the financiers, have been in favour either of cancellation or ruthless scaling down. But while nearly all the experts stood for one line of policy, governments, because they feared their electorates, pursued the exactly contrary line.

What is true of the attitude of the allied public to reparations in Europe is true of the attitude of the American public to European debt. All who know Washington know that the private view of very many senators and congressmen is for cancellation, but it is a view which they dare not express in public. To do so would be as much as their political position is worth. The two cases of Reparations and Debts are both noteworthy, in that bankers, financiers, capitalists—because it was their obvious interest so to do—have stood (after the first passionate explosions) for accommodation and workable terms, but have been unable to carry their point as against the public feeling. Indeed, it is part of the popular case in America against the bankers that they have "plotted" all along for cancellation of the

give time to allow the passion, the temper, and the ferocity of war to subside, so that you could finally adjudicate in a calmer atmosphere the claims between the various parties.

Mr. Maynard Keynes had commented a little earlier on the matter thus:

"Mr. Lloyd George took the responsibility for a Treaty of Peace that was not wise, which was partly impossible and which endangered the life of Europe. He may defend himself by saying that he knew it was not wise and was partly impossible and endangered the life of Europe; but that public passions and public ignorance play a part in the world of which he who aspires to lead a democracy must take account; that the Peace of Versailles was the best momentary settlement which the demands of the mob and character of the chief actors conjoined to permit.

European governmental debts in order to render their private investments safer. That may well be true, and the motives of the financiers as evil as you like, but their interests have plainly stood for a policy of appeasement while popular passion as plainly has stood against it. The whole story is an instructive one and has been dealt with by the present writer in several books. The popular passion—alike in America over debts and in Europe over Reparations—has been due in large part to sheer puzzlement and confusion.

The essence of the whole difficulty is that payment can only be made in goods and services, and at a time when unemployment is rife a people are in no mood to see the products of the industry by which they live come in floods from abroad. They want payment by the foreigner, but want also to keep out his goods. That is to demand mutually exclusive things. But because our education has not in the past given the millions who pass through its mills even the most rudimentary notions of economic science, those millions have never in fact understood why the demand to "pay in money, not goods" is, in these circumstances, contradictory. The puzzlement has added to the exasperation, to the exacerbation of tempers.

But this aspect of the post-war settlement and the role of popular feeling therein is only one part of the story, the story of the efforts to create after the appalling lessons of the war a world that should at last be based on sound and civilised foundations. Take the history of the League.

In dealing with the defects of the League, its relative impotence, the half-heartedness with which the states that constitute it pursue the policy it was founded to promote, it is common to blame the governments and to hold the people guiltless. One would assume from these criticisms that throughout the people had been prepared to take risks and responsibilities, in order to make their first great experiment at the scientific organisation of the world community a success. But the very first blow, which was also the very severest which the League received, the defection of the United States, was due to the fact that popular feeling failed to support the efforts of the government which brought the League into being. The head of that government gave his life in a last despairing effort to secure his people's support. The popular feeling, the tradition against any "entanglement with foreigners" was sufficiently strong to enable the enemies of Wilson to wreck his plans, to strike with semi-paralysis at the start this nascent world government.[1]

Popular feeling may have been right in its instinct thus to strangle at birth the first experiment at a real "parliament of man." That is not the question for the moment. The point is that we cannot ascribe the intention to strangle it to the government, the ruler, and the desire to save it to the people. The "people" (in so far as one can speak of them as an entity at all) were indifferent or hostile, lent themselves more easily to

---

[1] The United States Ambassador in London in an interview granted to the *Observer* (December 2nd, 1934), says:

"It is a commonplace of British and European comment on American diplomacy that the United States proposed the formation of a League of Nations, yet it did not join it; proposed the formation of a world court, yet did not adhere to it; in short, that, in the words of the old epigram, the American President proposes, but Congress disposes." That criticism was fair; but it no longer holds.

party and sectional intrigue than to the larger purposes of world organisation.

Again, the popular attitude is not due to any desire for war or indeed any indifference to peace, but to confusion as to the way in which peace may be obtained, the price which has to be paid for it. "Why need we bother with a League in order to have peace. Foreigners must know that we shall never attack them. In order to have peace in the world they have simply to refrain from attacking us." If the people are not prepared to pay the price of peace, it is mainly because it has never been made really clear what that price is.

Not that Britishers can be complacent about it; for if popular feeling in America has kept that country out of the League, popular feeling in Britain has gone far to make the institution impotent; to block, that is, the only kind of undertaking which can make any collective system workable. We find happening to the efforts of British governments, in lesser degree, exactly what happened to the efforts of President Wilson's administration. The representative of a government, meeting the representative of other governments in the conference room at Geneva or elsewhere, actually face to face with the problem, sees that, if peace is to be established, certain undertakings are necessary. The representative provisionally gives those undertakings—and they are promptly repudiated by the people at home.

Mr. Lloyd George, in order to induce the French to abandon the idea of a Rhine frontier, to give them confidence to make sufficient concessions to Germany in order to prevent the feeling which has actually since grown up in that country, offered France certain guarantees against German attack. Those undertakings failed of British ratification. The effort had to be made all over again in another form. Lord Cecil, after immense labour at Geneva, with the same general purpose of so meeting French misgiving as to make possible some disarmament and concession to Germany at last secured French agreement to the Treaty of Mutual Assistance. It was promptly repudiated by Parliament, a Labour government being then in office. The head of that government himself faced with the same problem Lord Cecil had faced, drew up with Herriot the Geneva Protocol (having a strong family resemblance to Lord Cecil's Treaty), which, when at last completed, a new British parliament (an election having meantime thrown the Labour government from power) promptly repudiated.

It is inadequately realized that neither a League of Nations nor any workable system outside it can possibly be a success unless (*a*) we, the British public, are prepared to assume certain obligations in respect of it and take certain risks; unless (*b*) the government of the day is aware that the public are ready to assume those obligations and risks, and unless (*c*) foreign nations are also aware that the British people will stand by the obligations which the Government has entered into.

For years certain journalists and politicians have insisted that sections of the Covenant (notably our obligations to make common cause with other states in resistance to a breaker of the peace) have become a dead letter; that our undertakings in the Locarno Treaty can bear an interpretation which, in fact, relieves us of any obligation at all. The Government, it is true, have stated on several occasions that this country stands by all its obligations. But side by side

[89]

with these official declarations are persistent statements in the Press, often by eminent men, which amount in effect to the declaration that these obligations are no longer binding and that if it came to a pinch the public would not honour any pledge which amounted to "mixing this country in the quarrels of other nations." Indeed, one group of papers has for years persistently declared that this country has changed its mind about the League as a whole, is sick of it, should withdraw from it and relieve itself of all obligations under it.

Does the British public really feel that way about the League? Have we, in fact, decided to reverse our policy?

No one really knows. One group of commentators say one thing, another group a quite contrary thing. Elections give little help in determining the mind of the public because of the multitude of other issues involved. Yet so long as this doubt on the part of foreign nations as to what our attitude in a critical situation would be exists, the very first purpose of the League cannot be achieved. That purpose is, of course, to substitute for the old international anarchy in which each seeks security by being stronger than his neighbour (thus depriving that neighbour of security) a more workable co-operative or collective system in which a great combination of states creates overwhelming power (diplomatic, political, economic, financial quite as much as military or naval) for peace as against warmaking tendencies in any one nation. If a given nation feels that it can depend in the long run on the operation of such a system, that it does not depend merely upon its own strength, it will not strive as a matter of life and death to be stronger than a neighbour. But if nations cannot depend on that system being applied at all, not even on its economic and financial side, then they will revert to the old competition of arms, with the old result, ultimately, of war. No collective or co-operative system of defence can possibly work unless there is belief on the part of each that the others really will fulfil their obligations.

Again, eminent and powerful people have been saying that so far as this nation is concerned it will certainly not fulfil any such pledge because it will henceforth take no part in such a system; that circumstances have so altered since the signature of the Covenant and Locarno Treaties that the country has not now any obligation for common action in the preservation of peace. They are able to make these statements without being charged with accusing our people of bad faith, because there is still a great deal of confusion in the public mind as to what the League is, attempts to be, must be, if it is to succeed. Our statesmen speak of "the collective system" as though there were common agreement as to what it is and what it involves. But there is no such agreement. In any assembly of a dozen persons you will get nearly a dozen views as to what the League is, what it involves in the way of national responsibilities, what is the minimum responsibility that ought to be assumed if it is to work as a peace-preserving instrument.

Two diametrically opposed policies are now presented to the British public. On the one side are great newspaper proprietors of enormous influence, controlling vast gramophones by which they can reach the public ear, urging with violence a policy of armed isolation or of competitive arming as the surest road to peace. On the other side are men—the names of Cecil and Lytton may be taken as illustrations—who, to put it at the lowest, are of equal authority in matters of public policy, urging what is known as the collective system as the only means by which effective national defence can be reconciled with peace.

The public has to choose between these two policies. They cannot both be right. If one leads to peace, the other leads to war, and the responsibility is with the ordinary man who cannot possibly avoid the choice.

In pointing out these facts, one runs the risk of appearing to imply that "the people are to blame." If such a phrase meant that the people, in any sense, want war, it would be utterly untrue. Since the Great War at least the mass of ordinary men and women alike in Europe and America have shown an increasingly deep and passionate desire for peace. If a general will-to-peace could stop war and armament, those evils would cease. But it is necessary at the various stages of the argument of this book to go on repeating two things: (1) that war does not come because men want it, or don't want peace, but because they insist on policies which are incompatible with peace, without realising that they are incompatible; and (2) that until the reasons for policies like those embodied in the League or Locarno are understood and have entered into the texture of commonplace thought, the experience which has been common alike to Wilson, to Lloyd George, to Cecil, to MacDonald, will go on being repeated. It is not new plans, new devices which are needed, but such understanding of those already in existence by the public as a whole which will enable governments to work them without being let down by their electorates at the crucial moment; electorates whose good will is unquestioned, but who have had litle chance really to understand the policies they so light-heartedly repudiate.

Albert Einstein has put the problem thus:

> The work of statesmen can succeed only if it is supported by the serious and determined will of the peoples.
>
> I know very many people who are willing to approve in principle opinions such as have been expressed here, but who will fall back the next moment into the ruts of ordinary political action. We . . . must be prepared to make sacrifices for our convictions.
>
> The sacrifice I am thinking of is the partial abandonment of state sovereignty by the separate States, and the yielding of the principle of egotism in favour of international security. Here lies the hope of Europe and the Western world.[1]

The "educated" have shown no whit more of wisdom in these matters than the simplest peasants and workers. Not infrequently they have shown much less. The conduct of the German nation to-day amazes the world; the German public acquiesce in policies which seem to carry us back to the Middle Ages. Yet they are an "educated" people. The worst of the Nazi hysteria and excesses come not from the fields and factories, but from the universities. That aspect of the question—the relation of learning (in the sense of erudition) to social and political capacity—is dealt with more fully later. The point for the moment is that public opinion, the feeling of the ordinary man, is the decisive factor in determining the nature of public policy; in the reten-

[1] *Sunday Chronicle,* March 4th, 1934.

tion of Nationalism, the refusal to apply to international
affairs principles of conduct which we know are indispensable to the creation of any decent society within
the nation; and that the errors which produce the
international chaos are not remedied by the extension
of "education" as we know it. In view of the fact that
pre-war diplomacy, the management of international
affairs (under the direction, it is true, of governments,
often obliged to obey public clamour) was in the hands
of highly educated upper classes, the mere extension to
others of the "educational advantages" they enjoyed is,
plainly, not going to advance us much.

How, then, is the unfortunate John Smith to face his
problem? How may he recognize the errors into which
he has fallen, and by what means may he hope to avoid
them in the future?

The next chapter will consider that point.

## Chapter VI

## A KEY TO COMPLEXITIES

This subject has become complex and technical and the specialists differ. So do specialists in medicine. Nevertheless the layman has so profited from medical knowledge as to transform the world by the abolition of dreadful pestilences—bubonic plague, cholera, leprosy—that used to curse it. He has done this by taking over from the medical expert the few truths about which no expert differs from another: To prevent pestilences sewage must be kept from drinking water. There are a few political and social truths, no more difficult to understand than the microbic theory of disease, which would enable the layman to eradicate the pestilence of war if he could see what they are. The purpose of this book is to disentangle from specialist knowledge those political truths which correspond in medicine to the transmission of disease by micro-organisms.

"IT IS all very well to say that Smith is to blame for clamouring for the wrong policy. But how is he to know what is the right policy, when even experts disagree?"

If doctors differ, what is the patient to do? If experts cannot agree as to the course which ought to be followed, how shall the relatively ignorant layman decide aright?

The ordinary citizen may well ask those questions in relation to the problem of preventing war; and the fact that he receives such diverse, and such conflicting counsel, when he approaches this subject furnishes better excuse, if excuse he seeks, for not concerning himself particularly with the matter than any argument of his so far dealt with. He is offered innumerable mutually exclusive solutions. To the slogan that "Armaments Mean War" others retort quite as definitely that "Armaments Mean Peace." Some invoke international co-operation as the sure basis of a peaceful world; others tell us that freedom from foreign entanglement is its first condition. Some tell us we must have common action against the aggressor; others that the attempt so to act will without doubt involve us in futile war. One school stands by Pacts for the Outlawry of War; another declares such Pacts to be little more than empty gestures. Some want us to create international sanctions; others urge us, above all, to avoid sanctions. There can be no hope of peace, says quite a large school, without the abolition of private property, of Capitalism. The growth of Communism, say others with conviction, will assuredly involve us in the bitterest of wars. There are large groups of economists who see in the growth of economic nationalism the greatest barrier both to peace and prosperity. But at least one eminent economist has declared that the chances of peace are improved by the development of economic nationalism. The real cause of war declare others—a growing section—is not private property or Capitalism, but the existing monetary system, and if the granting of credit is taken out of the hands of the banks, given a new direction and placed in the hands of the government operating a certain monetary system, war will cease automatically and the fallacies and tempers which are now so pregnant of evil become harmless. But other schools of monetary reformers reject these conclusions, and tell us that peace can only be achieved by the establishment of an entirely different system of currency. A very eminent adherent of the late Henry George devoted a large part of his life to attempting to show that the adoption of the Single Tax would stop war. As I write these lines I see on my desk among the day's mail a publication containing one of a series of articles designed to show that the eating of meat is the main cause of war, and that vegetarianism would, more than anything else, help to solve the world's problems and bring peace. The adherents of "British Israel" carry on an active (and expensive) campaign against the League of Nations for some reason connected with the Book of Revelations. . . .

In the midst of this confusion how does John Smith set about clearing up his own mind? If he is in the forties, he himself has seen the greatest war of history and may want to begin with the explanation and clarification of that. How does he begin? Several thousand books (a librarian once put them at ten thousand) have been written in English alone dealing with the Great War. If he wanted to form opinions well grounded in fact about that war, how would he set about tackling that mountain? Does he begin at number one and go on until the ten thousand have been consumed? Plainly not. Should he begin historically—find out who began it and why? But on that subject the documents are endless; whole libraries in themselves. And very contradictory. The account given by, say, German books, differs radically from that given by the French or the English or the American. But the French also differ from the English and the English from the American. And there are rival schools within the national groups. And this, remember, on the simpler questions of fact, what actually took place, who mobilised first, who refused arbitration, and so forth. When we come to causes, the differences are multiplied endlessly. Around the question has gathered a huge mountain of literature, usually very technical, often extremely controversial, covering the fields of diplomacy, history, military and naval science, economics, ethnography, anthropology, psychology, nationalism, international law, which, far from helping to clear up the confusions in the layman's mind, usually makes it worse confounded—whenever, that is, the layman attempts to tackle this Himalayan range of books; which commonly, of course, he never does. Indeed, it would not be physically possible for the ordinary citizen, preoccupied with his personal problems, to skirt even the foothills.

A working-man friend of mine during the war joined an organisation which had been formed to study its causes. The organisers sketched out for him a line of study tracing its historical background. He made a rough calculation that he and his fellow students would reach the problems of the peace treaty in the course of eighty years of constant study or thereabouts. So he joined another organization for the study of international problems and attended lectures which dealt with subjects ranging from the Ethnical Minorities of Transylvania to American-Filipino relations; from the Kuomintang to Sierra Leone, from the constitution of Iraq to the organisation of the International Wheat Market.

"I attend as many as I can," he writes pathetically, "but even now my mind is not really clear as to what caused the war and what I must do to prevent similar tragedies in the future." He adds:

I genuinely desire wisdom on this subject. My academic guides tell me that my conclusions must be on the basis of the facts, and they are always ready, through these agencies of libraries and study circles and institutes, to give me more and more facts. I suffocate in them. Ignorant as I am, at least I know this: that if I lived for hundreds of years and did nothing else, I could never make myself familiar with what they call "the facts of the situation." If, in order to know whether I should accept Lord Beaverbrook's advice to destroy the League, or Lord Cecil's advice to maintain it, I must explore completely the range of subjects about which I got odds and ends in the study circle and institute, cover the whole history of all the minorities of Europe, the full story of the struggles of the Poles, Magyars, Croats, Serbians, Slovenes, Slovaks, Ukrainians, Ruthenians, Czechs, and a score more; know the story of the religious and linguistic differences involved; combine that with a knowledge of the rights and wrongs of our own claims throughout the world; the facts of India and differences and disputes there; if I am to know all the facts in order to decide with wisdom, I shall never be able to decide. If I am to vote with knowledge, then I shall never vote. But my neighbour and his flapper daughters, who pride themselves on not worrying about such things at all, *will* vote.[1]

Well, what must he do?

If our education were really framed with a view to "teaching how to learn" it would offer some sort of guidance in that situation. But in fact the sort of education that our millions get in the schools offers no guidance whatever.

And yet the situation is not quite as hopeless as at first sight it might appear, and a certain analogy, which I have used elsewhere in this connection, may help us.

The science of medicine, like the science of society, is an inexact and at times a very doubtful one, with its experts giving contradictory counsel. Doctors of medicine differ, as every patient knows; and highly technical controversies rage between them.

[1] For a more complete account of this inquirer's intellectual adventures see my *Unseen Assassins* (Hamish Hamilton).

But does this mean that the inexpert layman has not been able to avail himself of medical knowledge? He has been able to make use of that knowledge to such purpose that we have managed to rid Western society of horrors as great as that of war itself, which once ravaged it—of plagues, pestilences, cholera, leprosy, ophthalmia, that were once a commonplace. No longer is one-third of the population of Great Britain leper, as it once was; no longer is the population of the country-side cut in half by Black Deaths; nor great cities made into charnel houses by bubonic plague. The work of getting rid of those horrors was the work of the inexpert layman using medical knowledge. In order so to use that knowledge the layman did not have to enter into the difficult, technical and disputed points of medicine. The layman of the West has achieved this amazing thing by taking over from medical science a few simple fundamental truths concerning which no doctor differs from another. The layman has discovered that the few things about which the doctors agree are in fact more important than those about which they differ. For doctors are agreed on this: broadly speaking, cholera, typhus, bubonic plague cannot be cured, but they can be avoided, prevented; for they are transmitted by micro-organisms. To avoid pestilence, keep sewage out of drinking water, infected vermin from houses. The layman has seen the point, and through the appropriate public bodies—sanitary authorities and so forth—he has applied this knowledge.

The layman did not enter into the controversies of the doctors. He could not have done so and did not need to. He managed to isolate the one or two truths about which there was, and (for anyone who can read evidence) could not be any difference of opinion, and has applied those truths.

Now, there are certain agreed truths in social science (we shall deal with them in the course of these pages), not any more disputable than the microbic theory of disease, nor inherently more difficult to understand. I suggest that if the layman could take over from social science these quite undisputed truths and apply them to public policy, then the pestilence of war in the form which it now threatens to engulf civilisation can be avoided much in the same way that the pestilence of bubonic plague has been avoided, without the public as a whole having to master the intricacies of the science which it uses.

Let us apply this analogy.

Suppose that in the years since the war the lay public had been able to see the reasons for, say, certain conclusions of economic science (as that, if Reparation and Debts are to be paid, the creditor nation must not refuse by tariffs or other devices to accept the debtor nation's goods), concerning which one can say (a) that they are no more difficult to understand than the microbic theory, and (b) are conclusions about which no competent economist in the world, whatever other differences there may be, differs from another. Had it acted upon that perception, then a large part of the economic pestilence which has come upon us would have been avoided; our problem, reduced in dimensions, would have been more nearly within the public capacity to handle, and the seeds of future war would not be so numerous nor so fertile. I have ventured elsewhere[1] the suggestion that peoples of the western nations, heir

[1] *From Chaos to Control.*

to all the learning of the ages, may wreck their civilisation from persistent failure to see the absurdity of propositions ("they must pay the cost of the war in money, not goods," "the way for nations to be rich is to sell more than they buy"; "the way for nations to be safe is to be stronger than their enemies"), which could be explained to an intelligent schoolboy in half an hour. The world threatens to drift to chaos, not from lack of knowledge in the sense that we lack the knowledge to cure cancer, but from failure to apply to public policy knowledge already possessed, which is of universal possession, often indeed self-evident.

§

Is the writer then about to present the reader with some magically easy solution of the whole problem? The reader will have followed the foregoing pages very inattentively if he has derived therefrom the impression that this author believes in solutions that are easy in the sense of asking nothing from the ordinary man.

Let us see just where the analogy I have drawn is valid and useful. Preventive medicine has not solved the whole problem of health. Though we no longer know leprosy, bubonic plague, cholera, we have other dreadful diseases (e.g. cancer) that far from being wiped away are increasing. But the abolition of the old pestilences has been (a) a tremendous achievement that has taken dreadful horrors from life; and (b) accomplished without demanding of the public miracles of understanding or miracles of social discipline, since the achievement is common to the West as a whole. To disparage any corresponding achievement in the field of politics on that ground that it is not worth while to wipe away leprosy or bubonic plague because you may die of cancer, is so silly as to strain human patience to the breaking-point. Yet in fact it is one of the commonest arguments used by the militarist in this connection. He usually resents suggestions for creating even the most rudimentary international society, on the ground that "you can never get rid of war." That settles it. Because you cannot cure all diseases, let us cure none. You get disease by the contamination of drinking water, but since disease of some kind is inevitable, we may as well drink sewage.

The problem which faces civilisation to-day, which must be solved on pain of utter destruction, is that of one particular type of war which arises between independent sovereign states—not as civil war arises because the accepted political system, the constitution, has broken down or been challenged, but because the accepted system is having its inevitable and logical result. To solve the problem of war between sovereign states would not solve the whole problem of international disorder or injustice, or even the whole problem of war and conflict. It would not settle the deeper question which underlies the possibility of civil war, or class war; of bitter feuds like those which mar the relations of religious groups, particularly in the East; of the bitter race relationships arising out of differences of colour (to say nothing of those just as bitter which arise out of extremely little differences or none). All this is true. Yet it is also true that the settlement of the international difficulty remains the major problem of our time. Unless it is settled the others can never be settled and its solution would make those others very much more manageable; just as the absence of periodic pestilences like cholera simplify the task of improving health in general. It would avoid a reef which will wreck the ship of civilisation if not avoided.

Now we know that this particular form of war arises as the logical result of the accepted method of defence in the international field: each sovereign unit uses power for the defence of its rights in such a way as automatically to deprive some other of *his* defence; the security of one is purchased at the price of the insecurity of another. History, repeated human experience, shows that this dilemma may be avoided by applying to the relations, whether of persons or of groups, another method of using force for defence: as the instrument of a rule or law, not necessarily perfectly just, or one which is even regarded by those who accept it as just, but sufficiently workable for the time being to be accepted provisionally; a principle which may be indicated roughly by saying that a litigant must not claim to be the judge and use his power to enforce judgment. All organised society is based on arming law in that sense, as opposed to arming the litigants. This fundamental principle of society the nations, in their relations with each other, disregard.

Now, the understanding of that principle is no more difficult than the understanding of the microbic theory of disease. But the understanding of the microbic theory is quite within the comprehension of people who disregard it, like the often very intelligent people of India and China. Although India possesses doctors and bacteriologists as competent as those of Europe, the mass of the population (whose potential capacity of understanding is just as great) refuse to apply available knowledge because its adequate understanding is hindered by countervailing theories of disease—fate, the anger of gods, devils, or scruples about the destruction of vermin—and because of certain habits of life and thought which militate against its application. These people do not want cholera, but neither do they want to change certain ancient sanitary habits. The habits would have to be changed to-day, while the cholera will only come in the future, or perhaps not at all. What happens in the East in respect of abolishing pestilence happens in the West in regard to abolishing war.

Smith is offered, as we have noted, a great variety of cures. But if he goes on the principle of making the utmost use of the known, commonplace, undoubted fact, which cannot be questioned, he will be able to eliminate a vast number of those alleged cures as not worth examination. The layman of mediaeval Europe was told that witches had the power to create pestilence; and that the cure for plague in his village was to drown the village witch. He finally shook himself free from that notion, not by reading Latin tomes on demonology (for the authors of those tomes were often the most ardent protagonists of that theory), but by applying to the problem knowledge which he possessed equally with the learned student of those tomes, but which the latter, sometimes by reason of his learning, failed to apply—such knowledge as that witches often themselves died of plague; that this old woman, alleged to be able to strike with death those whom she did not like, had for weeks been standing before a tribunal of judges threatening her with torture and death, and whom, therefore, she had no particular reason to like; and, accused of being able to pass through key-holes, had for weeks been imprisoned in a cell that contained a keyhole. If the layman had had to pass judgment upon all the various medical controversies, had been obliged for the purpose of deciding whether witches really did cause the Plague of London or the Black Death, to read Latin tomes on witchcraft and study Paracelsus, witch burning and bubonic plague would still rage in Europe and America. The layman did not follow that path at all. He said (often it is true without being conscious of the method which he was following) : "Let us take first what is certain and test the uncertain supposition by the known and certain fact." He applied Valery's description of philosophy, "An attempt to transmute what we know into what we should like to know."

So with Smith's decision about the cures of war which are offered to him. If he is able to reduce considerably the range of study he need undertake by eliminating those doctors who obviously have not yet made up their minds whether they want to cure the disease or not, he can reduce the range still more by eliminating the doctors whose cures are in conflict with what John Smith knows by his own experience to be true, in conflict with arithmetic and physical possibility. Indeed, by far the greatest amount of the literature urges cures which are based upon a disregard of arithmetic and physical possibility, as later we shall see.

The first fact to note, however, is that without any doubt we know the cause of war; we know, by repeated and unquestioned experience, what will stop it. Having established that point, we shall go on to inquire why the cure is not applied; how its application might be made possible.

## PART TWO

# WHAT WE KNOW OR MIGHT KNOW

# Chapter I

## WE KNOW THE CAUSE

Contrary to what seems general belief history gives us numberless examples of war being brought to an end over vast areas in which originally it had raged unchecked for untold generations; the Pax Romana, the Pax Germanica, the Pax Britannica, the Pax Italiana, to cite only a few. Where a group of sovereign and independent units combine into a federation for mutual defence, war ceases. The suggestive difference between the history of the British colonies of North America which learned how not to fight and of the Spanish colonies of South America which failed to learn shows that without certain antecedent political conditions neither psychological nor economic forces could normally produce war.

IT IS, we know, a dangerous thing to be ignorant of one's ignorance; it is just as dangerous to be ignorant of one's knowledge. Indeed, the former usually means the latter; means that one is ignorant of the commonplace knowledge which might check or correct an erroneous theory, a fallacious belief. The man in the old school tie who tells us gaily and with such assurance that efforts to stop war are futile or who elaborates weird and strange theories as to the cause of war, may not have much history, but he has sufficient, did he but apply it, to know that over vast areas of the earth where war had raged for centuries, it has been brought to an end, not once or twice, but again and again; and that this repeated experience of man enables us to know both the main cause and the main cure of war.

That knowledge does not of itself, of course, solve our problem. The application of the cure may involve at times a price we are justified in refusing to pay; may conceivably create a condition worse than the disease. Indeed, it may be said that we know the cause, we know the cure, but not how to induce the patient to take it. Let us start from the known.

War arises, and must arise, when separate groups, national or other, claim to be sovereign, independent of each other; each judge of its own rights in its relations with other similar groups, and each arming itself to enforce its own judgment, to "defend its rights." For if one sovereign unit is to be adequately armed for defence it must be stronger than any challenging its "rights." Then what becomes of the defence of that other? Security for one automatically destroys the security of the other. We describe this condition, in which each is his own defender of his own conception of his own rights, as anarchy, the absence of government or of organized society. Social theory would indicate, what experience proves, that out of that "principle of association" must inevitably come war.[1]

Anarchy may be ended—has often been ended—and law, a recognised rule of conduct, peace, established in one of two ways: by the extension of the authority of one powerful group or nation over less powerful ones, imposing the necessary rule; or by common agreement to observe the law, to give it authority. The first process we term, broadly, imperialism and the second federalism, although usually the process is partly compulsory and partly voluntary, and having begun in compulsion, may end in voluntary association (e.g., Canada beginning as a conquered state has developed

---

[1] From the political and economic point of view the chief cause of war is the organisation of society into national states each claiming complete sovereignty. And anything which would do away with the doctrine and practice of national sovereignty would go a long way towards preventing war. (Julian Huxley in *Challenge to Death,* Constable, London.)

into the freely co-operating member of a common-wealth).

History gives many instances of independent groups having contacts which provoke questions of conflicting rights being led to combine their power for mutual, co-operative, collective defence, so that any member which attempts to impose its judgment by force upon another faces, not merely the power of that other, but of the whole society. Common power stands behind a rule of conduct, law, designed to protect all.

The most striking example of the first method is, of course, the *Pax Romana*. It gave peace to the whole civilised world. We are apt to think of the civilised world as never having known peace—the prevention of war. It is quite untrue. For a period much longer than the history of the United States war between the nations of the known world came to an end.

Ludwig Friedlander[1] tells us that "the Empire gave two and a half centuries of peace, only occasionally and locally interrupted"; a condition since unrealised.

Contemporaries acknowledge these boons of peace, and security and regularity of intercourse. . . . Rome had similarly stayed the endless confusions of incessant war-ring states; she had united peoples and dynasties into one organisation of peace, one unbreakable ring. In the first two centuries after the death of the first Caesars the imperial revenue rose rapidly; and peace secured pros-perity. Hill and dale were cultivated; the mercantile marine increased, and trade between all countries. No-where were there wars, or battles, or bandits, or pirates. This was the majesty of the *Pax Romana*, which made

[1] *Roman Life and Manners*, translated by Leonard A. Magnus, Rout-ledge, p. 269.

Rome a sacred home, an eternal source of life, a secure anchorage; as though the gods had renewed the life of the world; all peoples prayed for the eternity of this gift of Rome.

As the common authority of Rome declined and the independence and sovereignty of separate groups developed, the Roman peace was replaced once more, of course, by war.

But the Roman experience was only one of many. In India, where sovereign nations or groups had fought endlessly for countless generations, the common authority of Britain for over a century has afforded peace between erstwhile warring states. It may be, of course, that the tyranny of Britain in India is such as to constitute too great a price to pay for peace between the Indian states. That is an entirely separate question. The fact is that the establishment of a common authority between formerly independent states has caused war to cease where once it raged.

We see the same fact—the creation of some common authority—explaining the disappearance of war when we examine the history of, say, the Italian states. So long as those states considered themselves sovereign and independent communities, they fought each other. The very cities, indeed, went to war with each other. Those wars were brought to an end by the Unification. In this case voluntary association as well as the growth of a central power played a part in the process. But the operating cause in the elimination of war is the same.

The history of Germany, which our grandfathers knew more commonly as "the Germanies," tells a similar story. For centuries wars raged between the independent principalities and kingdoms (at one time they numbered nearly three hundred). The German Union of 1871 secured peace between them.

The story of our own island enforces exactly the same lesson. For centuries the British islands were divided into separate kingdoms—once into very many independent kingdoms. When each was sovereign and independent they were continually at war—particularly the kingdoms into which that sister island, that now wants independence as a condition of peace, was divided. With the consolidation of the many sovereignties into one (which incidentally did not mean the disappearance of separate nationalities, languages, cultures, as witness the survival of the Welsh language and many aspects of Scottish nationality) there came peace.

The new world enforces the lesson no less insistently than the old; both in its negative aspect, when decay of a central authority provokes war where peace had existed previously; in its positive aspect, when the creation of a union brings peace where previously war had been. In South and Central America we see how the breakdown of the central authority of Spain gave rise to a number of independencies and thus to war between them; and in North America the inverse process of the creation between separate states of a common authority keeping the peace. This distinction between the course taken in the one case by the Spanish American and in the other by the English American states is singularly illuminating in this connection, and has a significance too little noted.

Spain's authority over her American colonies lasted for nearly three centuries. Her rule was incompetent and corrupt, involving gross oppressions and creating hardships and poverty beyond belief in the subject populations. But one colony or administrative area did not fight another. Over that vast area peace as between the separate colonies was maintained.

Comes the successful revolution of the Spanish colonies. Following that revolution, it was open to the separate colonies to follow the example set by the revolted colonies of Great Britain: to form some sort of federal bond, some agreement for common and mutual defence. But the main revolt of the Spanish colonies came half-a-century after the North American War of Independence, at a time when the doctrine of Nationalism was beginning to take a firm hold on the minds of men, and was already assuming an extremism which it had not developed in Washington's day. That explains partly, but only partly, as a subsequent chapter will show, why an area like Mexico and Central America, instead of becoming a federation, as the thirteen revolted colonies of Britain became, split into six separate republics, which immediately proceeded to go to war with each other and have been going to war with each other at frequent intervals ever since. Over a vast area which under a single sovereignty had known complete peace for two hundred and fifty years the fact of separation into independent units makes war endemic.

Mr. Aldous Huxley, whose researches into past civilisations has led him to study the history of Spanish America, has evidently been impressed, as this present writer[1] has so often been impressed, with the lessons in the subject which we may draw from Spanish-American history, especially when we compare it with the history

[1] Who, as a youth, travelled widely over Mexico and Central America.

of English-speaking America, which went through the same process of separation from the mother country. "If you would understand the politics of Europe," says Mr. Huxley somewhere, "study those of Central America." The hatreds between these artificially created states, the feuds and vendetta, have at times been as bitter as those which mark the history of, say, Germany and France. Speaking of the post-revolutionary history of Central America, Mr. Huxley says:[1]

> The newly fashionable idea of Nationalism was imported along with the idea of self-government. Applying the logic of this philosophy of hatred and division to their own immediate problems, the people of Central America tried to make each administrative district into an independent country. . . .
>
> The introduction of the nationalistic idea into Central America resulted in the dismemberment of a society which had hitherto been unquestionably one. Fellow subjects of the same king, speaking the same language, professing the same religion, and having every possible economic reason for remaining united, the Mexicans and Central Americans were constrained by the emotional logic of an imported theology of hatred to renounce all their ties of blood and culture.

What is true of the history of Central America is true in only slightly lesser degree of all Spanish America.

Compare this experience with that of the English colonies of North America, which have since become the United States, and which did manage to create a federal bond.

There was a period after the revolution of the thir-

[1] "Do We Require Orgies?" *The Yale Review*, Spring, 1934. pp. 140, 141.

teen American colonies of Great Britain in which it seemed exceedingly doubtful whether they would form a federation at all. There was nothing inevitable about their doing so. The Spanish-American colonies, when they revolted, did not; and the English-speaking colonies might not have done so, save for several fortuitous circumstances: the character and influence of this or that statesman amongst them, fear of the strength of the mother country. If Britain had been in reality a decadent state, or if Alexander Hamilton had not lived,[1] the revolted colonies would almost certainly have failed "to hang together in order not to hang separately."

If history had taken that turn, we might as easily have had a dozen nations (a French-speaking one, perhaps, on the St. Lawrence or in Louisiana; a Dutch-speaking one on the Hudson; a Spanish-speaking in California, etc.) just as we have a round dozen separate nations south of the Mexican border. We knew that if such independent nations had been formed in what is now the United States (especially with differences of language and culture), wars would have resulted, as they have between the independent nations formed from the Spanish American colonies, even though the latter have no differences of language and culture. (Note in passing that the national characteristics, linguistic and racial, which distinguish, say, Wales from England, and both from Scotland, are far greater than those which distinguish the Chileno and Peruvian, or the San Salvadorian and the Guatemalan.)

Put the illustration, as already suggested, in inverse form: Imagine that at some stage in the development

---

[1] And carried what our Marxians to-day would call the "Capitalist" view.

of Europe—at the breakdown, say, of the Western Empire—some degree of effective authority had grouped round, say, the Church, and the nations of Europe had become federalised states, like those of the American Union.[1] Then, though there might be civil war, as there has been civil war in the American Union, the problem of international war and that chaos in the international economic field as we know it to-day would not confront us.

§

Let us consider certain caveats that the reader will be disposed to enter.

He might claim that I am insisting upon what is a mere truism: "If there were no nations, nations would not go to war." We know, it may be argued, that if nations abandon their nationhood, their separate cultures and distinctive ways of life, we could have peace. But we also know, it may be added, that nations will not abandon their nationhood and cultural and traditional differences, so that the problem is not one in fact of abolishing anarchy, but of abolishing nationality.

This is a profound error. It is not the existence of nations, or the fact of nationality, or differences of language and culture which are the cause of war.

Separate nationalities have for centuries remained in undisturbed and unthreatened peace. Again and again it has been proved that cultural, racial and national

[1] Boniface VIII by a Bull claims that "all Kings, Emperors, and other sovereigns, whoever they may be, are subject, like all other men, to be summoned before the Apostolic Courts, for every sort of cause; for we, by the permission of God, command the whole Universe." (R. F. Wright, *Medieval Internationalism*, p. 89.)

[117]

differences are perfectly compatible with the maintenance of peace; and again and again it has been proved that identity of race, language and culture is no guarantee against war. The independent nation-states of Spanish America, which so readily go to war with each other, speak the same language, profess the same religion, inherit the same culture. The German states, which, when they were independent, went to war with each other so readily, shared a sufficiently common culture to be made to-day the basis of a passionate feeling of common nationality. This same sense of unity dominates in only less degree a group of Italian states which but yesterday, historically, constantly fought each other.

But while we thus see nation-states with a common language, culture, race, religion, historical background, waging, generation after generation, bitter wars with each other, we see peace maintained between most diverse cultural, racial or linguistic groups like those embraced within the frontiers respectively of India, Canada, South Africa, Switzerland, the British Isles.

When Wales and Scotland were politically independent, they fought with England. In many respects Scotland and England have remained nations, one clinging rather tenaciously to its separate tongue and the other to many peculiarities of law and tradition. But they recognize a common sovereignty, co-operate for mutual defence, and war between them has disappeared.

That the relations of nations should be constitutionally organized no more involves the disappearance or subjugation of national cultures than the fact that the changed political position of the Church involves the disappearance of religion.

# WE KNOW THE CAUSE

It may be true that the nation makes a corporate body, deeply rooted in psychological forces. But there are other such corporate bodies too: the church, the caste, the race, the clan; sometimes the trade union, the club, the political party. Some of these, like the church (the race, in certain circumstances, may be another), claim loyalties which in certain spheres transcend loyalty to any purely secular organisation. But even the church does not demand (though it did once, and the fact is significant) that it shall be the state and the only state; refusing to recognise a sovereignty outside the Church; insisting that its members obey no rules unless devised by Church authority, be ruled by none but themselves. It is a strange thing that different churches —forms of association representative of God on earth— can in matters outside their province submit to another sovereignty, can render unto Caesar the things that are Caesar's, but that the nation, so obviously human in origin, tends under the impulse of the nationalist idea to set up this claim to sovereignty in all things; to refuse any partnership with other similar bodies for the purpose of agreeing upon necessary rules of the road and a common means of defence.

Separate nationalities need no more produce war than separate churches need produce war (as they did in the past) once the corporate body of the nation, like that of the church, is prepared to surrender omnipresent sovereignty. War arises out of nationality only when we attach to it the claim for a form of independence and sovereignty which constitutes, as we shall see presently, a denial of right: The denial to others of the rights we claim for ourselves.

Some of the plainest facts of daily experience and

[119]

history show the utter invalidity of certain commonly accepted assumptions concerning alike the psychology and the economics of war.

We speak of the hatreds of nationalism as things inborn, as causes of war which, since they are psychological, no political device, or reform, or agitation can affect. In the same way we speak of the economic rivalry of states as something which no change of political ideas or political machinery can seriously modify.

Whereas, it is quite plain that neither the psychological nor the economic conflict would or could have arisen but for certain antecedent *political* conditions created by *political* ideas.

Guatemala hates Honduras with a hatred as deadly as that which characterises the attitude of France to Germany. But "Guatemala" is a purely political creation. For nearly three centuries those two groups did not make "nations" at all, and it no more entered the heads of the people of the Spanish province which is now Guatemala to entertain war feelings towards the people of the Spanish province which is now Honduras than it occurs to the people of Norfolk to nurse war feelings about the people of Suffolk. The political entity had to be created and the notion of separateness to gather round that creation before either the psychological or the economic conflict could arise at all. And history gives plenty of examples of the thing acting the other way on, of political union ending psychological feuds. Bavaria and Prussia were bitter enemies: pundits explained the hatred engendered by the rival patriotisms as due to deep psychological causes, beyond reason, beyond the domain of conscious theory or idea. To maintain this separateness was the first duty of the patriot on both sides. Comes Hitler with his conception of "one folk"—the one folk being, not Prussians on the one side or Bavarians on the other, but "Germany." The new political conception reverses completely the direction of the passion: the same passion which once stood *for* the separateness of Bavaria now inspires the energy directed towards abolishing the separateness. *That we should fight is perhaps part of our nature, our biological make-up. What we fight about is part of our nurture, is determined by the intellectual concepts which gain possession of our minds.*

Some similar truth underlies the notions of economic conflict, which undoubtedly have their part in the causation of war. Had Hamilton failed in his efforts to unify the Thirteen Colonies and had New England become one nation and Pennsylvania another, we should have heard endlessly of the competition of the trade of Pennsylvania with that of New England, of fights between them for markets, their rivalry of interest. As it is, if you were to talk to-day to a New Englander about the commercial competition of Pennsylvania, it would be as meaningless to him as to talk of the economic competition of the Baptists with the Episcopalians.

But he quite understands "the competition of Canada"; Canadian goods "compete" with his, and he has successfully demanded tariffs to keep them out. Some years ago there was an American movement, widely supported, for the annexation of Canada. It would have been considered by most economic nationalists a great gain. But the same goods which he now deems so harmful would, in the event of Canada being part of the United States, freely enter—the same goods made by the same people would then have to be regarded as being as harmless economically as those coming from Pennsylvania.

Again, the economic rivalry depends upon political separateness; the idea of rivalry cannot even be conceived until the political separateness has arisen.

§

Now, the practical question in our immediate problem is this: What degree of federalism, of co-operation between existing separate units is the indispensable minimum of peace? The United States represents to-day a very closely knit federative union. But peace can be maintained between units possessing a far larger measure of autonomy than that possessed by the individual state in the American Union, as the maintenance of peace between the separate nations of the British Commonwealth clearly shows. The Dominions have become, since the Statute of Westminster (which merely recognised and rendered official an already existing condition), independent nations with a nationalism which on its economic side is sometimes exceedingly strong. But they are federalised in one important particular, though the constitution which ensures federalisation in this particular is (like the British Constitution) an unwritten one, non-statutory.

The nations of the Commonwealth are in fact, though not in statutory form, federalised for defence. Japan is perfectly aware that in attacking Australia she would be faced by the British navy and British national resources, though that navy is not one which Australians (who have one of their own) help to maintain. The

British navy stands in fact for the defence of Dominions who do not contribute to its cost, because those Dominions, in case of need, stand for the defence of Britain, as their contributions in man power in the years 1914-1918 and the financial burdens then assumed clearly show.

The British Empire has no written constitution, no common parliament, no common tariff, no customs union, no common budget, no Imperial army, no Imperial navy, no Imperial police, no Imperial court. Its nations are for the most part economically autonomous and their relations are often marked by bitter economic rivalry and disagreement, as the Ottawa Conference clearly revealed. We see bitter racial and religious strife in India, Ireland, South Africa, and (less intensely) Canada. The bonds which unite the nations of the Empire are less formal than those which are supposed to unite the nations of the Geneva League. Yet the Empire is a great political reality. For, though it has federalised nothing else, it has in fact federalised defence. And for the purposes of peace between its parts that is all it needs to federalise. But that degree of federalisation is the indispensable minimum. The experience of the Empire indicates at what point understanding between the nations of the world as a whole needs to be brought about.

## Chapter II

## INDIVIDUAL DEFENCE DENIES RIGHT: THE DEMONSTRATION OF RECENT HISTORY

The War arose because a potential enemy claimed a preponderance of power that would have left us defenceless. We preferred to possess the preponderance which leaves him defenceless. Each thus puts his power, not behind right, as we may sincerely believe, but behind a denial of right, the denial to the other of that right of judgment or superior power we claim. We used our power of judgment after the war to make the Treaty of Versailles. The Germans now want power to make another treaty which will be worse, compelling us to unmake it, *da capo,* until civilisation has perished.

THE lesson of the last chapter amounts to this: International anarchy is the cause of war, and anarchy might be described most fittingly in this connection as the method of defence by which each political unit is its own defender, and refuses to assume any obligation on behalf of mutual or collective defence by support of a general law or rule by which all members of the combination may be protected. The degree of federalism necessary for peace as an alternative to the present anarchy can be extremely loose, permitting a great degree of independence for the constituent units. The federal bond or rule of partnership need cover one point only: that of defence, the restraint of war. The only thing we need to internationalise is defence. If each is left his own defender, has to depend purely upon his own power for his defence, war must result.

Let us see why.

The process can best be revealed by the study of the events of the last twenty years, the circumstances which preceded the war, the peace which followed it, and the situation which has followed the peace.

A British cabinet minister, in a speech to a gathering of Manchester merchants a year or so before the outbreak of the last war, said this:

> Gentlemen, there is just one way in which you can make your country secure and have peace, and that is to be so much stronger than your prospective enemy that he won't dare to attack you. This, I submit, is a self-evident proposition which should be the guiding light of our national policy.[1]

Several hundred eminent commercial men applauded this "self-evident" proposition to the echo.

Let us examine it.

Here are two nations or two alliances likely to quarrel. How shall both be secure and keep the peace? Our cabinet minister replies that they will be defended and keep the peace when each is stronger than the other. Defence for one is to be achieved by depriving the other of it. The security of one is the insecurity of the other.

Now that fact is controvertible. The self-evident proposition of our cabinet minister is a defiance of arithmetic, of physical fact. One would assume that the very first question to be asked by men accustomed to dealing with affairs, to thinking with the other man's mind, would be: "Can we expect the other party to go without defence, to accept a position of inferiority which we refuse to accept?"

But plainly that question is not asked, it is simply forgotten and ignored by those who would persuade us that, in order to avoid the outcome of the 1914 situa-

[1] I must apologise to the reader for having quoted this masterpiece about a thousand times.

tion, we have merely to pursue the same policy which produced it. There is plainly no realisation of the fact that defence by individual power involves the use of force to deny Right, to deny to another the right of defence we claim.

As these lines are being written, more than twenty years after that meeting and after the lessons of the war, exactly the same arguments are being used almost daily by half the newspapers in Britain in the demand for an air force "second to none," the arguments following the familiar line of the arguments about naval power before the war. "If we can get X squadrons of planes we shall be stronger than the other, and secure." The same bland disregard of the other party; the same assumption that the motives which animate us won't animate him. The truth being, of course, that by the time we have the X additional planes, he too will have added planes, and security will be as far off as ever. The late Lord Fisher was quite sure that the building of a Dreadnought would place the British fleet beyond challenge. It did nothing of the sort, of course. It started a competition which, by rendering obsolete the existing type of battleship in which Great Britain had an overwhelming superiority against the world, made the British fleet very much weaker than it had been before the Dreadnoughts were built. On the other side, Admiral Tirpitz, the German, used to publish calculations that by the addition of such and such units to the German fleet, Germany would reach "security" by a given date. His calculations never made any allowance for the fact that German building would provoke British reply, so that his date of "security" was always indefinitely receding. That method of defence

[126]

destroyed utterly the Germany that he set out to make "secure."

If advocates of this method of defence got as far as admitting that the other side would reply to increases, the next step of their argument was that when the resultant war was fought, the Germans—or the British— would have learned their lesson, and the world would have peace.[1]

The Germans don't seem to have learned the lesson. We are told—with truth—that they are a graver danger than ever, and the net outcome of the whole episode seems to have been to transfer the contest from the sea to the air.

§

It is true that we do not much like to talk of "preponderance" as we used to talk in naval discussions before the War and demand two and even three-power standards. We prefer to talk of equality, "parity" of armament as the best situation for defence. We discussed naval parity with America for a long time, France military parity with Italy and, at the moment of writing, we are in the midst of discussions of air parity. Parity has a more respectable sound. We shall be saved, as someone remarked, by Faith, Hope and Parity.

[1] Professor Headlam in his war-time book *The Issue* asks "When will Peace come?" And answers:

"It will come when Germany has learnt the lesson of the War, when it has learnt, as every other nation has had to learn, that the voice of Europe cannot be defied with impunity. . . . Men talk about the terms of peace. They matter little. With a Germany victorious no terms could secure the future of Europe, with a Germany defeated, no artificial securities will be wanted, for there will be a stronger security in the consciousness of defeat."

But the principle is just as impossible to work as was the other, for the simple reason that it is physically impossible to say when two nations *are* equal in power, to say what *is* parity. During the naval discussions we pointed out to the Americans that one proposed arrangement gave them more power in a certain category of ships. The Americans retorted: "Yes, but look at your coaling stations!" How many coaling stations go to how many ships? Nobody has ever been able, or ever will be able, to say. It was during that discussion that a still more elusive problem in the equation of varying factors of national power came up. Britain had built a new type of cruiser mounting an eight-inch gun, which the American experts were disposed to imitate, and the problem was to establish how the power of the cruiser mounting a six-inch gun compared with that mounting an eight-inch gun. The experts in Washington made an interesting discovery. In clear weather an eight-inch gun cruiser had undoubted superiority, because it could outrange the other. In foggy weather the six-inch gun cruiser had superiority, because, operating at close quarters, it could manœuvre more quickly. "Well, now," said the Americans, "consider the frequency of foggy weather on the British coasts compared with our weather. That gives your six-inch gun cruisers a power comparable to eight-inch gun cruisers on this side of the water, where weather is apt to be clearer. We really must take that climatic factor into consideration in the allocation of power." How much fog goes to how many cruisers? It prompted a senator in Washington at the time to say that among the factors we had to equate were fogs, bogs and hogs.

## DEFENCE AND RIGHT

A discussion along these lines could, of course, go on to the end of time, and the only purpose that it serves is to enable the experts of each nation to prove that, despite steadily enlarged budgets, his nation is still disgracefully under-armed because the other has more resources in fogs, or bogs, or hogs.

And if parity *could* be achieved it would not advance us the least in the world. For, assume that your two states have, after infinite technical difficulties, arrived at some sort of parity; then one of them goes and makes a new diplomatic alliance. That, of course, upsets the whole thing.

For whether our armament is adequate depends upon what it has to meet. A degree of naval armament completely adequate, if the enemy is, say, Finland, is quite inadequate if it has to meet, unaided, two or three great states. Unless the term "adequate," in respect of arms, is to be exactly as meaningless as talking of "the size of a piece of cheese," we must be able to say: "Adequate for what? Adequate to meet what enemy? To cope with what diplomatic situation? To enforce what policy?" Just as certainly as the phrase "enough money" must, if it is to mean anything at all, imply an answer to the question: "Enough for what—a cigar or a diamond, a lead pencil or a country estate?", so must the phrase "enough ships" or "enough aeroplanes" carry an implication of a given situation.

Yet it is a measure of the intelligence usually applied to the discussion of this problem that some admiral or general, speaking with all the authority and dogmatism of a specialist and technician, can stir the whole country, and lend himself to sensational newspaper exploitation by declaring, *ex cathedra,* that "we have not enough

[129]

ships," without even the vaguest hint of the size of the enemy, or the size of our allies, or the policy we propose to enforce. (The admiral would, of course, retort that those things depend upon the politicians, which is true, and which is also the reason why the admiral, as such, has no special competence to pronounce on the matter at all.)

Incidentally, that is why Isolationism is bound to break down sooner or later if it is an armed isolationism. Suppose we possess armament adequate to meet a state or an alliance that we regard as the potential enemy. We have parity. Then the potential enemy makes a new alliance. What do *we* do? Add to our armament to meet the power of the new unit? He makes another alliance. What do we do then? We too begin to make alliances. An alliance is an arm, like tanks or submarines. If the enemy resorts to it, we must. Isolation is possible if we don't compete in arms at all. If we do, then it must be very quickly abandoned.

At the time of the discussion of naval parity with America this present writer remarked, a little wearied with all the technical details involved: "I am rather less interested in the calibre of the guns than in the direction in which they are finally going to shoot. At us, or at a common enemy? It really makes a difference." That, of course, is the supreme question of all in this problem of effective defence: "Who is going to be with us and who against us?" And that depends on policy: upon what we shall regard as attack; upon what conduct on the part of foreigners will cause our power to be brought into the field against them.

§

To point that out usually occasions surprise. "But it is obvious," the usual retort comes, "what policy lies behind our armaments; it is the policy of defence." [1]

If you ask John Smith what he means by defence, his reply (it has been given to the present writer on scores of occasions) would be to the effect that he means by defence what the householder means by defence when he puts locks on his doors, or takes a poker to the burglar. "By defence, I mean that the foreigner shall kindly keep out."

Let us see.

In the last thousand years or so Britain has fought very many foreign wars. Since 1066 without any exception whatever they have had this peculiarity: they have all been fought in someone else's country. I once tried to make a list of those countries that have never seen the British army or the British navy in any form, and when I was through, the list was a short one consisting, I think, of two countries—Switzerland and Greenland. There is one country, however, where, for very nearly all those thousand years, our army has never fought a foreign foe: this country.

If defence really means what the householder means when he puts locks on his doors, what were we doing on all those occasions in other people's houses?

It does not mean that our numberless wars were

[1] "What this country can do is to set straightway about the task of becoming strong in arms. No country fears us as a possible aggressor. No country, on the other hand, will be inclined to launch an attack when there is every probability of a powerfully armed Britain being lined up with the defence. Our influence will be as placatory as that of a policeman in a crowd." *Sunday Dispatch*, 18th March, 1934.

aggressive wars because they were fought in other people's countries.  It means that defence cannot be
merely defence of the nation's soil; that there are very
many things besides invasion which we or any great
country would regard as attack and which would cause
us to fight.

Our history in that respect is not peculiar.  It is, on
the contrary, common to all great states.  Take America,
interesting because her declared policy is non-entangle-
ment, detachment from the affairs of the outside world,
isolation.  In her brief history as a foreign state she has
had quite a number of foreign wars and been near to
several more.  Again, not one was fought to repel
invasion.  They have all been fought in someone else's
country.  America had been independent for only a few
years when she was sending her navy into the Mediter-
ranean to fight the Barbary States; she nearly fought
France; she did, in 1812, fight Britain (the war beginning with the invasion of Canada) ; she fought Mexico,
China, Nicaragua, Spain, Germany.  Not one of these
was to "keep out the burglar," to repel invasion.  One
historian has calculated that American troops have
landed on foreign soil about one hundred times—and
her history does not yet go back two centuries.

Let us agree that not one of these wars was aggressive
or provocative on the part of either Britain or America.
(We are dealing with the two nations that typify the
non-aggressive, "saturated," satiated nations, favouring
the maintenance of the territorial *status quo*.)  Yet not
one was to repel invasion, or even, perhaps, a con-
templated invasion.

The meaning is plain: Defence must include very
many things besides the mere defence of the nation's

soil; it must include the defence of the nation's interests in such matters as those relating to access to undeveloped territory, the settlement of new land, free and assured use of this or that narrow strait, passage through that inter-oceanic canal, protection of citizens in disorderly countries, extra-territoriality in the Far East, capitulations in the Near East, rights on the High Seas . . . the list is endless.

Now, plainly there can be honest difference of opinion about such things, and wars arise precisely because the difference *is* honest, because nations disagree, sincerely, passionately, as to what their respective rights are in these matters.  Men cannot usually be persuaded to die for what they know to be wrong; nor to give their fortunes, their sons, their happiness in such a cause.  The more sincere, the more passionate each side is in believing its own view to be the just and right and honourable one, the greater is the likelihood of war arising out of the dispute.

The assumption that our rights are as self-evident, as settled, as agreed, as that the silver spoons Mr. John Smith has honestly bought and paid for belong to him and not to Mr. William Sykes, begs the whole of the question which constitutes the problem of war.

When educated men say: "Of course we shall defend our rights," and assume thereby that there can be no dispute as to what those rights are, one wonders whether they have spent even an hour in considering with an impartial mind the other side of any dispute in which our country has been involved: the dangerous disputes with America about sea rights, for instance, which led to one war and so very nearly to others; whether they have ever considered both sides of any of the numberless

[133]

territorial disputes of the Balkans and elsewhere. How is it possible, when going into the *pros* and *cons* of these interminable quarrels, to say that right and wrong is as clear as the ownership of the silver spoons which Mr. Sykes would take, that "national defence" approximates to the action of Mr. John Smith protecting his property with a poker, and that the issues involved are as simple?

But if defence means, as it must, defence of our rights in a dispute with others, note where the demand for preponderance of "power for defence" leads you. One state says to another:

> It is quite true that we ask for greater power than you. But we give you our most solemn assurance that that power will be used purely for defence. That is to say, when we get into a dispute with you as to what your rights are and ours are in a given matter, where it is a question of whether you are right or we are right, what we mean by defence is that we shall be in a position to be judge of that question, and so much stronger than you that you will have to accept our verdict without any possibility of resistance or appeal.

If a foreign nation should hold that language to us, what would be our retort? We should reply with perfect truth that the demand was outrageous, that it was the demand of one of the litigants to be the judge.

Then why do we ask foreigners to occupy a position which we refuse to occupy when they ask us?

This claim for preponderance means putting our might, not behind right, as we honestly believe, but behind the denial of right: the denial to the other party of that right of judgment which we claim for ourselves, the denial to him also of the means of defence we claim for ourselves.

Is that so or not?

For thirty years I have asked that question, and for thirty years been without an answer even pretending to justify on moral grounds the position which we all take. Englishmen reply sometimes to this effect:

> The dilemma is just a logician's artificial antithesis. Of course, when we ask for preponderance of power over another we do, in a sense, deny to him the right we claim. But let us face facts. The foreigner must know that our power will not be used for aggressive purposes. Why should it be? Have they anything we want? Haven't we got enough? For a century our navy was supreme. Was it ever used aggressively? Can any nation say that it wronged them? If, therefore, foreigners pretend that they fear our preponderant power will be used aggressively, they cannot be sincere, and must be themselves contemplating aggression, which is one reason the more why we should keep our end up.

Which, of course, is exactly the way that foreign nations—the American, the French, the German and Italian—talk, though no one of them will believe that the others are sincere in so doing.

Before the war there was a good deal that was plausible in the view just quoted. Our potential command of the sea did, it is true, ask foreigners to be content with an inferior position, did ask them to place their foreign trade at the mercy of our preponderant power, did put them in the position of being able to use the highway of the world only by our grace, and

not as of right, did ask an attitude of "playing second
fiddle," which, when suggested for ourselves, we
declared to be a craven one for any great people to
accept. But we did not abuse our position. We managed for nearly a century to avoid all but one continental war, and the acceptance of British naval
supremacy had become a habit with the nations. Had
not Admiral Tirpitz taken over lock, stock and barrel
the propaganda of our own Navy League, and Admiral
Fisher undermined our naval supremacy by introducing
the Dreadnought, we might have created a sort of
Monroe Doctrine of the sea that other nations would
have accepted (as the nations have accepted the American doctrine), and made of the British navy something
in the nature of a world police, a real factor for peace.

But the war, and still more the peace which followed,
has made any such solution for ever impossible.

Early in the present century we realised that sea-
power of itself was not defence enough. If, in the
impending Franco-German duel, France was utterly
overcome by Germany, France's colonies taken from
her, her channel ports transferred to Germany, then
indeed we should be reduced to defencelessness.

We argued:

Germany's victory over the French would make her
so preponderant that in any dispute we should simply
be at her mercy, in a position of complete defencelessness, having no means of effective resistance, no
means of defending our national rights. Our rights
would be at the mercy of her judgment, not ours.
She might, of course, use her preponderance of power
well; but then she might not.

If it is asked what we were defending when we declared war on Germany, the short answer is that we were defending the right to have any defence at all.

§

That is the true story of the war. The rest—the Belgian Treaty, the question of who mobilised first and so forth—is largely irrelevant, or incidental, secondary to the main purpose of preserving a position in the world which permitted the defence of our national interests and rights. The destruction of France would have left us defenceless. In defending France, as we said a thousand times during the war (and are beginning now in phrases, like Mr. Baldwin's "our frontier is the Rhine," to say again), we were defending ourselves. And given the fact of the international anarchy, it was a perfectly honourable position.

We said:

A state of national defencelessness, like that which German preponderance would involve, is a position no free people should consent to occupy. Rather should we die.

So far, we were undoubtedly right. Not quite so right when we added, as we did:

"We therefore propose that Germany shall occupy that position."

And to prove to her that she could with safety, so far as her national rights were concerned, accept our preponderance, that she could trust us to be judge of the dispute, though we were also litigant, we made the Treaty of Versailles. Would anyone in Britain to-day have the temerity to declare that that Treaty is an entirely just document? No one even pretends that it is just. Indeed, our isolationist papers which were, at the time of the making of the Treaty, most claimant in demanding that it be made still more severe, now cite it almost daily as one of the reasons why we should have nothing to do with the Continent and make no engagements that might involve us in the disputes arising from it.

§

Whenever one has occasion to point out that under the old system of defence by competitive power the defence of one automatically kills the defence of the other, there is almost always a feeling that the point is a purely theoretical one; that the preponderant British navy has always stood for justice and right throughout the world, and that on the basis of experience foreigners may fairly be asked to accept its preponderance. "When has it ever stood for anything but justice," asks the Briton, with indignant resentment at any implication to the contrary.

Yet such defenders of the old order are often extremely severe critics of the Treaty of Versailles. Do they face the fact at all that the British Navy made that Treaty—that is to say British naval plus French military power? Much that is at present incomprehensible to many sincere Englishmen, passionately convinced that British power could never be used to promote injustice, might perhaps be made understandable if they would face realistically the fact (which their minds might capitalise) that

### THE BRITISH NAVY MADE THE TREATY OF VERSAILLES

(And Americans might remember that their navy helped the British to do it.)

Had we been free to refuse the demands of French intransigence, we could doubtless have made a better treaty, or quietly amended in due course the one we did make. But we were not free. We had to "stand by our allies" ("Hats off to France" when she invades the Ruhr). It is part of the process of this method of defence that, in order to secure the necessary alliance, you have to agree to the ally's view of what he is entitled to, as he agrees to yours. We stand by France's view of her rights in Morocco as she stands by ours in the case of Germany's colonies. And, being compelled to "stand by our allies," we were not free to stand by any principle of right or workability unless that principle agreed with an ally's views. This inevitable feature of the competitive or Balance of Power Method, is dealt with more fully in a subsequent chapter.

In any case, those who now suffer under the Treaty regard it as the work of British naval power *plus* French military might. But for that combination it could never have been made.

The German argument now runs:

The Versailles Treaty shows what comes of being weaker than your opponent. You can never hope for justice unless you are stronger. We shall gather our strength for justice, and one day win it by the power of our right arm.

[139]

If and when Germany becomes sufficiently strong, as she will certainly become if we retire from any further concern in European affairs, she will make a new Treaty. Will it be any juster than the one we made? It will, of course, be still more unjust, for the Germans, particularly Hitlerised Germans, are no more fit than British or French to be judges in their own cause.

A *Times* correspondent writes from Germany:

> Although at present there is no intention of external war, yet National-Socialist Germany is determined to have her grievances redressed—if not by peace, then by war. These grievances are both territorial and denial of equality. As a young leader put it: "We must have a standing army, second to none, lining, fully equipped, our military frontiers which are the same as our political ones. These must be drawn *in accordance with what we Germans consider just and proper for the German race.*"

It would be extremely interesting to know what rearrangements General Goering, or even the author of *Mein Kampf,*[1] sitting as victors over a defeated Europe (defeated, it may be, because Britain had decided that she was unconcerned with what happened on the continent) would consider as doing justice to the German race.[2] Even if they took the present Treaty of Versailles

---

[1] In *Mein Kampf* Herr Hitler writes: "Oppressed lands are not brought back into the pale of a united Reich by fiery protests, but by the thrusts of a mighty sword . . . not by passionate appeals to Almighty God or by the fluent tongue of polished parliamentarians, but by the armed power of a polished sword and bloody combat!" (Pages 708-710 of the German edition but omitted from the English. See Mr. Robert Dell's *Germany Unmasked*.)

[2] Herr Wilhelm Stapel in a publication entitled *Der Christliche Staatsman* (!) writes: "We are Germans, and as Germans we are the best no matter whether we are in a minority or a majority. If there

and applied to its authors its general principles, we should get a result concerning which one may say with complete certitude this: Its victims would immediately set about preparing to liberate themselves from it by a new war. For, of course, settlements made by one of the parties to a dispute steadily get worse, as first one side is judge and then the other "gets even" by a new settlement when it is his turn to be victor. When Bismarck sat at Versailles (for that of 1919 is the second Franco-German settlement made there) he made a Treaty by all odds more moderate than the one Clemenceau, sitting in the same place nearly fifty years later, thought it wise to demand.

So, almost certainly, we should be among the victims of the second German-made Versailles Treaty and should then set about doing what Germany is now doing (with so much success) : Evade the disarmament provisions and get ready for the next "war for justice," (and though not a war *for* justice it would be a war against injustice). We might be successful in it. Then would be our turn to make a punitive Treaty. Would it be less severe than that of 1919? As much worse as there would be more wrongs to avenge than we could profess to have had in 1919. So that that Treaty would justify on the other side another "war against injustice" *da capo* . . . until all justice, all kindliness, all mercy, all civilisation have perished from the earth.

were only two Germans living in the whole of Poland they would be more than the millions of Poles, just because they were Germans" and this particular Christian statesman concludes therefore that the Germans would have the right, if they could, to subject the Poles to their domination.

The principle opens up interesting vistas for those countries where "two Germans" may happen to live.

And, again, each war *will* be truly a war against injustice, though never a war *for* justice. For its ultimate purpose will be to compel the other party to accept the very injustice against which each is fighting (i.e. no adequate defence); to compel the other to occupy a position of inferiority of power, which each declares he would rather die than accept for himself.

Defence by preponderance of the nation's individual power must, with however little intention, constitute a denial of justice, a denial of right.

There is the dilemma at the heart of the international anarchy. In the use of force in the international field, we turn upside down the principles of justice and right which we apply within the nation and there know to be indispensable to any workable society.

To remedy that anomoly is the first step; and the minimum. So long as that fundamental anarchy exists one can say that war does not arise from obscure and hidden motives, but is the natural and to be expected result of something obviously and definitely wrong in the political organisation of society.

Let us be quite clear where the error lies.

## Chapter III

# PLEDGES AND PEACE: THE WAR'S LESSON

Most of the twenty-two states that entered the war were free from any commitment so to do. Freedom from commitment (e.g. the United States' position) did not keep them out; commitment *would* have kept them out, since if Germany had known that by following a certain line twenty states would range themselves against her, she would not have followed that line and there would have been no war. The lesson is therefore that if states arm they must make known beforehand what will cause them to fight. Unless a state will so commit itself arms can never be an effective instrument of defence.

THE most significant as well as the most undeniable lessons of the Great War are those most commonly overlooked, evaded, or turned upside down.

The first is this:

*Freedom from pledges to go to war did not keep out great states that were drawn in. Commitment would have kept them out. For if Germany had known that by following a certain line twenty states would have entered the war against her, she would not have followed that line, and there would have been no war. The power of most of the states that fought Germany was therefore bereft of peace-keeping effect. It did not act as a deterrent to aggression because the potential aggressor was unaware that he would have to meet it.*

Let us look dispassionately at the facts.

Britain was pledged under the Belgian treaty to resist violation of Belgian neutrality. But up to the very last moment Germany did not know whether by keeping out of Belgium she would keep Britain out of the war; and had some ground for believing that Britain would enter the war in any case one day, whatever Germany's policy in this or other matters might be.  British power as a means of securing respect for the law of Belgian neutrality, or any law, was therefore neutralized since Germany felt that she would incur the penalties whether she obeyed the law or not.  The fact that we were not free to withhold the penalties if the law were respected deprived those penalties of force as sanctions of that law.  Our semi-pledges to Allies deprived our pledges to the law of deterrent effect.

Most of the states opposed to Germany had no previously accepted obligation to take action against her; America had not, Japan had not, Italy had not, Roumania had not, China had not.  None of the belligerent states had commitments similar to those of Article XVI of the Covenant, which now so disturb its critics.  Yet despite freedom from such pledges, more than a score of belligerents were quickly entangled.

Non-commitment did not keep these states out; for they were not committed and they were drawn in.

Certain allies, it is true, had obligations to each other, but neither of the opposing sides knew what conduct on its part would ensure the support—or opposition—of others.

Not merely did the potential power of nations in the position of the United States, or Italy, or Japan, fail to check any aggressive tendencies of Germany, but it could not possibly have had that effect in the absence of predetermined policy touching its use, since Germany was unaware that her designs would encounter the hostility of those nations and that she would have to meet their opposition.  Italian power before the War did not check Germany's war purpose, and could not have done so, because Italy before the war was Germany's Ally, and

Germany had hoped to have Italian force on her side. American power did not and could not have checked German aggression in the years before the war, because no one living had the faintest idea that it would be brought into the field against Germany's political schemes. And even to the last German statesmen were evidently, in view of the indecision of British policy, gambling on the hope that Britain would keep out of the war.[1] In any case, the pre-war potential power of states in the position of America and Italy was as a deterrent of German aggression obviously, in view of the absence of any exact knowledge of where they would stand, exactly *nil*.

But had Germany known for a virtual certainty beforehand that by following a certain line of policy she would bring into the field against her, not merely France and Russia, but also Britain, Italy, Japan, the United States and a whole gathering of lesser states, she would have modified that line and the war would, in all human probability, have been avoided. If, in other words, public opinion on the Allied side had been ready to accept as a matter of deliberate policy *only those involvements which events a year or two later were destined to compel it to accept* then it is reasonable to assume that there would have been no war. It would not, in fact, have meant an increase of commitment or entanglement because very soon the nations were fully committed and entangled. But if, instead of being com-

---

[1] I have seen a letter from a very highly-placed German personality, in the confidence of the Kaiser and his ministers, stating: "I give it as my considered opinion that if early in July 1914 Germany had known for certain that Britain would support France unequivocally, there would have been no war."

mitted after the event, they had been committed beforehand, the war would have been avoided. The
difference between the two situations would have been
not the degree of real entanglement but the degree of
pre-commitment. A situation involving pre-commitment would have made avoidance of war possible, a
hand-to-mouth situation, dealing with each step as it
came up, made war inevitable.

That type of sanction, of diplomatic pre-commitment,
is the minimum which the world must accept if it is
(a) to rest defence successfully upon arms at all, and
(b) to prevent the possession of arms leading ultimately
to war.

This is the most vital, the most tragic lesson of the
whole vast episode. And it is usually either unperceived, disregarded, or misinterpreted.

§

Many of the most vocal defenders of the Allies
evidently still believe that the British or Allied case is so
weak that it cannot be justified without distortion of
plain fact, without persistent implication that but for
the Belgian issue, or but for the fact that Germany was
directly attacking us, we should never have gone into
the war; that that accounted for our entrance; that
though states as distant as America and Japan were
brought in, we should have stayed out if Belgium had
not been invaded, or Germany about to invade us. If
such is to be the degree of intellectual rectitude with
which we approach a subject like this, then we must
abandon any hope of profiting by experience at all.

For we shall not be able to see what the lessons of that experience are.

Given the international anarchy as it existed in 1914, our action may well have been entirely justified and the part played noble and honourable, but it is quite plain that we should have gone into the war whether Belgium had been invaded or not, and we did not go in because Germany was directly attacking us, or proposing just then to invade this country. (For some years the Press had been full of lurid stories of German "plots" of invasion.)

We were not directly attacked, Germany was not invading Britain, not proposing so to do. It was to Germany's supreme interest to secure at that time our complete neutrality. We, like most of the Allies, became a belligerent, because German victory would have been a standing menace to our security. The thing for which, ultimately, we were fighting, as indicated in the last chapter, was the right to have any national defence at all.

This, after all, was perfectly well recognised by all respectable authorities at the time. A *Times* leading article (March 8, 1915), voices the common attitude thus:

> Our honour and interest must have compelled us to join France and Russia even if Germany had scrupulously respected the rights of her small neighbours and had sought to hack her way through the Eastern fortresses. The German Chancellor has insisted more than once upon this truth. He has fancied apparently that he was making an argumentative point against us by establishing it. That, like so much more, only shows his complete misunderstanding of our attitude and our character. . . .

We reverted to our historical policy of the Balance of Power.

Five years later (July, 31, 1920), the same position is insisted upon:

It needed more than two years of actual warfare to render the British people wholly conscious that they were fighting not a quixotic fight for Belgium and France, but a desperate battle for their own existence.

The fact that the principle of the "Balance" compelled us to support France, whether Germany respected the Belgian Treaty of 1839 or not, and so deprived our power of any value as a restraint upon German military designs against Belgium, that there was in fact a conflict of obligations emerges very clearly from the story of the negotiations, A great English lawyer who followed these negotiations, has brought out their meaning in an account which he wrote at the time.[1]

Sir Edward Grey's story of the stage at which the question of Belgium was raised is quite clear and simple. The German ambassador asked him "whether if Germany gave a promise not to violate Belgian neutrality, we would engage to remain neutral." "I replied," writes Sir Edward, "that I could not say what our attitude should be. I did not think that we could give a promise of neutrality on that condition alone. The ambassador pressed me as to whether I could not formulate conditions on which we would remain neutral. He even suggested that the integrity of France and her colonies might be guaranteed. I said that I felt obliged to refuse definitely any promise to remain neutral on

[1] *How the War Came,* by Lord Loreburn.

[148]

similar terms, and I could only say that we must keep our hands free."

"If language means anything," comments Lord Loreburn, "this means that whereas Mr. Gladstone bound this country to war in order to safeguard Belgian neutrality, Sir Edward would not even bind this country to neutrality to save Belgium. He may have been right, but it was not for the sake of Belgium interests that he refused."

Compare our experience and the attitude of Sir Edward Grey in 1914, when we were concerned to maintain the Balance of Power, with our experience and Mr. Gladstone's behaviour when precisely the same problem of protecting Belgium was raised in 1870. In these circumstances Mr. Gladstone proposed both to France and to Prussia a treaty by which Great Britain undertook that, if either of the belligerents should in the course of that war violate the neutrality of Belgium, Great Britain would co-operate with the other belligerent in defence of the same, "employing for that purpose her naval and military forces to ensure its observance." In this way both France and Germany knew, and the whole world knew, that invasion of Belgium meant war with Great Britain. Whichever belligerent violated the neutrality must reckon with the consequences. Both France and Prussia signed that Treaty. Belgium was saved.

Lord Loreborn (*How the War Came*) says of the incident:

> This policy, which proved a complete success in 1870, indicated the way in which British power could effectively protect Belgium against an unscrupulous neighbour. But then it is a policy which cannot be adopted

unless this country is itself prepared to make war against either of the belligerents which shall molest Belgium. For the inducement to each of such belligerents is the knowledge that he will have Great Britain as an enemy if he invades Belgium, and as an Ally if his enemy attacks him through Belgian territory. And that cannot be a security unless Great Britain keeps herself free to give armed assistance to either, should the other violate the Treaty. The whole leverage would obviously disappear if we took sides in the war on other grounds.[1]

This, then, is an illustration of the truth above insisted upon: to employ our force for the maintenance of the Balance of Power is to deprive it of the necessary impartiality for the maintenance of Right.

Other witnesses tell the same story. In Mr. Harold Nicholson's life of his father, Lord Carnock, a whole series of despatches reveal that (a) Germany was struggling to the last to keep us out of the war, and (b) the protection of France was a far more vital consideration than the neutrality of Belgium.

If, in fact, the purpose of our power was to secure the neutrality of Belgium, then we sacrificed that purpose to other purposes. Our half-pledge to support France nullified completely the deterrent force of our power in restraining Germany from, say, violation of the neutrality in Belgium.

---

[1] Lord Loreburn adds: "But Sir Edward Grey in 1914 did not and could not offer similar treaties to France and Germany, because our relations with France and the conduct of Germany were such, that for us to join Germany in any event was unthinkable. And he did not proclaim our neutrality because our relations with France, as described in his own speech, were such that he could not in honour refuse to join France in the war. Therefore the example of 1870 could not be followed in 1914, and Belgium was not saved but destroyed."

For the prospect of punishment to deter the criminal it does not suffice that he should know that he will be punished if he commits the crime. He must also know that he won't be punished if he keeps the law. If he is going to be arrested in any case, he does not give two straws for the law which imprisonment is designed to protect.

§

It is common ground that the purpose of our power is to prevent attack.

What is attack? We were not attacked in the direct sense in August 1914. Germany would have made very great sacrifices to have kept us neutral. Doubtless later on she would have destroyed us utterly. Our entrance into the war may well have been completely justified in every moral sense. But let us face the quite obvious and undeniable fact she did not want us in at the moment and would have done a great deal to keep us out, and that nevertheless we joined her enemies. We interpreted "attack" as something quite other than invasion or any kind of military action against *us*.

Attack did not mean that with us in 1914. It did not mean that with Italy, nor with Japan, nor with Roumania, nor Brazil, nor the United States.

Shall we in the future act as they did or not? What shall we regard as attack?

Lord Lothian and many other distinguished men tell us that any attempt to "upset the Balance of Power" will certainly be regarded as attack.[1] But Lord Beaverbrook

[1] In a letter to *The Times* of May 9th, 1934, Lord Lothian writes: "The root of the present tension is that Europe is passing from a system of stability through the military preponderance of France and her

and others as eminent say that in the future Britain will not care two straws about the Balance of Power on the Continent—say so repeatedly, emphatically. Lord Beaverbrook, whose views have wide and popular support, tells us that the Balance of Power policy has no longer any importance for us, because the victor in a continental war is not likely to be more powerful as the result of victory but weaker, and so not to be feared by us.

It is an interesting theory, but suppose that he is wrong? It is not likely that Germany shares that view. She at least expects to emerge more powerful as the result of victory. When Britain later on in any continental war discovers, as America discovered quite a long time after the war began, that German victory would be a danger, will that situation constitute "attack"?

Now, there is nothing academic or remote in that question of what we shall regard as attack or what foreign nations think we shall regard as attack. In view of our determination to build up a great air force it has tragic and urgent importance.

It is common ground to-day that there is no defence against air attack except the fear of retaliation. We must, as Mr. Baldwin has declared, kill more women and children more quickly than the enemy. It is all but unanimously conceded that you cannot, in certain conditions of fog and mist, stop aeroplanes from bombing your aerodromes, transport centres, electricity and gas

associates to one of stability by balance. Once that balance is reached, as it is being reached, there will be no competition in armament unless and until some great power attempts to upset the existing order by force, as Germany did when she set out to build a superior navy before the war. If that happens in the distant future there will be once more, as in 1908, a general combination against it."

stations, water reservoirs. All that your air arm can do is to make it plain to the enemy that if he does these things, they will be done in even greater degree to him (which incidentally, of course, assumes that he has not done it very effectively first. For in that case you won't be in a position to do it.)

We say in effect to Germany or any other prospective enemy: "If you attack us we shall blow your cities to pieces."

But, again, is "attack" to mean what Italy interpreted as attack when she entered the war, or Roumania, or Japan, or America?

In the absence of any certainty concerning the British attitude, the fear that like Italy, America, Roumania and others in the last war, Britain may decide to come in later on would certainly prompt an enemy to argue:

> Sooner or later Britain will come in, however scrupulous we are in leaving her alone. Her public men have warned us that any attempt to "upset the Balance of Power" will bring her in. But our victory will certainly upset the balance—it cannot achieve its purpose unless it does. So let us by surprise attack dispose of British power, since it is likely to be used against us.

It is clear that the threat of retaliation loses all its effect if the enemy gets it into his head that in the end you are going to fight him in any case. If he believes that whether he attacks us first or not we shall be brought in ultimately against him in any case, his obvious interest is to dispose of us when he can take us unawares. If he can do so successfully we shall not be able to retaliate. Unless he knows what the purpose of

[153]

our power is, what it is intended to prevent him doing, what act of his would leave us indifferent and what would make him our enemy, threats of "punishment" are likely to be perfectly ineffective, for he will retort: "We are convinced that you will punish us in any case."

So when we threaten that we shall blow the German cities to pieces if she "attack" us, Germany must know whether, for instance, we shall regard attack upon France as attack upon Britain. Uncertainty of our attitude in that respect will put a direct premium upon Germany "getting her blow in first." The existence of a large British air force would increase not diminish the temptation so to do.

Yet in presence, not only of these facts, but of the even plainer fact that states, like America, Japan, Italy, though obviously uncommitted, were in the last war drawn in, in presence of the fact that freedom from pledges did *not* keep them out, the British public to-day says: "The lesson of the war is that in future we must be neutral; that we must give no pledges."

This is the view put forward particularly with daily persistence by the organs of all the great newspaper trusts. One great newspaper magnate demands incessantly the complete tearing up of every shred of commitment—the Covenant, Locarno, the old Belgian Treaty. But the same views extend far beyond the popular Press. It is probable that the majority alike of Tories and Liberals, militarists and Pacifists, admirals and Quakers, join hands in demanding that we give no commitment to fight, "as we gave in 1914." The majority of those divers groups are agreed that whatever happens about armament or disarmament, League or no League, at least this country shall never give a firm undertaking to fight for any cause but "its own defence."

There is proceeding as I write an active Press campaign, not merely for increased armaments—which conceivably (though improbably) might be a factor for peace—but just as emphatically a campaign against these armaments being made part of an international arrangement, an instrument of law; and *for* their remaining an instrument of purely national policy.

The essence of the agitation carried on by papers like the *Daily Mail,* the *Daily Express,* the *Morning Post* is that it is not so much *for* arms as *against* the League or any collective system of defence. Lord Rothermere says, "Armaments mean Peace," but only if they are purely national instruments. Whenever the government shows a tendency to make the armaments the instrument of international institutions, to enter into agreements with other nations to make common cause against the aggressor, the war maker, then the denunciation of such proposals is even more bitter than the denunciation of disarmament and Pacifism.[1]

The contrary view, that pledges designed to make us part of a system of mutual and collective defence should be stiffened, not weakened, is held, it is true, by important sections in all political groups, but it is the view rather of specialists, of those who have made a more

---

[1] It is noteworthy that while writers like Major Yeats-Brown condemn Pacifists as anti-Christian because he thinks they won't fight, the Rothermere and Beaverbrook Press has of late taken to girding at the "Geneva fists" for being ready to drag us into war to fight "for foreigners." "Our bloodthirsty Pacifists" is now the phrase by which, mainly, the effort towards the creation of a system of collective defence is condemned.

than superficial study of the question; it is not yet the view of the big public.

These pages suggest that peace depends upon it becoming the general view; that so far and so long as national armed forces are retained at all, they must be publicly pledged to the international purpose of common resistance to the war-maker, or their presence will, in the end, inevitably provoke war. If it be true, as so many suggest, that a pledge to make such common cause would not be kept, then the way out is not simply to accept that fact as final and to go on with the competitive arming, but either persuade our people to give the pledge or drop the arming. It is for the peace-maker to decide which is the easier course. But without one or the other we shall get war.

One young man, a Conservative, the advocate of a Great British navy and air force, who professes to know (as perhaps he does) the feeling of his generation on this matter, says emphatically that nothing will ever persuade them to fight for any such purpose as "the ending of war." He adds:

> If this country were itself attacked it might be another matter. But that they would fight in a quarrel with which primarily they had no concern, I simply do not believe. My generation differs about many things. But I think (although I do not wholly agree with them) that in this at least my contemporaries are tolerably well united.

He goes on to say that for his generation the one outstanding lesson of the war is that "in future we must be neutral, we must not fight, and we must not promise to fight. . . . The policy of pledges has been tried and has failed. It failed in 1914." Which is an extremely curious reading of history.

To describe a situation in which we see half a world which has no pledges at all drawn gradually into a conflict, as due to a policy of clear, previously-given pledges, is to play with words and play with truth.

One wonders whether the authority I have quoted would apply his generalisation to the case of America. Was it the policy of pledges which brought *her* into the war?

The American case is only an extreme form of a general case, a rather more emphatic and striking illustration of what was in fact true of most of the other Allies who, though standing outside the orbit of formal military alliances like those which bound France and Russia, were nevertheless involved. But while it is obviously, patently true in the light of experience that an isolationism of policy even as complete as that which has always marked America's foreign policy does *not* enable a state to remain out of war, a policy of clear pledges (of the right kind) would, with a certainty as great as that for which we can ever ask in human relations, have kept us out by avoiding the war.

I have heard "with my own ears" an eminent American admiral say (as reason for a stronger American navy) this:

> If only the American navy had been twice as large in 1914 there would have been no war because Germany would have feared to attack.[1]

[1] Just as one may read any day in the Press such statements as this actual one taken from letter published in October 1933: "Germany attacked us because she knew that we were unprepared for war."

What in fact would have been the effect of a great increase in the American Navy in the years preceding the war?

The historic enemy of America in naval matters was not Germany but Britain. Disputes about sea rights had already provoked one war between Britain and America and had come near to provoking others. The Americans had for generations nursed historical grievances on that score, had talked of the "freedom of the seas," subserviency of American trade to foreign arrogance. . . . If in the early years of the century, when those disputes were still rife, America had begun to build up a navy to overtop that of Britain, Germany would have rejoiced. That fact would quite certainly have diverted Britain's enmity to the other side of the Atlantic. In naval matters, in all questions of sea rights before the war, those relating to capture at sea notably, Germany and the United States stood together on one side as against the position taken by Britain on the other. How in this circumstance could an increase of the American navy have been interpreted as a warning to *Germany?* Germany, if indeed she was then contemplating aggression upon Britain, would have welcomed this addition to the forces which she would have every reason to believe would stand on her side of the dispute.

So with the equivalent British statement that war would have been prevented if Britain had been more "prepared."

One recalls those demands for greater "preparedness" in the early years of the century, particularly the demands for universal military service. They first became audible in Britain at the end of the last century and the beginning of this. We needed a great army—in order to fight France, our hereditary foe, shortly to challenge our empire. If at that date we had gone in for immense military preparation, it is not Germany that would have been disturbed, but France. Even the *Daily Mail* in its early years spoke of "rolling France in the blood and mud where she belonged," and spoke of Germany as our potential ally. In those circumstances would military preparations have restrained *Germany*, German action against France?

If power is to restrain or deter the potential criminal, he must at least know whether power is directed at him or at another; he must know what the offence is which will involve punishment. To say to a man "If you do certain things I shall kill you," and when he wants to know "What things," you say "I don't know until you do them," how can your threat possibly deter him? Further, the party you desire to deter by your threat must know, not only that he will incur penalties if he does those things, but that he will be exempt from the penalties if he does not.

But there are certain other indispensable conditions of effective defence and of peace which the war and the events of the post-war period have revealed, which are all but universally ignored and which it is well to explore.

# Chapter IV

## DEFENCE MUST BE CO-OPERATIVE

A state dependent solely upon its own power for defence of its rights must be stronger than any likely to challenge them; which automatically deprives that other of similar defence. The only egress from this dilemma is for the defence of each to become the function of all, which is the method operating within the frontiers of each nation. International relations stumble towards that method, hampered, however, by general misunderstanding of the issues by a public confused as to the choice of risks. A note on the nature of the police function in the international field, and on grievances as the cause of war.

NOTE how the issue of defence is usually misconceived.

Debating this question some time ago, an objector put to me as indicating by analogy the fundamental issue, this question:

"Would you take a poker to the burglar if he were to enter your house?"

and he asked me to consider the political significance of the fact that in old-fashioned bedsteads there was a place where the householder kept a blunderbuss wherewith to greet the highwayman.

I replied that I *would* take a poker to the burglar if nothing better were handy; that I *had* considered the political significance of the blunderbuss, which I thought was this: that in the days when every householder had a blunderbuss as a matter of course, highwaymen were much commoner than they are now, when not one householder in a thousand has a firearm on the place. It is therefore plainly not the individual blunderbuss which has achieved security for him. It is the organisation of collective defence by society as a whole. So long as the highwayman had merely to take into account the individual householder, he could argue that a bandit gang stronger than one household could ravage the country. That is not the situation to-day. We all of us say in effect to the potential gangster that if he attempts his tricks, it is not merely John Smith, quaking with a poker or even a blunderbuss, that he will have to meet, but the whole apparatus of organised society—legislatures, laws, magistrates, courts, police, detectives, goals. . . . The certainty that the bandit would encounter all these makes banditry as a career less attractive that it might be otherwise. Sometimes society fails, as witness Al Capone. But collective action for mutual defence, not individual action, is nevertheless the very basis of our security.

If analogies there must be, one can say that it is not a question of whether you would take a poker to the burglar, but whether you would pay your police rate *for the protection of others,* including the perfectly loathsome person next door. If you won't pay for his protection through law, he won't pay for yours, and there can be no law, no police, no organised society. If, when a murder is committed, we as taxpayers argued that our money ought not to be spent in finding out the murderer since we were not concerned in the quarrel, didn't know the victim, that it was none of our affair ("let him attend to his business and we will attend to ours") —if that were the common argument, none of us would be safe. Which means that if independence and sovereignty, "each his own judge," is incompatible with organised society, equally so is "neutrality."

The principle is not less true if applied to the international field. It is much more true, as the result of the Disarmament Conference proves.

For some years we have been asking certain states (e.g. France) to disarm. One of them says to us, to the community of nations: "I fear certain of my neighbours. If one of them attacks me, what are you, society, the world, civilisation going to do about it?" And if the reply is: "Nothing at all; it is no business of ours," then the state in question says: "This means that I have nothing but my own power to depend upon. I shall, therefore, in order to be secure, make that power greater than that of the neighbour who may attack me." The neighbour employs the same argument, and we are back once again to the futilities and impossibilities of "each being stronger than the other."

Let us explore a little further the mechanism of defence.

You have a dispute with your neighbour about a right of way across his garden, and go to him saying:

"This dispute has gone on long enough. I am passionately convinced I am right. I shall therefore burn down your fence, those buildings, and make a road across your garden."

He telephones for the police. When they come, they do not settle the matter. They say:

"We know nothing about your dispute. If you have a grievance, take it to the Court. If the judgment goes in your favour, and your neighbour then does what you are now proposing to do—takes the law into his own hands and uses his own force to become his own judge—we shall restrain him, as we now propose to restrain you."

The function of the police there is to prevent the litigant being the judge, to prevent force being used as the means of settlement. But, as we saw from the his-

torical see-saw just indicated, the whole purpose of
national power under the isolationist system is to enable
the individual nation to be its own judge of its own
interests and rights in a dispute with another and so to
deny to the other the same right of judgment. The purpose of police is to *prevent* the litigant being the judge;
the purpose of the army and navy in the international
anarchy is to *enable* the litigant to be the judge. Under
such a system, force can never be an instrument of
justice.

The police is the arm of the law (say, the law of arbitration, the law that no one shall go to war in order to
impose his own judgment); the national force is the
arm of the litigant. By the police method both parties
are ensured equality of right, third party judgment
which, whatever its disadvantages, is the same for both.
The other method means that there can be no equality
of right.

During the war it pleased us to call the Allied Powers
the League of Peace. To a certain statesman who used
that phrase I put the question: "If, after the war, one of
our Allies attacks Germany, shall we do what we can to
restrain that Ally and defend Germany." He stared at
me in amazement. "Our business," he said, "is to stand
by our friends and to punish Germany, not defend her."
Then I ventured to suggest that the alliance was not a
League of Peace and could not be, until it afforded some
prospect of protection as well as punishment to the defeated.

§

Simple and self-evident as are the social principles
outlined in the last few pages, they are usually ignored

[ 163 ]

in the voluminous discussions of the problem of defence which goes on in our Press, in books, in public speeches, Air League publications, newspaper editorials, campaigns......

One may hear, daily, educated men talk about the army or the navy (using the words in a purely national as distinct from an international sense) being needed "just as we need police."

Lord Rothermere talks to us of the strong man armed keeping his goods in peace[1] and tells us that the question is whether we shall have defence for the national house or go without it.

After fifteen years of post-war discussion there is still extremely little popular recognition of the fact that if arms are to be retained at all "for defence" and are not to involve the competitive arming which must end in war, then their retention must be coupled with obligation to protect others by protecting the law, the law that there shall be no more war. The vital truth in this matter, which is an almost self-evident one, is also the most neglected. Still do we commonly say:

"We will fight, but only if we are attacked. If each observes that rule there can be no more war even though the nations are heavily armed."

Smith believes that each for himself would work if each would respect the rights of others, which implies that rights are obvious, established, unmistakable, whereas the essence of the problem is that each side

---

[1] The usual quotation gets no farther than "the strong man armed." But the text goes on to suggest what happens when a *stronger* man than the householder comes along. The passage is quite plainly intended to bring home the inadequacy of purely individual defence and the whole purpose of the parable is turned upside down. See quotation p. 309.

quite honestly and sincerely believes that the other is wrong; and that "what is right" is precisely the question in dispute.

The public quite inadequately recognise—if indeed they recognise the fact at all—that the international anarchy is a moral anarchy; that the demand for "force second to none" denies to the other the right we claim, making defence by the individual method incompatible with justice. They insist upon a system of defence which defies alike arithmetic and ethics with no real consciousness that it does either. Smith will not surrender armed defence which might solve the whole problem; he will not assume the burdens of a co-operative or collective armed defence which might work and would certainly avoid the dilemmas of the armed anarchy.

Almost can I hear the discerning reader at this point exclaim:

But the man is making the very error on the other side of the fence of which he has just been complaining in the case of the public. If it be true that armies do not have the same function as the police, if the analogy between an army and a police force is false, just as false is the implication that an international force (to which his argument seems to be pointing) can operate against the national force of a great state with the same ease, or in the same way, that the police, backed by the whole power of the community can against a person or a mob within the state.

The use of such words as "police function," "police power," "police force" in relation to the international problem, probably conjures up a vision in the mind of the reader of some composite, piebald body based upon

Geneva or the Hague, composed of Czecho-Slovaks, Albanians, Negroes, Chileans or Swiss, commanded by a Lithuanian generalissimo. I have no such vision in my mind. If the public are prepared to accept the organisation of an international police force along those lines, well and good, but it is possible to secure police action, that is to say, common action in support of law and in restraint of the peace breaker, without that particular form of international organisation. That is to say the great nations can, while retaining the national forces as now organised, put those forces behind a common purpose; as the last war showed. Twenty nations acted in common.

Imagine that the great states of the world have agreed that in future their foreign policy, the mutual obligations of their alliance-undertakings, is to be guided by one main principle: the creation of overwhelming power against the nation which refuses peaceful settlement of its dispute and goes to war. It is not more complicated or difficult, it is less complicated to organise alliances on the basis of a publicly declared policy of that kind than upon the secret, semi-secret, double crossing "re-insurance" arrangements for despoiling a third party which have so often marked the old diplomatic arrangements. (And remember that the old method, as exemplified in the last war, involved most elaborate international organisation covering the whole world in the ramifications of its economic and financial restrictions, naval and military operations.) From the moment that the governments are guided by the former policy, and their armies and navies are its instrument, then those forces, *as now organised,* have become the police force of civilisation, have become the embodiment of

[166]

the power of the community, having a common purpose standing behind a law which offers protection to all by restraining the breaker of the peace.

The difference between military force as "an instrument of national policy" and police force is not a difference of organisation or of weapons; it is a difference of purpose, of function. If we internationalise sufficiently the purpose and function of power we do not necessarily need to internationalise its organisation.[1]

The disquisition on the nature of police power was introduced, not because the writer supposes for a moment that armies and navies can operate with the same simplicity that a domestic police force can, but because a very prevalent view grossly confuses and misinterprets the function respectively of army and police, and because there arises from this confusion a prevalent misunderstanding of the issues involved. The analogy between "police" and the collective power of the world used as an instrument to restrain the disturber of the peace applies to the function, not the form of organisation. While confusions as to the respective functions remain we run the risks of using force to deny right under the sincere impression we are doing the contrary. The analogies between the police and the collective system are intended to clarify a principle. The principle of gravity is the same whether applied to an apple or a planet; and to perceive the nature of the principle in

---

[1] Armies, of course, sometimes perform police functions: the French army in Boulevard Riots, the British on the North West Frontier. But those are not the purposes which create the international situation or threaten Armageddon. Nor is it the forces created for those purposes which set up a race in armaments. A police force is for a city's protection; but one city does not become disturbed if another increases its force; and police forces don't arrest each other.

the case of an apple enables us to perceive how it applies to planets.

Let us briefly summarise:

(1) In a situation in which we and other states honestly differ as to what our respective rights are, in which the question is whether we are right or the other is right, we ask for power "adequate for defence," meaning sufficient to enable us always to be in a position to decide the question. We ask the other to accept our judgment, although we would refuse to accept his.

We think to avoid this dilemma by "always being just"; by the feeling that no nation need fear that we should abuse our position of judge, litigant, executioner, all in one. Even if it were historically true (which in view of the Versailles Treaty it is not) that our judgments in disputes with others were always just, we still deny the right of judgment we claim. There is, and can be, no equality of right where one party to the dispute is, because of his superior power, the judge. It is not a question of grievances or any injustices which the superior party may or may not inflict. We had no grievances against Germany in 1914; we were not suffering an imposed Treaty of Versailles. Yet we went into the war (and would have gone in, as our statesman admitted, even if the Belgian issue had not arisen) because any increase of German power would have placed us at her mercy. Why should we expect Germany to continue at ours? (Germany's supreme grievance to-day is precisely that she has not equality of power.) It is a real, not a fanciful dilemma. Under this system, might *cannot* stand behind right, however just the litigant who decides the dispute may try to be. The right in question is the right to be free from the judgment of the other litigant, however just he may be.

(2) To put power behind the principle of third party judgment does ensure some rough approximation to equality of right. Whatever the disadvantages, they are in the long run about equal for both. Experience as old as written history shows that there is only one way out of the dilemma of competitive arming: to make power an instrument of a law, of the impartial judge, not of the rival litigants fighting it out.

(3) This function of upholding in common an agreed law is the function which distinguishes police power from power as now exercised by nations in the international field. The function of the police is to restrain the individual who has a grievance against another—dispute about property, rights of way,—from "taking the law into his own hands" and being his own judge. The purpose of a nation's military power is to *enable* it to be its own judge of its own rights in a dispute with another. The function of police forces is the exact contrary of the purpose of armies and navies as we have known them in the past.

(4) This police function can only be organised when the community realises that defence cannot be an individual function, that it must be collective, co-operative, mutual, if it is to be effective at all; that if in organised society the individual will take no responsibility to defend others, then he cannot possibly defend himself. Law becomes powerful, not primarily because it punishes, but because it protects: the punishment is a mere incident of its main function of protection.

§

Within the last five or six years there have appeared some scores of books dealing with the injustices of the Versailles Treaty and pointing to them as lying at the root of Europe's unrest and as probable cause of the next war. To avoid war we must revise the Treaty.— though in fact it is just as true to say at this moment that any attempt to revise the Treaty, would, almost certainly cause war.

Several of these books call for a "just settlement" of the respective claims of the nations concerned. It is as though one should say: "Why cannot the Republicans and Democrats in America and the Conservatives and Labour Party in England come once for all to a settlement, then shut up Parliament or Congress and let the country have peace."

Grievances can never be settled. What is satisfactory to-day would be unsatisfactory to-morrow, to say nothing of the fact that it is a physical impossibility to "settle" Europe on a basis of separate independent nationalities, which is the main demand of some of the most vocal grievances. In many places in Europe we have three or four nationalities in the same street. It is a physical impossibility to grant a sovereign and independent government to each. And it is of the very nature of nationalism as we know it to make no concessions; to show no give and take. And if it were physically possible to create a Europe on the basis of independent nationalities, it would make its economic life impossible and bring us to economic as well as political chaos.

Revision and change are assuredly indispensable to

peace, and to devise machinery and means for making such changes is one of its problems. But we shall fail to reach the heart of the difficulty altogether if we assume that revision, settlement of grievances, would be a reliable preventive of war, even if we could assume the settlement of many of them being possible (which it is not, since they embody mutually exclusive claims).

How little mere "revision," or settlement of specific grievances, would constitute a solution, is revealed by one fact of the war itself which is usually overlooked and which is of the very first importance.

Germany, whom we on our side regard as the author or chief author of the war, was not in 1914 the *victim* of a Treaty of Versailles. She was the beneficiary of a Treaty she herself, as victor, had imposed at Versailles half a century before; was the possessor of great territories in Eastern Europe and in Africa which she has now lost.

And so far as the "unredeemed nationalities" were concerned—the Poles, Czechs, Southern Slavs—very many were fighting *for* Germany. Pilsudski, the present dictator of Poland, was a general in the *German* army, and the main element in the new Poland are people who fought for Austria. And on the other side, few of the Allied states who entered the war had specific grievances against Germany. Of the states which entered the war against Germany, neither the United States, nor Russia, nor Britain, nor Italy, nor Roumania, nor Japan, were suffering under a Treaty of Versailles. The war did not come as the result of unredressed grievances on the part of Germany's opponents, of claims made by the Allies which Germany had refused to accord. In the years of bickering which preceded the war, what claim

had we made on Germany which by 1914 she had refused to grant? Or, for that matter, what were the
claims which Germany was making that we had refused
to grant?[1] Germany had made no such claims either
upon us, or Italy, or France, or America. It might well
be that, having obtained preponderant power, she would
then have presented claims which we should refuse to
grant; or we might fear that such would be the case.
That indeed is a fact which brings us much nearer to
fundamental causes. But that is also something very
different indeed from the theme developed in the books
on revision just referred to, and a problem which the
remedying of the grievances they discuss would in no
wise meet.

Neither we, nor America, nor Russia, nor Italy, nor
in fact any of the other Allies had any grievance of a
nature which we felt would have justified our joining
in the war against Germany, except this supreme grievance: Germany was becoming so powerful that she
threatened to deprive us of all means of defending ourselves. What we were fighting for was, in the last analysis, as indicated in the last chapter, the right to have
any defence at all.

The war of 1914 arose out of a struggle for power,
power adequate for defence. To say that, indeed, is
to come near to enunciating a truism, for all war is a
struggle for power, power on the part of one party to
do something which the other resists—to possess a
province, occupy a territory, what not. If the power of
one side is completely and unquestionably prepon-

---

[1] "As a matter of fact, the relations between Great Britain and Germany were never better than on the eve of the War."—Mr. Winston
Churchill, in the House of Commons, 30th July 1934.

derant it can usually impose its will without war. But in that case the weaker has, in the present order of things, lost its means of defence; it is at the mercy of the more powerful.

In 1914 the enemies of Germany would not accept the prospect of her becoming a state so powerful that they would be unquestionably at her mercy, so that to them her will would be law. Nor would we be ready to accept such a position to-day, unless we are ready to abdicate defence by arms altogether.

To say that it does not matter how strong a foreign combination may become, is to say that it does not matter whether our navy and army is able to match its potential enemy or not, and is to make nonsense of all that we have been doing since the war and are doing to-day more energetically than ever in the way of building up an "air power second to none," increasing our navy and so forth. If we are prepared to accept the creation of a state at our very doors overwhelmingly more powerful than we are, then what in heaven's name is the sense of talking about "adequate" forces, or forces "second to none"?

It is true that certain British isolationists argue that in the event of the conquest of France by Germany, the latter would not be a powerful state, but emerge so shattered by war that we need not fear her and that this reason has deprived the old Balance of Power policy of such virtue as it may once have had.

But that overlooks completely the way in which in the international anarchy armed power is used. For the defence of a nation's interests "War," the wet warfare of the battlefield, is not in question during the first phase at all. But power is, potential power. One has only to cast one's mind back over the incidents of the last generation or so—our efforts to secure our lines of communication to India and the antipodes by the Suez Canal, and the conflict with France that it brought; the occupation of Egypt, the partitioning of Equatorial Africa; *l'Affaire* Stokes; the Sudan; Fashoda; the Boer war—to see how impossible is the armed defence of a world-wide empire from the moment we say: No alliances. When, at some diplomatic gathering or international conference issues such as those involved in the above mentioned incidents are in question, no one wants war. But groups form; each attempts to secure for his own claim such preponderance of *potential* power that it will not be worth while for the others to challenge it. An empire like Britain, defending what it may regard as indispensable lines of communication, is confronted by a diplomatic combination of hostile states which say in effect: "We desire your withdrawal from ——," Egypt, or Fashoda, or some Asiatic frontier position. It may be true that things would never be pushed to the point of war. But one can never tell. And if the diplomatic combination against one is overwhelming one cannot risk it. One must yield, yield because of the inability to confront a hostile diplomatic combination with a similar combination. The modern diplomat in fact adopts the technique which was that of the petty sovereigns of the eighteenth century, who fought wars without battles: "The Marshal has the honour to point out that he is able to command at this moment two thousand more men and twenty more cannon than are at the disposal of your Excellency, and would therefore request your Excellency's withdrawal"—which was usually forthcoming. This sort of strategy prompted

[174]

Marechal Saxe to say that the perfect war would have no battles.

Where the preponderance of power against you is clear, you yield. Where it is doubtful you weigh the stakes against the hazards of war. Behind it, in the background, is the danger that the implied challenge may be accepted. In the end it always is accepted.

Those who believe that a world-wide empire can disregard the alignment of power which goes on in the rest of the world, must read history in curious fashion. There has never been a single century in the twenty that have followed Caesar's invasion in which we have not been drawn into the affairs of continental Europe. We are now asked to believe that when Tokio and Melbourne are far nearer to London than York was in the days of the Roman, and when "Britain" is no longer an unknown island off the North West coast of Europe but stretches across the entire world—that we can in these circumstances adopt an "isolationist" policy of defence which was not possible when Julius Caesar ruled in Rome.

As these lines are being written certain eminent leaders in our national life are engaged in agitating for very great increases in our naval and air power, and one of those leaders who has been notable for an agitation against the commitments of the Locarno Treaty writes:

"Germany, even if she has been re-arming for some time past, is in no position as yet to fight against the might of steel-girded France. So there will be peace, and the peace will be the result of no disarmament counsels, but of France's brave and steady realism of these long ten years.

"Once again has France shown Europe that equi-

[175]

librium can be secured by decisive overweight no less than by balance of power. . . .

"England's friendship and sympathy with France remain. We understand her difficulties and we are fully alive to the possibility that circumstances might arise in which we should feel ourselves bound to come to her aid. But at the same time we would overwhelmingly prefer—and, indeed, demand—that we ourselves should be the judges of whether these circumstances had arisen."[1]

In other words, the internationally organised power is to be used as the instrument of the litigant, or one group of litigants as against the other, to enable one side to be its own judge, thus depriving the other of equal right, instead of being the instrument of equal rights for all, beginning with, say, the right to arbitration, third party judgment.

That is the essential difference. Power is still to be used; war is still in the background as an instrument of coercion; our own paraphernalia of war are to be increased; and if and when we go to war the coercion to be exercised will not be that merely of our own national power, it will be the combined power of ourselves and allies, an international sanction. But the sanction will be applied for the purpose of enforcing our view of our interests and rights in any given dispute. Meantime peace rests upon the preponderance of one party, at whose mercy the other must remain. Peace will remain so long as one party accepts, or can be made to accept a position which those who urge the policy declare our own nation should never accept, that no proud nation ever should accept; a position of inferiority of right.

[1] Lord Lloyd, *Daily Mail,* 20th October, 1933.

[ 176 ]

The right to preponderance which one side claims, denies by its very terms a similar right to the other.

Now Europe during the last ten years had been slowly, clumsily, getting away from that stultifying policy. Haltingly and with many set-backs there had been going on a process of shifting power from the disputants to the European community as a whole; using it for the purpose of ensuring respect for certain rules, or rights, which should be equal for all. The Versailles Treaty (an example of what happens when one of the parties to the dispute pronounces the verdict), was being rapidly though informally revised. The "Geneva atmosphere," the habit of contact and international co-operation, had rendered a large part of the Treaty a dead letter, and that revision by tacit consent would have continued if international institutions and the spirit that goes with their growth, had been allowed to develop by gradually linking them to the power held by the constituent states, by throwing upon impartial international authority to an increasing degree, the function of determining how the common power of the nations should be used. France herself desired that development. It has been a continual reproach to her that she tried to "use the League for enforcing the Treaty of Versailles" for "crystallising the *status quo*." But if that Treaty was to be one continually subject to quiet and peaceful revision, as it has been, what the reproach really comes to is that France wanted to use the League for the purpose of preventing the alteration of the *status quo* by war. Which is precisely what the League was established to achieve. Change by war means that new settlement is dictated by the aggrieved party, certain to be as unjust on one side

[177]

as the previous settlement was on the other. The Germans if victorious won't make a better Treaty than that of Versailles; they will make a worse. The new Treaty in its turn will have to be revised by war, to be followed by a peace just as evilly one sided . . . until the end of civilisation. France, to do her bare justice, has seen something of what this process must lead to, and has been ready to base her defence upon the principle that the keeping of the peace—not the forbidding of change—shall be made an international obligation. If that could have been achieved, if Europe's power could have been pooled and put behind the keeping of the common peace, international institutions would have developed, that development would have afforded means of peaceful change, and national defence would then have become what it must be in order to be effective, a co-operative process, the function of the community; "sanctions" and "defence" would have been almost synonymous terms; power would not be, as it must be in the international anarchy, the instrument by which we deny to others the right we claim for ourselves, but the instrument for ensuring equality of right. Might and Right would not be in opposite camps as they must be when Might is used for making each judge in his own cause; they would be in the same camp—that of equal law.

## PART THREE

# ECONOMIC FACTORS

# Chapter I

## THE ILLUSION OF NATIONAL "POSSESSION"

Instead of conceiving of wealth as based on processes which must be co-operatively maintained, we commonly conceive it as being a definitely limited quantity of land or material which if one nation possesses another is deprived of. This fundamentally fallacious conception largely explains our preference for anarchy over order; for preferring competition for preponderant power to the pooling of power in partnership.

WHEN, to the pre-war generation, I put the question why war was inevitable, the commonest reply was typified by one actually given by the then editor of the *National Review* in these terms:

War is rooted in biological need. It is the ultimate struggle for bread. Take the present case of Germany. She has born to her every year a million children. Every year that extra million babies are crying out for more room. Germany needs the wheat of Canada and the wool of Australia wherewith to feed and clothe them. But these resources belong to us British whose duty it is to keep them for our children, our posterity. Colonies fit to receive the German surplus population are the greatest need of Germany. We have no right to surrender our heritage for the benefit of foreigners; our first duty is to our own people. The same struggle for life and space, which more than a thousand years ago drove one Teutonic wave after another across the Rhine and the Alps, is now once more a compelling force. It is out of these vital needs, which no paper guarantees can dispose of, that the fateful struggle will come.[1]

[1] In *Mein Kampf* (p. 731) Hitler writes: "The aim of Nazi foreign policy is to secure to the German people on this earth the territory and soil that are its due, that is, that will provide for the large Ger-

[ 181 ]

Now, if that is a true statement of the problem, or (which is just as much to the point) if the parties in the case believe it to be true, though in fact it is false, war is inevitable. Nations will not commit what they believe to be suicide, condemn their children to the miseries of starvation, on behalf of the higher morality. It is as though one cannibal were to say to another:

> It is plain that either I must eat you or you must eat me. Let's come to a friendly agreement about it.

They won't come to a friendly agreement about it, they will fight. And they will fight even though as a matter of fact there is plenty of food for both, if only one cannibal would stand on the shoulders of the other in order to reach the fat coconuts on the branches out of reach of either acting alone. ("Which is a parable.") They will fight, that is, so long as each is firmly convinced, however wrongly, that the only source of food for himself and family consists in the body of the other.

The belief that in the most vital sense war does indeed "pay" is deeply rooted in our profoundest convictions, in what we would probably call "instinct," an "instinct" buttressed by nationalist and patriotic suggestion which plays upon us in a hundred unnoticed ways. We believe that benefits to be derived from the possession of preponderant national power enormously outweigh the benefits of international co-operation, the pooling of our power with that of other nations to

man population and enable it to expand. Only this aim makes it justifiable before God and our German posterity to risk the loss of German lives. The Nazis must have the courage, without regard for tradition or prejudices, to gather together all the forces of our people to march forward on the path that will take it out of the narrow space on which it lives to-day and lead it towards new territories."

secure co-operative support of law, a collective and co-operative system of defence.

So long as men hold to that belief—as they do—effective international co-operation will be impossible.

With reference to the case as stated in the quotation just given, I suggest four things.

(1) The theory outlined in the quotation is in its main implication almost entirely false, the child of a terminology so grossly inaccurate as utterly to distort our thought.

(2) In the sense, and to the extent to which it is true, successful war constitutes no solution of the problem involved in that partial truth.

(3) The argument would never have been used at all, had there not been at the back of the critic's mind a certain moral assumption, namely, that foreigners have no rights, not even the right to existence.

(4) While such moral assumptions mark our political morality in the international field, not only can there be no permanent peace, but we shall never establish any relationship between nations which will make possible the creation of that body of law which is *indispensable to the life of Britain.*

Let us take these points *seriatim.*

*Point No.* 1. It is not true, given the continuance of even the pre-war economic internationalism, that Germany had to expand politically in order to feed her population. She fed them in part by the "exploitation" of territory—North America, South America, Russia—which she did not own, and did not need to own, by the same method which we use in feeding our population. She needed the wheat of Canada or the wool of Australia wherewith to feed and clothe her excess population. Would political conquest of these Dominions enable her to get those things without payment—the same payment which secures them now? You, the English reader, "own" Canada and Australia (a fact which, when your credit is exhausted at the bank, you might recall to the recalcitrant manager). Does this political "ownership" enable you to secure a single sack of Canadian wheat without paying for it like any miserable foreigner? You can get it by one means, and one means alone: by giving something in exchange. It was open to the Germans to do so on the same terms, without conquest or political control. And if the German, as a result of conquest, were to occupy your position, he would still have to obtain wheat by the exact means which were available without conquest. In other words, the change in political relationship would not alter the fundamental economic relationship at all. When we use arguments of this kind, we are tricked, as I have said, by a terminology so hopelessly false and misleading as utterly to befuddle our minds.

More, is not the rhetoric about the "Teutonic Waves" and the "struggle for life" mere bombastic theory divorced from the realities of present-day politics? Is our problem the difficulty of obtaining wheat or wool? Do nations tend to withhold their produce from others? Why, the complaint everywhere is not that wheat and wool and other primary products are inaccessible, are withheld, but that they are "dumped" too readily. Every nation is engaged, not in trying to seize bread or raiment, but in trying to keep those things from its shores.

But the divorce from reality gets worse as we go on. The implication is that while Australia and Canada are

[184]

of the British miner, who goes without both the coffee and the wheat. The trouble is plainly due to dislocation, a failure of world co-ordination and co-operation, a failure caused mainly by war and the spirit which underlies war. The truth is not "Fight or Starve," but "Stop Fighting or Starve," a truth which even Japan will not be able to ignore. The cure for insufficiency is better co-operation. War makes better co-operation impossible.

§

Never were creatures of prey so mischievous, never diplomatists so cunning, never poisons so deadly, as these masked words. They are the unjust stewards of all men's ideas. . . . The word comes at last to have an infinite power over him, and you cannot get at him but by its ministry.

Thus Ruskin. Most truly can words be evil tyrants as well as unjust stewards.

I once called a book "The Great Illusion"[1] (prompted by a line of Milton's "this great illusion of the benefits of war"). It might perhaps as appropriately have been called "The Masked Words," for the illusion with which it dealt has been born in large part of a terminology of

---

[1] Which for years critics who had not read the book insisted on interpreting as meaning that war could not take place, or that bankers could not finance it. There is not from first to last in the book a word which justifies such conclusion. Its purpose was to reveal war as the inevitable outcome of commonly accepted assumptions. This misrepresentation still continues. Thus the *Syracuse Journal* (28th June, 1934) and other Hearst papers of the same date in a leading article: "During the years preceding the war many books were written to prove that important wars could never occur again. As Sir Norman Angell declared in his work *The Great Illusion;* 'The nations could not finance a serious conflict.'" He declared nothing of the sort.

international politics so loose, inaccurate, misleading as to betray men's thoughts upon the whole subject.

Note some of these masked words.

The victor in war "captures" a province, or a colony, "takes" territory that previously "belonged" to the vanquished, and is "enriched by the spoils of war." There has been a transfer of "property" from one group of owners to another. Taxes, previously collected by the vanquished nation, are now, to his enrichment, collected by the victor. "Markets" and trade are captured with equal simplicity, once victory is assured. Trade follows the victorious battleship or the army. But for the might of the British navy foreigners would "take" our trade; our riches are a constant temptation to powerful states who would certainly "seize" them if once our weakness gave them opportunity.

These words and phrases occur, not merely in the leading articles of popular papers where in the clamour of daily journalism—particularly the stress of drumming up a panic about the inadequacy of our navy or air force—terms cannot always be very carefully considered, but are employed by the authors of most pretentious political treatises as meaning just what they say. In *The Great Illusion* itself I have quoted from first to last some dozens of pages—and could have quoted hundreds —from then current political literature showing that, in the minds of the writers, the spoils which go to the victor are real spoils, that there is indeed without any question a transfer of property from one group of owners to another.

The acceptance of this proposition is not confined to any one school of thought: it was, and is, accepted, often without any qualification or question, by very many in nearly every school of political thought.[1] Before the war the idea that victory meant definite economic advantage was advanced more forcibly and emphatically, by the militarist type of mind, by those who stood by bourgeois and capitalist conceptions of society, than by Socialists who were apt to question the proposition severely. Since the war, the reverse is perhaps the truth. Most informed Capitalists, particularly bankers and financiers, do really believe that another war will smash their system, smash civilisation, and must at all costs be avoided. But as against that, most Socialists now (much more than previously) aver that Capitalism is irresistibly pushed to war by the competition for markets, that the home market being inadequate, Capitalism must "seize" or "capture" foreign markets by war, or go under. This has become one of the major themes of modern Marxian Socialists— indeed of most Socialists—who, like their pre-war intellectual predecessors on the bourgeois side, accept as self-evident, not even needing discussion or explana-

---

[1] The editor of an American paper during the discussion of the Debt problem suggested that Britain might settle her debt by "selling Canada to the United States." Lord Lloyd, speaking at Blackpool on February 23rd, 1934, after fifteen years of unsuccessful attempts to seize anything whatever from Germany, said: "We do not want war, but we are presenting to an unregenerate world to-day the biggest block of undefended plunder that has ever been known in the history of the world."

Mr. Winston Churchill, speaking in the House of Commons, 30th July 1934:

"We were a rich and easy prey. No country was so vulnerable, and no country would better repay pillage. This rich metropolis, the greatest target in the world, was a kind of valuable great cow. tied up to attract a beast of prey."

tion, the proposition that a Capitalist state, having won a war, can, by means of that victory, "take" markets which otherwise it could not.

Some thirty years ago this writer suggested in summary of his thesis that:

When a victorious nation "captures" a province (as Germany captured Alsace-Lorraine) there is no transfer of property from one group of owners to another. There is a change of government, of political administration which may be good, bad, or indifferent; worth dying to resist or not greatly worth bothering about. But speaking broadly there is no transfer of property from one group of owners to another: the land, the houses, farms, factories, bonds, shares, furniture, clothes, remain in the same possession after the war as before.

This was not always so (e.g. the Vikings *did* seize actual goods; the Normans turned out Saxons and put in new owners of land). The change is not due to increasing virtue but to the changed nature of wealth which, as the result of an infinitely complicated division of labour is now dependent upon an uninterrupted process of exchange, itself dependent upon monetary and credit devices which confiscation or military seizure disastrously interrupts. An invader who simply "seized" property in the old Viking fashion would probably find that the banks of his own nation held the debentures or mortgages, his own nationals the shares, his own insurance companies the insurance.

Apart from that, nations don't want the goods of foreigners: every nation is busily engaged doing its best by ever increasing tariffs to keep them out.

For reasons related to these facts a vanquished enemy's trade cannot be seized or transferred to the victor. To prevent Germany from selling her hardware to South America may well be to prevent her buying Indian jute or Australian wool which, unsold, prevents India or Australia from paying the interest on their debts to London.

Conquest does not solve or for long even ease the Capitalist dilemma of the output of surplus goods, for to find money wherewith to buy the victor's goods the conquered people must itself sell goods which automatically add to the surplus to the extent that the money derived from their sale relieves it. Lancashire has suffered more from the industrialisation of India brought about largely by the investment of British capital in the British Empire than it has by the competition of Japan. All attempts to compel a conquered province to buy without selling produces much more rapidly than ever before monetary dislocations disastrous to economic stability, to trade and industry.

It is not necessary to own territory in order economically to exploit it: in the nineteenth century the United States was a richer field of investment for British Capital than any of the British colonies; a single foreign state like Brazil was worth more to Germany than the whole of the German colonies combined.

If it were true that addition of territory added to a nation's wealth, then the people living in big countries would be richer than the people living in the small. But the Swede is not poorer than the German nor the Swiss than the Italian. The idea that addition of territory means added wealth to the existing population is about as sound as the proposition that when a city takes in a suburb the annexing body acquires the suburbanites' property. If in 1873 Germany collected taxes collected in 1870 by France, the "Germany" of 1873 included the Alsatians. Those receiving the taxes were increased in exact proportion to those paying them.

No indemnity commensurate with the cost of modern war will be paid by the vanquished in future since, payable only ultimately in goods or services, too great a dislocation would be caused to the victor's own economic process by the attempt to receive them.

§

Such were the typical propositions of *The Great Illusion*.

An attempt was made to show the bearing of certain obvious changes in the nature of wealth upon the problem of its defence. The Vikings of old would ravage our coasts for goods and carry them away. If we could imagine the compliment now being returned and some British Anlaf attempting to give employment to our idle merchant ships by taking them into the Baltic and loading them up with butter, bacon, eggs, timber and bringing them back to Britain, what would happen? Every Protectionist in the House of Commons would clamour for an emergency tariff at all costs to keep those goods out and our farmers would insist that they got it. These are complications which the ninth century Viking did not have to meet.

But these would not be the only complications that book suggests which would follow upon a raid into the Baltic and wholesale confiscation by invading hordes. The British coal trade with Scandinavia and the Baltic is an extremely important one, and on that trade depends also much of our shipping industry. It is the fact of taking our coal and getting a cargo both ways that has given to us so much of the carrying trade of the world, and if our modern sea rovers began sacking Stockholm or Copenhagen or Christiania, they would in fact be sacking the working-class homes of Newcastle or Barrow or Cardiff almost as disastrously, reducing to unemployment and starvation British miners, British factory hands, British shipbuilders, British sailors.

"I doubt whether, when Anlaf sacked Maldon or Colchester, the Scandinavian carrying trade was greatly affected, or the unemployment rate increased. But this is only the beginning of the complications with the modern Anlaf. British insurance companies have insured the very buildings that our British Vikings would be burning, the shares of our businesses now sacked are held by British investors, British banks have lent money to the now ruined merchants, or discounted their bills, or lent money to the merchants who had discounted the bills. I have not studied Viking history very carefully, but I doubt very much whether Scandinavian stock exchanges were greatly affected when Anlaf ravaged Essex."[1]

Material in the modern world is only wealth if you can get rid of it. The miner cannot eat his coal, or even build his house with it. If it is to mean food and shelter and clothing he must exchange it, exchange it in practice for money. But the purchaser must somehow get that money, and there is only one way he can do so in the long run—by getting rid of his material to someone who has money, who can only have money by getting rid in his turn of his material to someone who has money, who can only have money by getting rid in his turn . . . round the world.

In other words, wealth is a flow, a process, a keeping of the traffic moving on the commercial highways of the world. If the traffic is blocked by the obstacles

[1] *The Great Illusion*, 1933, p. 139.

with which the history of the last fifteen years has made us so familiar and which always follow in the wake of war, unpayable debts creating, by the maldistribution of monetary gold, exchange difficulties, economic nationalism, so that the traffic stops, then the material ceases to be wealth.

If we conceive of this problem of making secure the means of civilised life as, broadly speaking, the problem of ensuring the smooth working of an intricate, world-wide co-operative process, we shall stand inevitably for co-operative methods of defence; conceive of defence mainly as the means of securing observance of necessary rules, laws, which will permit all to live. If, however, we conceive of prosperity as based upon the exclusive possession of materials, things, limited in amount; of a nation's wealth as consisting of goods and chattels that can be taken, as a burglar might take a householder's plate, then we shall think of defence in terms of isolated power, as a problem of defending the nation's soil from marauders, as a man locks his door to prevent robbery. This last case would even be stronger still—conclusive indeed—if it were true (evidence given in these pages shows that it is still the prevailing view) that a nation's economic opportunities throughout the world depend upon its power, by military or naval preponderance, to enforce its economic claims against the claims, similarly presented, of others; if the view that the competition for power is, in fact, the struggle of expanding populations for sustenance, for their due share of the limited resources of the world. So long as these assumptions—unexpressed, it may be, or vaguely and hazily held—dominate the public mind, the public the world over will stand for the maintenance of its nation's arms; and oppose any collective or co-operative system of defence.

But as against that view this author presents another, which can be outlined in part as follows:

*Defence, the security of the nation, its people, wealth, trade, prosperity, cultural rights, civilisation, demands mainly, not the defence of materials or soil from predatory seizure by others—all nations in the modern world are actually far more concerned to exclude than to seize the goods of others—but the organisation of processes analogous to the maintenance of unimpeded traffic on the highways. While Big Navy organisations are demanding more cruisers to "protect our trade routes," half that trade disappears in a few years, and our ships lie idle in port, successfully blockaded by economic collapse. What is the Navy doing? Vital trades in great industrial cities of the North are ruined by the tariffs of our own Dominions. How does the Navy protect it? An admiral once said that, but for our Navy, foreigners would "loot the cellars of the Bank of England." We were pushed off the gold standard through a raid by foreigners upon our gold reserves. How could the Navy prevent it? If in fact the livelihood—the life—of our nation is dependent upon the maintenance of a flow or process, analogous to traffic regulation, then defence of that life can only be secured by co-operation with others. To attempt to ensure safety and smooth travel by the method of each having a bigger car than any he is likely to collide with, and to drive as he sees fit with no regard to general rule, must by its nature fail. It can only produce chaos and disaster, as indeed it has in the international field. You cannot possibly ensure anybody's defence by the isolated action of each user of the road.*

*Defence, safety, must be organised by the community, or there can be none at all.*

The book thus summarised did not discuss merely or mainly the question whether war "paid." It discussed whether the reasons underlying the policy which all nations follow, the pursuit of power, were valid reasons; whether preponderance of national power "paid," was effective, that is, for the purposes of political and economic security; whether annexation paid, really added to the wealth of a people; whether trade could be promoted or transferred by dominant armies or navies; asked what we really meant when we talked of our navy "protecting our trade"; whether the wealth and resources of the modern world were of a fixed and limited quantity, any share of which, seized by one nation, was lost to others, thus making of war "a struggle for bread," or whether the quantity of wealth available depended upon the efficiency of that co-operation by which it was produced; whether the effectiveness of that co-operation was not incalculably reduced by the international situation which preparation for war necessarily produces; what was the real function of force in the organisation of these co-operations; what were the conditions of its social employment and where it became self-defeating and anti-social; how, in other words, we might hope to make national power effective for national defence. In the final analysis its purpose came to this:

*To examine the assumptions which caused the nations to adopt a method of defence which is self-defeating; and to make plain the fallacy of those assumptions in terms of the obvious facts of the modern world.*

The question of how best to secure defence necessarily includes the question of what it is we want to defend; how far the problem includes the defence of life, civilisation, social order, and the things necessary thereto, as well as moral freedoms, cultural possessions, nationality, political independence; the relation of our economic organization to those things.

Had those arguments, not a mere vague acquiescence in the proposition that "war does not pay," really entered into public consciousness, it is certain that a large part of the mess in which we have entangled ourselves would have been avoided. We should, for instance have done early in the matter of the Reparations embroglio what in any case we were obliged to do at long last at Lausanne in 1932, and so would not have had during ten years that proportion of the economic disorder, confusion and uncertainty which has resulted from the maintenance during that period of impossible claims; should not now be faced by a possible repetition of the futility in the case of the American Debts; would be more ready to co-operate effectively in the international arrangements which alone can make our Disarmament, or World Economic Conferences, successful; and we should not have had the Treaty of Versailles.

That Treaty seems to have embodied almost every fallacy which the author's book of 1908 indicted. Yet the Treaty was imposed by a public opinion (for many witnesses have testified that some of its most dubious clauses were inserted, not because the governments and actual treaty-makers believed them to be feasible, but because public opinion demanded them) honestly desirous to have done with war, weary of it; by a public which proclaimed sincerely enough that its intention in making a treaty of that kind was precisely to make this the war that should end war. That indeed was the slogan of the time. No one wanted war any more. No one believed that war paid. But the terms of the Treaty are proof that everybody wanted to annex new territory, wanted economic self-sufficiency, a weakening of trade competition, desired preponderant power, strategic frontiers, to pursue, that is, the policy which produced the war. We may not have believed that war paid, but quite plainly we believed that annexation paid, that the impoverishment of neighbours paid, and particularly that power paid.

Nowhere do we see reflected in that Treaty the belief that our prosperity is dependant upon that of our neighbours, that economic stability can only be secured by an international co-operation which must be based upon equality of right and which continued competition for preponderance of power must make impossible.

The typical propositions of *The Great Illusion* are largely statements of the obvious; completely so when they point out that a Germany which annexes an Alsace-Lorraine and takes the taxes, is also a Germany which then includes the population of Alsace-Lorraine, who get the taxes; that those who receive are increased in exact proportion to those who pay. The reader may well wonder whether it is necessary thus to go on stating the obvious. But consider the significance of experience such as this: When, in the course of lectures, academic or otherwise, or in the course of conversation, it has been my business to point out that "capture" of territory does not mean transfer of property, and I make no mention of taxes, then invariably (the thing has happened not merely once or twice or on a dozen occasions, but on hundreds) comes the objection: "But you have forgotten the taxes—the conqueror collects the taxes."[1]

The obvious is not obvious when it comes into conflict with words or symbols that have by long habit embedded themselves in our minds.

Perhaps a personal experience may be forgiven in this connection since it bears upon the problem of why the public does not see the facts.

When the propositions just outlined were first elaborated by the present writer in a little booklet written about 1905 and published a year or so later, I sent a copy to the editor of a certain high-brow publication for review. No review appeared, and I asked the editor why. He replied: "I looked at it myself and dropped it after reading the outline of the proposition which the book set out to prove. I take it to be one of those 'clever' things based upon turning the plain truth upside down and making it appear false. The whole thing is obvious rubbish. To say that a nation does not add to its wealth when it captures valuable territory is neither more nor less true than to say that my family would not be better off if my uncle left them his estate in Devonshire." He was neither stupid nor uneducated, but his state of mind in respect of the book's main proposition was that of a peasant told for the first time that the earth is round, he "knowing from the evidence of his senses" that it's flat, and that, if round, the people on the other side are standing on their heads, which is funny but obviously not true. I saw then that "masked words" and the habit of thought they engendered con-

---

[1] An early newspaper critic (in the *Daily Mail*) went to the extent of working out at considerable length the cash value of the taxes which Germany acquired when she took over Alsace-Lorraine.

stitute an obstacle to the perception of social truth as powerful as that which "the evidence of their senses" must have constituted for those who first heard of the rotundity of the earth. That obstacle can readily enough be overcome in the case of a physical fact capable of visual demonstration. It can be overcome in the case of the social truth also, but probably with more difficulty, for the demonstration must be spread over generations. I persuaded my friend to read the book. He did so, and became a "convert," and rather an enthusiastic one. But for years he came to me at intervals with "difficulties," some argument he had been unable to answer. And almost always was the difficulty rooted in the loose use of words, in confusion between the symbol and the thing for which it stood.

Yet his education had been mainly literary and linguistic, a dealing with words; suggesting a point concerning which it will be useful to say a little in due course.

## Chapter II

# CAPITALISM, SOCIALISM AND PEACE

When a Capitalist state has had, and won, its "war for markets" it cannot use victory to get the market, as witness victorious Great Britain, much less able to dispose of its surplus after its successful war than it was before. Another war would destroy both markets and capitalism. In promoting war, as they sometimes do, capitalists, being subject to the same errors and passions as the bulk of mankind, think and act as nationalists or militarists not as economists. Socialism does not emerge from chaos: Fascism emerges. Socialists and Capitalists have as much a common interest in the creation of an international order as in the maintenance of a sewage system or of rules of the road.

In the post-war period the economic explanation of war has, with an increasing number, taken a line different from that dealt with in the preceding chapter. Not pressure of population, the struggle of peoples for life and sustenance, but Property, Capitalism, the struggle for profits is the cause of war.

We are, therefore, told that if peace is to be established at all, "Capitalism must be swept utterly away, the institutions of private property abolished, the whole world become Socialist or Communist." Or, as Mr. Brailsford puts it, *"Property or Peace."* You cannot, he assures us, have both:

> War in the modern world is the outgrowth of the system of property. When men will to banish war, they must abandon the exclusive and monopolistic institution of property . . .
> Socialism offers in the modern world the one sure road of escape from war. It alone can arrest the logical movement by which property generates it.[1]

[1] *Property or Peace,* H. N. Brailsford, p. 261.

[203]

This means, of course, that nothing can be changed until everything is changed, that Socialists and Capitalists can have no ground for common action on behalf of peace, no common political interests, cannot co-operate in the maintenance of international order and the suppression of anarchy.

Mr. Brailsford, representing a widely held Socialist view, does not balk at that conclusion. He writes:

> Our goal of order and peace can be reached only by a relentless concentration on the single purpose of abolishing private property in the means of life. It asks from us the hardest of all things for intelligent men to concede—a deliberate narrowing of ourselves, a set fanaticism that will neither pause nor capitulate till its central purpose is achieved.[1]

Others of this school of thought make it quite clear that even if peace could be obtained by co-operation or "compromise" with the existing order, they would not purchase it at that price. Thus the secretary of the No More War Movement criticises me[2] severely for failing, in his view, to recognize that fact. He writes:

[1] *Property or Peace*, H. N. Brailsford, p. 245.

[2] From a letter in *The Manchester Guardian*. I replied in another letter as follows:

"But it is not only at Geneva that the judge and jury are the representatives of what your correspondent regards as a criminal system of society. The judge and jury in Britain are equally representatives of that society. Does the secretary of the No More War Movement think in consequence that we should do better without the courts, that it would be better for the litigants to 'shoot it out,' and for everyone to defend himself as best he could without the aid of the police? Even if the Geneva system is under the domination of an Imperialist society, are the alternative anarchy and the resulting wars any less under that domination? Is it better to have an imperfect system of law which can be gradually changed or no law at all? Does the existing anarchy ensure justice and freedom?

. . . the judge and jury at Geneva are all representatives of a system of society which many of us regard as criminal in itself . . . where the vast majority live under Governments such as those of India or Italy.

We do not regard a League of Governments as having any moral authority whatsoever. . . . It behoves us to consider what sort of peace do we want—peace based upon freedom and justice or peace based upon a dictatorship of the Secretariat at Geneva.

The world to-day is riddled with Imperialism with which we can never willingly co-operate or compromise.

That means breaking with "practical politics," for if continuity is to be held a virtue, then the way to end

"I have not the slightest hesitation in answering the questions the general secretary puts to me; nor, if I may say so, have I ever had.

"I do not in the least suppose that every judgment given by Geneva would be impartial or just; I am pretty sure indeed that many would often be unjust. But I would regard the verdict of even a bad court as to be preferred to the decision of the best war; occasional injustice under law as infinitely better than no law. If we have to choose between peaceful judgments by such Governments as we have got, an unjust peace if you will, and war, I choose the unjust peace and take such chance as the world presents of eliminating progressively the injustices of peace.

"But I am not at all sure that the general secretary of the No More War Movement makes that choice.

"The implication of his letter plainly is that even if Geneva could secure us peace, he does not want it because it would be an Imperialist or anti-democratic peace. Well, there is something to be said for preferring war to a bad peace, and militarists of all ages have said it. But it is indeed strange to hear the general secretary of a No More War Movement saying it.

"If for the attainment of peace, of any system of law as an alternative to anarchy, we have to wait until all Governments have become democratic (this would demand considerable changes in Russia) ; until Governments, like Britain, have ceased all Imperialism; France become pacifist; Italy has had a new revolution and repudiated Fascism; Germany repudiated Hitler; Poland, Pilsudski; until all laws are just, all systems of society equitable and democratic—well, we shall have to wait a very long time indeed."

cannibalism would be to encourage cannibals eating ten men per week to reduce to nine, eight and so forth. We who break from the old social standards have no use for "practical politicians" who have brought us only war and misery. There is nothing in their system that we wish to continue.

This same Peace Movement official, speaking at a conference of The War Resister's International, gives precision to the above view in these terms:

> Defence of the existing order of society is not peace, it is the maintenance of a war-motivated civilisation; where violence is the moral basis of the state itself. . . .

How serious such a view may be in dividing peace forces and frustrating peace effort is evident enough.

The average man, knowing too well the difficulty of securing even small reforms, apt to be put off by the complexity and difficulty of any public question, is told that it is no good attempting to do anything whatsoever about peace unless and until he is prepared to transform the whole social and economic fabric from top to bottom. In so far as this view influences the attitude of the ordinary man at all, it confirms his predisposition to regard himself and his opinions as in no way responsible for war, and in so far as it prompts the politically minded to oppose or disparage the League, it allies the extreme Left of Communists and Socialists with the extreme Right of Militarists and Jingoes, who also oppose Geneva.

I suggest, in respect of the assumptions which underlie the various propositions quoted above,

(1) That Capitalism as an economic system neither needs nor benefits by war; that it cannot use successful

war in the modern world as a means of disposing of the surplus of its production, acquiring new markets, increasing its profits; that, on the contrary—as the position of the victorious Capitalist states after a completely successful war abundantly demonstrates—Capitalism has suffered disastrously and been incalculably weakened by war and that another like the last will, as enlightened Capitalists are aware, probably destroy it altogether.

(2) That the Socialist refusal to co-operate with bourgeois efforts towards a better international order, the systematic disparagement of all such efforts, persistent "crabbing" of the League and similar institutions, is profoundly bad strategy from the point of view of all sound social reform and an ill service to Socialism itself; that it puts the cart before the horse in that Socialism needs peace in order to come into being at all in Western Europe, and that the refusal to co-operate with a Capitalist order to maintain peace will end in a chaos which while destroying Capitalism, will fail to produce Socialism, as that chaos has failed so to do anywhere in Western Europe; that Socialists have as much a common interest with Capitalists in the suppression of war as they have in the suppression of cholera or any other pestilence equally evil for Capitalist or Socialist.

Let us take the last point first.

The views of the English Socialists from whom I have quoted were, of course, the views promulgated officially and persistently by the Russian government until the eve of its entrance into the League of Nations. That entrance was itself an avowal of fundamental change of policy on that point—a change prompted, doubtless, not only by the Japanese menace, but by an intelligent appreciation of post-war events. In no single case west of Russia has Socialism anywhere emerged out of the numberless upheavals which were the legacy of the war. Out of the chaos produced by the war has come, not Socialism, but Fascism: not "the Social Revolution" of the Marxian prognosis, but counter-revolution, the destruction of the fruits of the French Revolution.

That fact—the fact that Capitalist society *could* produce a counter-revolution—has itself been commonly ignored until the present. It is something, indeed, which the pre-war Socialist could not have understood. We have been in the habit heretofore of talking of "the" revolution, and of groups known as "revolutionaries," assuming as a matter of course that any revolution must be from below, any revolutionary change for the advantage of "the exploited mass" who had "nothing to lose but their chains." The fact that there could be such a thing as a bourgeois revolution, designed deliberately to undo the work of the French Revolution, to repudiate its doctrines, to deny the Enlightenment, was something never envisaged by the pre-war Socialist or even by the post-war Marxian. It is indeed something which runs directly counter to the orthodox Marxian interpretation of history.

The Soviet leaders had themselves accepted, after the War, the assumption that "revolution" in Capitalist countries must mean a Socialist revolution, and proceeded on the approved Marxian principle of supporting "revolution" in general. For some time now, of course, Moscow has abandoned the policy (though not perhaps the slogan) of "world revolution," and accepted the principle of co-operation with non-Socialist states for certain common political ends.

The whole post-war tendency illustrates how very much the policy of refusing to co-operate with "Capitalist" plans of peace, to regard Socialism as the sole road to peace, is to put the cart before the horse. It is probably true to say that unless Socialists can help to prevent Capitalists from going to war, Socialism will be destroyed—together with Capitalism. The post-war history leaves little doubt upon that point.

For what does Russia's membership of the League imply? It means that the "Capitalist" organisation she has so consistently disparaged can serve a purpose in helping to prevent the destruction by war of the first great Socialist experiment of history. If Russia's action does not mean that, then it is meaningless.

It is common ground that Russia's object in joining the League is to enlarge as much as possible the obstacles to war in the East, a war provoked by Japan, and the result of which might well be the downfall of Russian Communism. It is equally common ground that Russia's membership of the League will render Japanese aggression, in which Russian Socialism might perish, more difficult. If the League, as enlarged by Russia's membership, does help to prevent that Japanese aggression, then its first great achievement will have been the saving of Socialism in Russia. (Such are the strange humours of history.)

Russia wants peace, peace to go on with her Socialist effort without the diversion of resources, energies, attention, effort, which war would involve. She plainly believes that the existence of the League and her membership in it helps towards that end. She recognizes

that however the economic purpose of a bourgeois or
Capitalist state and a Socialist one may diverge, there
may well be a large field of other purposes, even political purposes, which they may have in common, interests
for the defence of which they may co-operate.[1]  As
things have turned out, the maintenance of peace within
the framework of the present economic system is indispensable to the establishment in Western Europe of any
form of Socialism which aims at welfare as distinct from
the militarist mystic, racialism or nationalism of German or Italian Fascism.  Even Socialists admit that if

[1] In January, M. Molotoff, speaking at the meeting of the Executive
of the Communist Party, said: "It seems that the League is an em-
barrassment to the enemies of peace—as is shown by the exit of Germany and Japan.  The world knows we have no intrinsic respect for
the League, but in so far as it is a brake upon or impediment to war
danger, we cannot fail to appreciate its services."  And on Christmas
Day M. Stalin gave an interview to the correspondent of an American
newspaper (Published in the *New York Times* of December 28th,
1933) in which he said that, "If the League is only the tiniest bump,
somewhat to slow down the drive towards war and help peace, then
we are not against the League . . . and it is not excluded that we
should support it, despite its colossal deficiencies."  Finally, M. Litvinoff made an even more important statement on December 29th to the
All-Union Executive Committee, when he said: "We are now on the
point of transition between two eras. . . . There are . . . bourgeois
States . . . which are interested for the immediate future in the maintenance of peace . . . a fact which is highly valuable to us. . . . It
may be assumed that in the League of Nations that tendency will win
which is interested in preserving peace. . . . We have never objected,
and do not object, to organised international co-operation which aims
at strengthening peace.  Not being doctrinaires, we do not refuse to
make use of existing or future international combinations and organisations, providing we have now, or in the future, reason to believe that
they would serve the cause of peace. . . ."  It is interesting to note
that only on December 6th, M. Litvinoff, then in Rome, had informed
the Press that "there is no question of the U.S.S.R. joining the League
under any contingency that can be foreseen."

war comes Capitalism may be destroyed.[1]  But we can be quite sure that if war comes, or the preparation for it goes on in Western Europe, Socialism will just as certainly be destroyed.

Possible bases of co-operation have already been revealed by the revival of the Franco-Russian military alliance.  The French *bourgeoisie* plainly fears German military nationalism more than it fears Russian Communism, and is prepared to co-operate with the latter for protection against the former, and the Communist state realises that there are degrees of Capitalist wickedness; that the Nazi or Japanese type is more immediately dangerous, to put it at its lowest, than the French or American type.

That is to say, as an indispensable condition of the security of the greatest Socialist experiment in history, as an indispensable condition of the right to carry it on at all, we are, surprisingly, thrust back into reliance in the international field on that very doctrine of liberal co-operation between rival systems which has during these recent years been so much disparaged by certain Socialist writers.

Let us push this analysis a little further.

In his book, *Property or Peace,* Mr. Brailsford criticises the League because it "merely reproduced on a

---

[1] "Nor are Great Britain and France, the two leading parliamentary countries, in any danger of military defeat in the near future, provided that they stand together . . . these countries do not want war, though it may be forced upon them, and though they could rely on winning it in a military sense.  Their Governments want peace, both because they know that their populations want peace, and because war would very likely mean the end of Capitalism and the establishment of a Socialist system."  *What Marx Really Meant,* by G. D. H. Cole, pp. 162-3.

great scale the old-world police state, limited to the function of preserving order . . . as a king might call his quarrelling feudatories to their allegiance," and did not from the start tackle the economic task of currency control, adjustment of the world price level, organisation of the world market for primary products, control of the flow of population and emigration. "These Liberals of Versailles were politicians for whom economics hardly existed."

But does not history and the plain logic of the problem before us indicate clearly that the economic task cannot possibly be undertaken at all until the "police state" exist; that without a basis of political order no large scale economic planning is possible at all. If that political order must arise, *in the first instance,* out of voluntary co-operation between independent units, must not one begin with the purposes about which there is the greatest measure of agreement, rather than with those which provoke the greatest measure of disagreement?

Until the quarrelling feudatories *were* brought into some sort of agreement or common allegiance, no British state capable of organising unemployment benefit, old age pensions, health insurance, free and universal education, could possibly have come into being, and one can hardly imagine feudal chiefs being brought into very active co-operation for the specific purpose of abolishing feudal privileges. In so far as the development towards a common sovereignty was voluntary at all, its motive was primarily self-preservation, protection, defence, security of "rights" broadly, as Feudal society saw them; recognition of the fact that while acquiescence in law was not as good as complete mastery or independence, it was better than the alternative destruction or chaos. The very fact that bourgeois, individualist society of the early nineteenth century in supporting certain political and legal changes did *not* intend the particular economic outcome which resulted, is surely ground for hope that a similar political beginning in the international field may have a similar economic outcome. Had the Reform Bill—or for that matter the Charter of 1838—embodied all of Owen's Socialism, it is quite certain we should not have got Parliamentary Reform, and extremely unlikely that we should have got the body of social legislation which we have. For, as we now know, if the Chartist demonstrations under O'Connor had developed into a clash with the forces under Wellington, the Chartists would have been hopelessly beaten, and democracy, both political and economic, have received an immense setback.

"Capitalism" does not support Geneva with anything like the unanimity that it supports the apparatus of our own British law, the courts, police, parliament. Does this mean that because Capitalism supports—and uses—those institutions, Socialists ought to oppose them? That Socialism would have a better chance if law courts and police did not exist and should therefore set out to destroy them? It is not Socialism that would emerge out of the anarchy, any more than Socialism has emerged anywhere in Western Europe out of the post-war chaos.

The assumption that Capitalism by its nature must oppose the establishment of the police system, of law, internationally, has no warrant in history and no warrant in economic science. Which brings us to the more fundamental assumption underlying the attitude of some Socialists.

On what ground is it stated, usually so emphatically and dogmatically, that "Capitalism is the cause of war"? The case has been stated most ably, moderately and clearly perhaps by Professor Harold J. Laski, and I cannot do better than quote his summary.  He says:

> Once, after the 'eighties, the drift towards economic imperialism had begun, it brought with it inescapable consequences.  The discovery that the exporters of capital could use the state as the collectors of the interest on their debt transformed the whole psychology of trading relationships.  It necessitated a strong state; and this, in its turn, involved a state whose physical power was adequate to its pretensions.  It is not accident that the enormous increase in military and naval expenditure occurred *pari passu* with the need to protect investments abroad. . . .
>
> The economic imperialist puts forward a simple case. He points out that we live by our power to export manufacturers and capital; we must therefore have markets as the condition of our survival.  We need them the more because our productive powers, through scientific discovery, continually expand, competition glows ever more keen, and if we cannot sell abroad, the dependence of our people on foreign supplies of food would mean an inability to maintain our population at its present level. To secure markets must therefore be the essential objective of our policy. . . .
>
> The root fact from which we have to start is the accumulation in states of a developed character of surplus capital more rapidly than the opportunity of its domestic employment.  It emigrates because it cannot find the security or the rate of profit which foreign investment

offers; and, when it emigrates, it looks to the state to protect it from risk as best it can. *The Intelligent Man's Way to Prevent War.* pp. 508-16.

The whole of that theoretical arch rests upon one keystone, the assumption that the Capitalist state, needing to expand its markets for the sale of its surplus products, can acquire those markets by the use of military power, either through the seizure of territory whose population can in some way be compelled to buy goods, or by preventing competitors from having access to those markets; or, in respect of financial operations, that war can be used to open fields of investment or to collect the dividends or repayment of loans when the investment has been made. First and last the assumption is that military power can compel these things, that they can be made to follow upon conquest and that conquest is the instrument. If that is not true the whole elaborate thesis falls to the ground.

It is not true. The abundant, the overwhelming experience of the post-war years proves that it is not true, and reveals war to us, not as the outcome of forces necessarily inherent in Capitalism, but as the outcome mainly of certain political errors inevitably productive of anarchy; errors shared by the Capitalists themselves, who are as liable as others to misinterpret their interests, and often to think and feel as nationalists rather than as economists,[1] a conclusion which makes our problem

[1] But not always. A student of international finance (Mr. H. Powys Greenwood) writes:

"Mr. Lloyd George records in his *War Memoirs*—and nobody can have been in a better position to know the facts—that in July 1914 the supposedly puppet-pulling financiers were almost without exception in a state of panic which baffles description. Their whole vastly

very different in character from that which the Marxian suggests.

It in no way substantiates the proposition which Professor Laski outlines to cite cases where important Capitalist interests have gained by war. The charge is that the working of the system as a system generates war. Very important Capitalist interests would most certainly profit by another Great Fire of London—profit enormously. That does not prove that Capitalism inevitably generates arson, nor makes arson a "Capitalist interest." Even if arson were pretty frequent (as it is), it would be quite inadequate to point to such cases to prove that "arson was inherent in Capitalism" and could only be grappled with by bringing that pernicious system to an end. To prove such a proposition, to indict Capitalist society on these grounds, it would be necessary to show the *process* by which Capitalist society benefited, or was pushed by the nature of its mechanism to arson.

What is supposed to be the *modus operandi* by which finance and industry hope to dispose of surplus products and ease the glut problem by the winning of modern wars, knowing what modern war involves? The rationale of the thing is never clearly indicated by these critics. They usually assume as self-evident that a Capitalist state that wins a war is then in a better position to dis-

complicated world was tumbling about their ears. The Governor of the Bank of England wept copiously in the Chancellor of the Exchequer's parlour. Most international bankers and financiers made heavy losses during the war, whereas many industrialists made fortunes. If international finance plotted Armageddon it must have been demented." *The Contemporary Review.* July 1934. p. 26.

pose of its surplus, and can use victory to force markets open.[1]

We are able to say now, with dogmatism, that a Capitalist state, having gone to war and won it, cannot use its victory for disposing of its surplus products.

Circumspice!

We live in a Capitalist nation that has just achieved complete military victory, and is obviously unable to use it for the purpose of enabling her to dispose of her surplus, for no crisis experienced by capitalism was ever so severe as in this moment of complete victory, one of the greatest victories of history—victory over a highly organised industrial state that used to be described as Britain's most redoubtable commercial and industrial rival. Britain has added as the result of that victory vast territories to her Empire. Never was her power more complete, never conquest in the military sense so overwhelming, never her Empire so great. And never her financial and economic difficulties so immense.

If ever a Capitalist state needed markets, or finance needed really secure and profitable investment, it is now. If ever a Capitalist state had complete victory over its "rival," free use of that instrument of military force which, the Socialist tells us, Capitalism uses for the expansion of markets, it has it now. Then why is the instrument not used for that purpose for which, we are told, it has been forged?

---

[1] "The only finally tenable basis for life is a fair exchange between both individuals and peoples. The capitalist must deny this, for his very being depends upon his getting the better part of every bargain, and since in the logic of the case he cannot dispose of his surplus within his own area, he must have exterior markets which can be forced to buy from him. 'Forced' is the key word." Mr. Geoffrey West in *Adelphi*, January, 1934.

Where are the new markets of the victorious states?

Germany, before the war, had a very large foreign trade. Our Press did indeed in the early years of the war talk a great deal of the transfer of this trade to us. We conquered Germany completely, we took over her colonies, embodied all sorts of economic provisions in the Treaty of Peace. Where is the resultant expansion of British markets?

If ever we had abundant proof that military power can *not* be used for enabling a Capitalist state to acquire new markets, get rid of its surplus products, find new fields for its investments, that proof has been before our eyes in the years which followed the Great War.

Our foreign sales are in volume about half what they were before the war, the markets of many of our stable industries a good deal less than half; some seem to be on the road to disappearance.

The crisis which war has meant for Capitalism is not confined to trade and industry.

The war multiplied our national debt by about ten, destroyed many of our investments, made collection of many debts due to us impossible, made it impossible to pay some of our debts, caused breakdown of our whole monetary system, pushed us twice off the gold standard, undermined our home markets, and was the main factor in causing world depression, revolutions, dictatorships, and disorders, which have had repercussions here, gravely disturbing Capitalism as an institution.

It has involved, not a crisis, but a series of shattering crises which are world-wide. They apply as much to great powerful states, nations covering a continent like the United States, as to lesser states mainly interested in primary products, like the Argentine, Brazil, Australia, or the Scandinavian states, Denmark, Norway, or more industrialised states like Belgium or Switzerland. None has escaped the economic blizzard.

Foreign investment? But there is hardly a banker in the world who does not tell you that the investment of capital abroad is finished, dead, done for; that it will never be revived on the old scale.[1]

In one of the passages from Professor Laski, quoted above, he describes one of the factors of imperialism as the discovery by Capitalists "that the exporters of capital can use the state as the collectors of the interest on their debt." Well, if there is one economic fact which stands out in the history of the post-war world more clearly than any other, it is that military power cannot now possibly be used for the collection of debt. This era might figure in financial history as "The Debt Repudiation Age" as in other historical spheres we speak of the Stone Age. It is, moreover, Repudiation with Impunity. The weakest state can refuse to pay its debts and the strongest is impotent to compel it. For years a powerless and disarmed Germany has owed Britain enormous sums, both in the form of government and private debts. Most extraordinary measures, amounting to what might be described as the financial occupation of the country, were taken to ensure the collection of those debts. Militarily Germany was impotent and her enemies all powerful. Those enemies were at times

---

[1] Sir Arthur Salter in *The Times* of September 24th, 1934, says: ". . . foreign lending . . . is a principal condition of any substantial expansion of foreign trade. After years of default and continued political uncertainty it is evident that foreign investment will only gradually revive: it will take new forms, require new precautions and, for very many years be on a smaller scale than in the years preceding the depression."

ready to employ utter ruthlessness, as the French did in the occupation of the Ruhr. Yet the whole process proved to be absolutely sterile. Nothing could be collected. The military instrument having failed completely as an instrument of collection, financial means were employed. Germany's creditors began lending her money for the purpose of paying the debts she owed. In other words, old debts were cancelled by the creation of new. But Germany continued always to win on the deal, with the result to-day that she has paid in Reparations, for instance, far less than the money which has been lent to her since her defeat for the purpose of making payment possible. And this does not refer merely to the government debts. As these lines are being written a Commission is in Germany trying to arrange for the payment of commercial debts and the sums due for material supplied to Germany within the last year or so, and failing to get the money.

But this phenomenon is not peculiar to the relations of Germany and the Allies. It characterises the relations between all great states, and great states to little ones. Great Britain has just announced that she cannot continue the payment of interest on the loans contracted in America during the war. Even supposing that the United States had a tremendous preponderance of power, how would that country, in view of the above story of debt collection, proceed to recover the sums which Britain owes? Leon Trotsky prophesied some years ago very dogmatically that a war between Britain and America was inevitable, owing to this very situation, the determination of the Americans to collect their debts. Imagine Trotsky to be a true prophet; the war having taken place; the United States victorious. How would that country then proceed to collect debts? What unknown measure would she employ as against Britain which we have failed to employ as against Germany?

But what is true in the relations of these countries is true also of very many small states that owe debts to very great ones and which the latter are quite unable to collect. One aspect of what at the time was described as characteristically American imperialism was the lavish lending by American bankers to a number of South and Central American states. At the moment of writing the states in default include Argentina, Bolivia, Brazil, Chile, Columbia, Costa Rica, Cuba, San Salvador, Mexico, Panama, Peru, Uraguay. American financiers have written off most of those loans as bad debts. They never will be paid. Yet America certainly does not lack preponderance of power. The bankers are aware that these debts cannot be collected, whatever military power America might apply to the task.

Now, we are dealing here with facts which throw light on what is perhaps the major count in the Socialist indictment of Capitalism as the main cause of war: The use of power to secure fields of investment and to make sure that the dividends are collected. Professor Laski, for instance, does not rest his case merely upon the fact that there are isolated instances—Egypt, Newfoundland —in which it could in a sense be said that battleships played a role in the collection of debt. His major point is that the process of using military power in order to extend markets and secure fields for investment and insuring that the loans are repaid, is not an occasional or incidental feature of imperialism, but its tap root, inherent in the whole system. One would have assumed, therefore, especially in view of the amazing and obviously relevant experience of the last twenty years, that the question of whether, in the conditions of the world as we know it, power *can* be used for debt collection would be very fully examined. Here are features to which one would suppose Socialist writers would devote a large part of their investigation. Yet these amazing economic episodes, characteristic of the last twenty years, are very rarely mentioned by the Socialist. In the essay by Professor Laski, from which I have quoted, long, detailed, exhaustive, there is only the most casual reference to the actual experiences, going on before our eyes, which bear so vitally upon the theory of the relation of Capitalism to war.

Let us note the facts which bear on certain outstanding Marxian arguments, particularly these:

(1) *War results from the struggle for raw material.*

A state possessing raw material has one purpose: to sell it. It is quite unnecessary to go to war to get it. Britain did not need to "capture" Louisiana in order to build upon its raw cotton the greatest of all British industries. As things are, the problem of capitalism is not shortage of raw material which has to be politically "captured" by wars that dislocate fatally the whole economic and financial system, but the far greater problem of over-production, surplus.

(2) *War results from the struggle for markets wherein to dispose of the surplus that cannot be sold at home.*

Military force, latent or active, the power to dominate another country in a military sense, does not enable a capitalist state to "force" its goods on that country in defiance of economic or financial difficulties such as those indicated below. The nations of the Empire, including India, which Britain is supposed to dominate have a fiscal autonomy which they employ to exclude British goods, to compete with British trade and industry just as though they were foreign states. Their tariffs are often no less damaging to British trade.

The fact of investing capital abroad does not solve that dilemma with which the Marxian deals. Interest on investment—the dividends on the railroads or the harbour works—can only be paid by the production of goods which accentuate the general world glut of goods, just as much as if the investment were made at home. Indeed, the dislocations caused by the glut of wheat, wool, cotton, coffee, coal . . . obviously is not to be overcome by conquering more territory for the purpose of producing more of those things. In so far as the theory put forward assumes that the purchasers in the markets so conquered are to be made "to pay in money not goods," it is merely a new manifestation of the old mercantilist illusion. Payments simply cannot for long be made in "money" by a country which is not exporting goods and the attempt to compel payment, creates devastating exchange and monetary dislocations more rapidly and more surely than ever before in history.

(3) *War results from the struggle for new areas of investment.*

Investment normally does not require military action. It is not necessary for investors to press their government to conquer a particular territory in which they desire to invest, as witness our very heavy investments in countries like the Argentine, Brazil, the United States; and the heavy investments of the United States in Canada, the South American States already mentioned, and in Europe. The shares of enterprises (e.g. South African Gold Mines) can be purchased by the capitalists of any nation on any stock exchange.

(4) *War results from the efforts of bond holders to collect debts.*

Military force does not enable a capitalist state to

collect the interest on its bonds or investments, despite certain isolated cases of the pre-War era; the proof of this in the post-War world is overwhelming and un-challengeable.

One Socialist writer tells us that "Capitalism is forced into war as a solution, even if only a temporary one, of the dilemmas and contradictions inherent in the Capitalist system."

Let us see.

Capitalism has never before faced such a degree of difficulty as it is encountering to-day in what is the most characteristically Capitalist state, America. Capitalists there would certainly turn to any means of easing the pressure. Now, if ever, is the time to apply the imperialist solution, if solution it be. Are they doing so?

Forty years ago the United States annexed the Philippines, not as the result of any economic need or motive, but as the by-product of an emotional explosion which led to the Spanish-American War. There has recently passed through the congress of the United States an act granting complete independence to the Philippines within ten years.[1] If the motive for annexation were

[1] A despatch from Manila published in *The Times* of August 31st, 1934, says:

". . . During the last two years there has been growing steadily a conviction that the Philippines have ceased to be either a political or an economic asset to the United States, and have become a liability burdensome both to American capital and labour interests and also a possible national danger. . . . Sugar can now be obtained more cheaply from Cuba, where American capital is more extensively engaged, and in addition Americans are convinced that national interests are best served by producing beet sugar at home. Copra also competes with the products of the American farmer. The coconut oil which is obtained in copra is used in manufactures for which vegetable and animal fats produced in the United States

[ 224 ]

mainly emotional, it is quite clear that that for *dis*annexation it is at least largely economic—the competition of Philippine sugar and other products with those of home producers.

American Capitalism has, as all the world knows, very profound troubles at this moment, and many and varied anxieties—grave problems of monetary policy, the gold standard, currency and exchange stabilisation, banking legislation, government control of banking operations, of the stock exchange, of the discount rate, labour troubles, social legislation. . . . Would anyone, who knows anything whatever at first hand of Capitalist mentality, suggest that "Wall Street" is really concocting "imperialist plots" as a solution of Capitalism's difficulties, the conquest of more territory, the subjugation of foreign peoples? Suggest to an "international financier" at this moment, when his house is falling about his ears as the result of the dislocations of the last war, that it is he who is fomenting a new one, is behind the unrest of the world, and he would regard you as an imbecile.

Incidentally, this reaction from imperialist expansion is to be noted on this side of the Atlantic as well. We have witnessed Press agitations against the assumption

might be used. . . . Formerly the political advantage of retaining the Philippines could be pleaded against these sectional interests. An opinion, however, has spread that a connection with these islands will drag the United States into whatever trouble may arise in the Far East, although the national interests might not be in any way involved. . . . The commercial interests, which at one time assuaged anti-Imperial opinion and defeated the efforts of the Independence Party by insisting on the incapacity of the Filipinas to govern themselves and the necessity of America having a military base in the East, are now outvoted by the interests which proclaim the Filipinas fully capable of looking after themselves, and emphasize the dangers of commitments in the Far East."

[225]

by Great Britain of the Palestinian mandate; against the continued occupation of Mesopotamia; for the withdrawal from Egypt. Again, the motives were Capitalist and economic. The burden on our finances of the Mesopotamian occupation was dreaded, despite the talk of "oil in Iraq." In a world in which there was already too much oil, and in which Capitalists at home were beginning to be interested in the production of oil from coal, an expensively administrated province, even if it does contain oil, loses its attraction. In fact, the organisation which finally took over oil concessions was a combination of American, Dutch, French and British Capitalists. The shares of such undertakings can be purchased by any Capitalist on any stock exchange without his government being antecedently obliged to go to war.

No case is perhaps more frequently quoted by the Socialists than that of India. India, we are told, over and over again, is a typical case where Capitalism pushes to the conquest or retention of markets by military means. We have conquered India. We developed that possession, invested money therein. With two results: (1) A great development of Indian industry which has been more severely competitive with certain of our own industries, like that of cotton, than even the competition of states like Japan. (For every five yards of cotton lost to Lancashire mills, Japan only supplies one.) (2) The Westernisation of India has resulted in its obtaining its fiscal autonomy with results, not only in high tariffs against British goods, but such devices as bounties to Indian-produced iron and steel which still further embarrass Britain's industry.

Manchuria may yet prove Japan's India in this respect, with the difference that the intensification of world unrest which Japanese action in Manchuria has involved may well mean for Japan a far more serious loss of trade, owing to continued economic and financial instability throughout the world, than any corresponding loss suffered by Britain in the eighteenth and nineteenth centuries as an offset to her Indian venture. The world is now more interdependent, more sensitive to disturbance anywhere. On balance, Japanese trade is more likely to lose than gain by adventures like that in Manchuria.

What, after all, is the nature of the difficulties which Capitalism faces, difficulties which must be as apparent to Capitalists as to Socialists? They are above all troubles which come from dislocation, disequilibrium, maldistribution. "Capitalist" economists have certainly never minimised the part played by war in throwing the whole thing out of gear.

Professor Clay,[1] for instance, notes:

Before the war the world's industry was in a state of balance. The different industrial groups in the world were so proportioned to one another that exchange went along smoothly. The war destroyed this balance and the world's industries have never found a new equilibrium. In retrospect, it is obvious enough that war must have this result; but we are so accustomed to rely on the recuperative power of the industrial organisation that we find it hard to conceive of a shock from which it might not recover.

The war involved the diversion of resources in men and equipment to war service and munitions production.

[1] *The World's Economic Crisis.* The Halley Stewart Lectures for 1931. (Allen & Unwin).

[227]

In the latter part of the war no less than half of the country's economic resources must have been absorbed in meeting war needs.  After the war it was necessary to divert them back into channels in which they could meet the normal demands of peace.  The task of rediversion was greater than that of organising them for war, not only because there was no dominating object by reference to which the movement could be controlled, but because the other channels from which they had been drawn were many of them closed by the war. . . .

The United States expanded its wheat acreage to fill the place left vacant by the loss of Russia's exports; the mills of Japan and India were expanded to supply the markets that Lancashire could not supply.  But this diversion of trade involved a duplication of capacity; for the war did not permanently contract Russia's capacity to supply the world with wheat, or Lancashire's capacity to supply it with cotton manufactures. . . .

The nationalist economic policies of post-war Governments after the war continued the good work of the war.

Australia decided to build up her own woollen industry by putting a prohibitive duty on imported manufactures, and just as the depressed Yorkshire industry was recovering, her next best market, Canada, decided to do the same.  Now England follows suit, and French spinners are looking for mills in England in which to duplicate the already excessive capacity for woollen spinning and weaving from which the industry in every country is suffering.  The story of cotton is the same.  In every country the industry has been depressed, even when other industries were active, because in the world as a whole there is more machinery than the total demand will employ.  The coal industry's troubles are rooted in the same policy.  When the Silesian boundary was under discussion the delegates of Poland and Germany both insisted that the coal-field was essential to their national life; a few years later negotiations over a commercial treaty between the two countries were held up, not for months but for years, because the Germans refused to admit any Polish coal, and the Poles insisted that they must be allowed to export to Germany this essential of their own national life.

The truth is that the popular Marxian interpretation of the relation of war to Capitalism is out of date.

At an earlier stage in the economic development of the world, for all the reasons which the present writer has elaborated elsewhere,[1] there was an economic case for imperialism. Modern conditions have rendered it very largely invalid. Both Capitalists and Socialists inadequately appreciate the change of condition.

In his *Imperialism and World Politics,* a post-war book, Mr. Parker Moon, after urging that all the facts of our world economy would, even from the point of view of those whose interests are rooted in the existing system, point to world co-operation, adds:

> Nations hesitate to take the step, inevitable as it may be, because public opinion and public sentiment cling to doctrines which were formulated to fit the economic facts of a generation or two generations ago. It takes so long to convert the public to a new doctrine that often the doctrine is out of date before it wins general acceptance. Men were slow to accept the gospel of imperialism which a few professors, business men, and journalists began to preach in the seventies and eighties of the last century, as a solution of the economic problems of their day; but in the end imperialism spread. Now it is being

[1] *The Great Illusion.*

applied, a mid-Victorian policy in a very un-Victorian age.

It is this survival of mid-Victorianism that makes it so difficult to perceive the plain facts of the present situation. We see not the facts but a mid-Victorian mirage.[1]

This author is all for simplicity. But the Marxian theme that "Capitalism" or "property" is the sole or main cause of war is simplification of the wrong kind, and ignores forces of psychology and politics which cannot be ignored, if we are to understand this problem. Those forces of themselves invalidate the commonly accepted Marxian thesis. Let us see what they are.

[1] *Imperialism and World Politics*, by Parker T. Moon, p. 558.

# PART IV
# PSYCHOLOGICAL FACTORS

# Chapter I

## THE INTER-ACTION OF POLITICS, ECONOMICS AND PSYCHOLOGY

Motives which we commonly regard as economic very often prove to be, when examined, political and psychological in character. The conditions which create economic rivalry are often conditions which have arisen out of circumstances that have not an economic origin.

IN THE quotation from Mr. Parker T. Moon's book on Imperialism, cited at the close of the last chapter, the remark is made that the economic ideas that still animate world politics are ideas which belong to the Victorian age which, economically speaking, has passed away. But it might be said with truth that the Marxian has taken over in common with the Capitalist, conceptions which go farther back than the Victorian age—to the conception of the state, a political or administrative unit, as also an economic unit, an "estate," a conception which has hardly responded to the facts since feudal times. A feudal chief had to conquer with his armies a neighbour's territory if he was to draw tribute therefrom. A Capitalist can draw tribute from the mines of Mexico or Peru without political conquest at all.

Much of the economic rivalry we discuss is conditioned by purely economic facts. Thus except for a *political* fact—the union of the German states—we should not, indeed could not, have thought of "German" trade at all. We should talk of Bavarian trade or Prussian trade; and the Bavarian Capitalist would have been accused (perhaps with truth) of plotting war against Prussia. But the condition necessary for war to take place at all would be a *political* separateness. Without that *political* condition the economic factors, surplus and all the rest of it, could not possibly lead to war.

Stranger things have happened of late than that the German Union should dissolve, as the Austrian has already done. (The disruptive nationalist tendency to small political entities is in fact far stronger than the imperialist tendency—as witness a round dozen of new states and nearly ten thousand miles of new tariff barriers since the war. This is far more characteristic of our time than that of political amalgamation.) The political fact would set up new economic hostilities which did not previously exist as the Anglo-Irish tariff war has arisen from new political conditions. The motives behind conflicts which we regard as purely economic are plainly often political in nature. Before the war the textile industries of Northern France agitated violently for a tariff upon Alsatian textiles, free admission of which they declared would be fatal to the industries of the Northern Departments. Alsace is annexed. The same goods, made by the same people in the same factories, are now admitted without let or hindrance—and the textile industries of the French Northern Departments have not a word to say. But if the goods were evil before, does the baptising of them French make them innocuous? If Mr. de Valera makes a republic, becomes a foreign state, we shall be told that the foreign butter, bacon, eggs and cattle throw British agricultural workers out of employment. If the Free State reverted to its original position (or even if Mr. de Valera by taking the oath automatically makes Ireland a Dominion) then we should accept that agricultural produce as having no deleterious effect upon

British farming. But it would be the same butter and eggs.

Are the motives here political or economic? Does the political fact make the economic conflict or the economic the political?

Recall, for the elucidation of this question the illustration of an earlier chapter.

The thirteen British colonies of North America nearly failed to create a federation; nearly went the way which Spanish colonies went later—into separate republics. If Pennsylvania had been one political independency and Ohio another, each with its separate and competitive tariff, currency, currency regulations, each its own army, own navy, wrangles about access to sea or lakes, sooner or later there would have been war. Would its ultimate cause have been Capitalist and economic? Then why don't they fight now? Capitalism is rife in both States. They don't fight because of a political fact—federal union. Only by virtue of a certain political condition —separateness—can Capitalism produce war.

Look further south. For nearly three hundred years there was complete peace between the provinces of Central America. Abject poverty, but peace. Those provinces lose their unifying bond of common authority, become separate nations, and lo! where for three centuries there had been peace war becomes chronic, never-ending. Let Mr. Aldous Huxley (who reminds us that "Central America, being just Europe in miniature and with the lid off, is the ideal laboratory in which to study the behaviour of the Great Powers") complete the story from which a quotation was made in an earlier chapter. He says:

[235]

The most striking fact about the wars of Central America is that none of them has had an origin which would possibly be interpreted as economic. There has never been any question of capturing markets, destroying dangerous commercial competitors, seizing provinces for the sake of their industrially valuable resources. The wars of the Five Republics have been wars between Conservatives and Liberals, between Clerical and Anti-Clericals, between those who desired a single federal republic and those who claimed sovereign independence for each state. They have not been wars of interest, but of "political principle"—in other words, wars of pure passion. The wars of Europe are not essentially different.

The theorists of the left proclaim it almost as an axiom that, where there is private profit-taking, there of necessity must also be periodical war. But this is clearly untrue. If capitalists were interested only in the efficient exploitation of their victims (as would to heaven they had the sense to be!) they would not waste their resources in fighting one another; they would combine to work out the most efficient scheme for squeezing profits out of the entire planet. That they do not do—or do so only spasmodically and inadequately—is due to the fact that the exploiters are as much the slaves of the passions aroused by nationalism as the exploited. They own and use the instruments of propaganda, but are themselves the first to believe in, and to act upon, the nonsense they broadcast.[1]

But there is a further point not covered by the above. The proposition that the behaviour of a class is determined by its economic interest implies, of course, that in such a case that class must correctly interpret its interest. But classes as a rule do nothing of the sort.

[1] *Beyond the Mexique Bay.*

Again and again they grossly misinterpret their interest, a fact which for some reason the Marxian refuses to admit. For him the Capitalist is a person of steel-like brain, never deflected from the straight course of his hunt for "dividends," "profits," a purely money motive. Such a picture is pure fantasy. Mr. Huxley corrects such over-simplification. Dealing with the point that Capitalists make and threaten wars on the Machiavellian principle, that foreign dangers give the ruler an opportunity for strengthening his position at home, he says:

> But what is this power compared with the power that would be wielded by an oligarchy of world rulers? And compared with the profits to be derived from a world-system of economy, how poor are the profits earned under a mere nationalist system! Moreover, modern war is demonstrably ruinous to economic activity and disruptive of social order. So far from enriching and strengthening himself by war on the present scale, the capitalist ruler is likely to lose in the convulsion most of such money and power as he possesses. In spite of which, our rulers insist that the political and economic system shall remain (to their own manifest disadvantage) nationalistic. Safe and profitable, internationalism is yet rejected. Why? Because all capitalist rulers are bound by a theology of passion that prevents them from rationally calculating their profits and losses. And so long as such a theology continues to be accepted by rulers, it makes no difference whether these are private profit-makers or bureaucrats representing "the People." The development of nationalistic state-socialism is not only possible; at the present moment, it actually seems a probability.

The truth is that our so-called wars of interest are really wars of passion, like those of Central America. To find a war of pure interest one must go far afield. The Opium War between England and China was one of the very few whose causes were purely and unadulterately economic. "All for Hate," is the title of every great international tragedy of modern times, "or the World Well Lost."[1]

It is true that, once you have got the political conditions which set the course towards war, then exasperation resulting from poverty may accelerate the pace. There could be no war between Prussia and Bavaria in 1934 as there was in the last century, whatever the degree of poverty, because the union ended the political conditions, which made war possible. But the inflation and the depression and economic stress undoubtedly helped in producing bellicose Nazism, which has increased the likelihood of war between Germany and other states, made European peace harder to maintain and any sort of organised European society harder to set up. But that brings us back to what is ultimately a psychological problem: the behaviour of peoples under the stress of certain irritations and exasperations.

Note, however, one feature in that history of the formation of the North American union to which reference has been made in a previous chapter. The forces which prevented the formation of separate republics in the North, and so prevented war, were "Capitalist"

---

[1] A critic of Mr. Huxley's point of view (*New Britain*, April 25th, 1934) says that the hates which produce war are the result of poverty. But nearly the whole point of the South American illustration is that centuries of complete peace were compatible with dire poverty, gross tyranny and gross economic exploitation of the masses. War came not with any increase of poverty (which was diminished at about the time of the struggle for independence) but with the splitting up of the larger national units into smaller ones.

forces, those of finance and "big business" represented by Alexander Hamilton; the forces which stood consistently against union and for separateness were the popular forces, the forces of nascent nationalism. For years the separate colonies refused to yield one iota of independence and sovereignty in order to create a common authority. "The jealousies and dislike of any central governing body seemed insuperable" writes Truslow Adams. In his life of Alexander Hamilton, Oliver writes that, "rather than part with or delegate a single shred of local sovereignty to clothe the shivering and naked form of federal government," the states would face any poverty, any financial and economic misery. "The prosperity which all men affected to desire was only to be had on terms which the states could not bring themselves to pay." All the familiar characteristics of nationalism had already come into being. Oliver writes:

> The Thirteen States proceeded to indulge themselves in the costly luxury of an internecine tariff war. The states with seaports preyed upon their land-locked brethren and provoked a boycott in return. Pennsylvania attacked Delaware. Connecticut was oppressed by Rhode Island and New York. New Jersey, lying between New York on the one hand and Pennsylvania on the other, was compared to a cask tapped at both ends; North Carolina, between South Carolina and Virginia, to a patient bleeding at both stumps. . . . Wherever there is a boundary there are apt to be disputes, and the political conditions being what they were, it was not likely that this copious source of ill-feeling would run dry. The barbarities of the Pennsylvanians under Patterson, in the valley of Wyoming, outdid even the legend of British atrocities and left a wrangling memory in Connecticut.

At one time war between Vermont, New Hampshire and New York seemed all but inevitable.

The dignified entreaties of Washington, the unanswerable reasoning of Hamilton, says Oliver, "failed to move their light minds." The citizens preferred "to endure the murrain, the locusts and the darkness, rather than abandon their mean jealousies, their rivalries, at once sordid and malicious. Finally, in their madness they fell one upon the other; each at the beginning looking merely for advantage to itself in injury to its neighbours, but as time went on seeking injury to its neighbours even as an end desirable in itself."

Nevertheless Hamilton succeeded. Why? Why were the North American colonies of Great Britain able to create and maintain a form of association between separate political units which has since, with one exception, enabled them to maintain peace over a continent; while the Spanish colonies, despite so many sporadic efforts, were unable to create a political union, with the result that war between the separate political groups has been frequent, bitter and destructive? Certainly not because there was "Capitalism" in South America but not in North. Nor is it true that the efforts at political unity failed in South America and succeeded in the North because in the latter case the influence of the propertied classes was defeated. Again the facts are all the other way. It is altogether probable that in the ten years bitter fight which intervened between the Declaration of Independence and the formation of a federal union, the interest of the propertied classes in the creation of that union would not have been sufficient to prevail against the sectional influence but for a political consideration which cut athwart the separatist tendencies of the masses. The two economic groups had a common political objective—independence of Britain—and a common feeling of danger. For while it is true those who fought the early battles on behalf of the American Union were bitterly opposed by the popular "isolationists" of their time ("isolation" then meaning, of course, the isolation of Massachusetts, Virginia, Pennsylvania), and while the various states then resented deeply the idea of giving power to the centre, it was also true that the thirteen colonies had "to hang together or hang separately." The country was drifting to anarchy. "The men in country taverns on a Saturday night might declaim about liberty till they were hoarse or asleep, but if the states were to leave their debts unpaid, become a mere pack of small republics, quarrelling among themselves until gobbled up singly by some European Power, there would be little liberty worth declaiming about," writes Adams. Had Great Britain been really an impotent and decadent state—as obviously impotent as Spain was after the Napoleonic defeat—the fear of a common and still powerful enemy would not have been present to furnish a strong powerful motive for cohesion. The fact that the British colonies did not go the way of the Spanish was due partly to the influence of men like Hamilton, but more potently to the fact that if they had fought among themselves Britain would still have been in a position to reconquer them. The Spanish colonies had much less reason to fear reconquest. In both cases the dominating impulse was political, "freedom," "independence." But the independence of what area? What unit? And freedom from what? The North American Union saw that it must be the independence of a large unit, or it would not be independence at all; the South American, freed from any pressing sense of danger from the mother country, asked for independence, not only from Spain, but the independence of each province from the other provinces; and sometimes indeed the independence of a department in a province.

The various parties in the English colonies saw the folly of pushing "liberty and independence" to those extremes. But they only thus stopped short of self-defeating folly by reason of a factor in this complex of causes which is perhaps the most important of all as bearing upon our problem in the eighteenth century "nationalism" was still qualified by eighteenth century rationalism. Both groups were acting under the impulsion of a dominating idea, "independence," but the Spanish colonies applying it in the nineteenth century did so with a logic which was often in complete disregard of administrative workability, economic fact, welfare, political sense. The English colonies often indulged in rhetorical fustian about liberty or death and independence, but they at least did not so apply it as to defeat its purpose.

President Murray Butler, of Columbia University, has drawn a parallel between those events and the present condition of Europe. You have only, he says, to strike out "Vermont, New Hampshire and New York," and insert "France, Great Britain and Germany," and you pass from 1783 to 1934. He reminds us of the "tariff wars" recorded by John Fiske:

A single instance which occurred early in 1787 may serve as an illustration. The City of New York, with its population then of thirty thousand souls, had long been supplied with firewood from Connecticut, and with butter and cheese, chickens, and garden vegetables from the thrifty farms of New Jersey. This trade, it was observed carried thousands of dollars out of the city and into the pockets of detested Yankees and despised Jerseymen.

Embargoes, retaliations duly follow. Yet finally the various "classes" of the colonies ended by seeing that, however their economic interest might clash, they had a common political interest in unity. They showed an intelligent comprehension of their own interests, a political insight, which the privileged classes, aristocracies and Capitalists of later Europe (or America) have for the most part failed to reveal. These latter failed to support the policies of international co-operation which were in fact indispensable to their welfare, to support the pre-war efforts to prevent collision. For the most part (there were notable exceptions, particularly in the banking world) they bitterly opposed those efforts. "Which proves," the Marxist is apt to argue, "that war is to the interest of Capitalists." It proves nothing of the sort. It could only be proof of such interest if we assumed first of all that Capitalists always interpreted their interests correctly, whereas the facts are all the other way. A Capitalist is just as capable of folly as a coalheaver, though it is the anti-capitalist who is usually the last to admit it.

The utter chaos and disintegration, the losses and miseries suffered by the privileged orders in Europe this last twenty years, have not been inflicted by revolutionists from below. They are the result, the inevitable result, of policies for which the privileged orders themselves have been mainly responsible. It was as much to the interest of European commerce and industry to establish some stable political order in Europe during the nineteenth century, to prevent the economic disintegration which would inevitably follow a great war, as it was to the interest of the American property owners at the end of the eighteenth century to create a federal bond between the colonies. But while the influence of the privileged classes of America was thrown on the side of that policy, the influence of the privileged order in Europe has been thrown, on the whole, with a few isolated exceptions, decisively against it.

§

A final word on this aspect of the subject to the Socialist who believes that he cannot have a common political interest with the Capitalist.

Extend the analogy just drawn between the situation of the eighteenth century American colonies and the states of Europe to-day.

Imagine that a Socialist movement had existed when Hamilton was attempting to form his League of North American nations. Would it have been wise for Socialists to have opposed him because he was not ready to charge the nascent Federal government with the task of abolishing property and other similar economic problems when it was not yet strong enough even to assume its "policing" task? Would that economic planning which Franklin Roosevelt is now undertaking have been easier or more difficult, if what is now the United States resembled South America in being half-a-dozen different states? And, comparing the standards of life in the United States and those which have obtained for the last hundred years in Central and South America, should we say that political federalism aided or hampered the economic welfare of the people?

*Chapter II*

# PSYCHOLOGY, EDUCATION AND WAR

Despite the importance attached by some psychologists to finding a "moral equivalent" for war, it is doubtful whether civilised folk feel the need of the particular type of "orgy" which modern war involves. Yet psychology could play an important role in throwing more light on the phenomenon of human obtuseness to the self-evident, or the all but self-evident. For it is not the facts which govern conduct (pace the materialist interpretation of history) but men's opinion about them, which is often an entirely wrong opinion. Peace advocates have at times ignored very simple psychological truths.

MUCH energy has been expended by psychologists upon problems such as that of finding a "moral equivalent" for war—some peace-time substitute for some of its excitements, hates, hostilities, orgies; or upon such questions as whether children ought to be given lead soldiers, youngsters encouraged to join the O.T.C., and upon the nature of the unconscious motives that are said to provoke war.

It is an aspect of the problem which the present writer has dealt with fairly fully elsewhere.[1] More recently Mr. Aldous Huxley has analysed some of the psychological attractions of war. He points out that man is a profoundly social being and derives enormous satisfactions from feeling himself at one with the other members of his group. "War strengthens all the ties that bind the individual to the group and heightens his sense of group solidarity to the point of intoxication." Most of the tasks in our modern world seem dull and pointless; war comes along and dignifies even the

[1] *The Fruits of Victory,* and in an earlier book, *Patriotism under Three Flags: a Plea for Rationalism in Politics,* now out of print.

dreariest routine with the name of patriotic work. "War, moreover, produces a certain simplification in the social structure; and there seems to be no doubt that men are on the whole happier in a simple than in a complicated society." Finally,

> War begets and justifies all manner of emotional excitement. People like excitement and are grateful for any excuse to express their feelings—particularly those feelings which education has taught their conscious minds to disapprove of. War justifies hatred, hallows violence, sanctifies delight in destruction—baptises with the sacred name of patriotism all the anti-social tendencies we have been so carefully trained to repress. At the same time it provides the non-combatant with endless opportunities for enjoying this savage emancipation vicariously and without danger, in his daily newspaper. The barbarian and the unconscious sadist are strong within us. So strong, that even in peace time newspaper proprietors find it worth their while to devote a large proportion of their valuable space to the description of crimes. In war time half of every morning's paper deals with slaughter and most of the rest consists of incitements to hatred on the one hand and group solidarity on the other.

The patriot, adds Mr. Huxley, is allowed to indulge with a good conscience in vanity and hatred—vanity in regard to his own group, hatred in regard to all other groups.

"The pleasures of hatred are certainly not greater than the pleasures of love; but for most people they are greater than the pleasures of abstract and impersonal benevolence. People can get more pleasure out of hating foreigners they have never seen than out of vaguely wishing them well and trying, through their official representatives, to co-operate with them. The number of men and women who feel wildly enthusiastic about the League of Nations is very small. The number of those who whole-heartedly loathe the foreigner, or the Jew, or the Capitalist, or the Communist, is enormous. Hatred and vanity pay a higher dividend in psychological satisfaction than do impersonal benevolence and reasonableness."

Certain facts are to be noted. It is sometimes argued that the intense passions of war-time do at least give greater solidarity to the nations engaged; add to the sense of being "members one of another," and so provide a useful, indeed, indispensable social cement.

In a previous book[1] I have tried to show that the effect, such as it is, is too temporary to be on balance an advantage. Pugnacities become so intensified in war that when the war is over and they can no longer be vented upon the foreign enemy, enemies have to be discovered at home, and the same emotion which, while war against a foreign enemy was going on, did indeed make the country one, operates when the war is over to split the country itself into rival "herds." There must be something to hate; if not a foreign enemy, then a rival social or economic class. For the Socialist, the Capitalist becomes an enemy to be fought with actual guns, just like the foreign enemy; for the Capitalist, the Socialist. Or completely new enemies, like the "non-Ayrian" are discovered. After all, it was the countries that were supposed to have been most welded and unified by war that revealed the most disruptive tendencies, the revolutions and upheavals, after the war.

We may here find an explanation of what seems

[1] *Fruits of Victory.*

otherwise enigmatical: why just *after* a war, universally lauded as a means of national unity, "bringing all classes together," the country is distraught by bitter social chaos, amounting to revolutionary menace; why the fashionable lady, capable of sincere self-sacrifice (scrubbing hospital floors and tending canteens) for her countrymen when they are soldiers, becomes completely indifferent to the same countrymen when they have returned to civil life (often dangerous and hard, as in mining and fishing). This may explain why countries frequently at war—the Spanish American Republics or the Balkan States—are also countries where group rivalries are fiercest, whereas states less engaged in war with one another—the Scandinavian States, for instance—show less tendency to internecine strife within their borders.

That comparison raises the question whether men suffer much psychologically by the loss of war "orgies." Does the Dane or Swede or Swiss have a sense of frustration, a sense that he has been deprived of the advantages which the Albanian, the Bulgarian, the Macedonian, with his feuds, enjoys in such full measure? Or does the North American, living in relatively peaceful Illinois or Massachusetts, feel the lack of the advantages enjoyed by the Haitian, the Guatemalan, or the Mexican?

Once a political condition has put war out of the question, do we really feel its psychological need? The same plea could have been made for the inter-tribal wars of Africa or the inter-clan feuds of Scotland or Ireland as for modern war. The modern Macdonald seems to manage pretty well without his periodical raid against the Campbells and to suffer no psychological injury from their cessation.

Is it not possible that the larger and more varied life which urbanised standards give itself satisfies whatever the excitement of war may give, provided that there is not always present the powerful suggestion which "danger of war" sets up. We have in our midst states for whom war is and has been for generations by reason of their political situation out of the question—nations like Sweden, Denmark, Norway, Holland, Switzerland. These are very civilised people, with a standard of life quite as high as that enjoyed by the peoples of the great states like Germany and France. One may doubt whether the former group really envy the war and post-war experience of the latter.

There may be some value in these researches for a peace time equivalent of war, but given political conditions which exclude war, as they do in the case of the lesser states like Norway, Sweden, Denmark, Holland, Switzerland, neither the psychological urge to war nor the deprivation of its orgies seem to possess much importance.

There are, however, other fields of psychological inquiry connected with war well worth investigation. Let us recall the main factors of our problem.

First, a real and general will to peace exists. It is extremely doubtful whether the mass of men do find the idea of war anything like as attractive as it may once have been. Not only is modern war a dull and dirty business, but on the whole it is recognized as being a dull and dirty business. Yet war is the result of the ideas and feelings, the scale of values of the mass of men—such ideas and values as those which give us a

Balkanised Europe of rival nationalisms. The nationalist does not primarily want war; he wants independence and sovereignty for his nation, and then domination of others as the only way to make it "secure," and fails to see that such a policy must produce war. The question is *not*: "Why does he choose war?" because he does not choose war; he wants peace. The question is: "Why does he choose, anarchy, independence, and expect to make it compatible with peace?" Why does he fail to see that the two are incompatible? That, obviously, is a psychological problem, having some relation, doubtless, to the inquiries we have just discussed, but plainly distinct therefrom. That the failure of the average man to see that his claim for "absolute independence" must make peace impossible, is due to the fact that if he did make the admission he would have to surrender certain temperamental satisfactions which he desires to retain, may well be true and related to the "orgy" question. But it is clearly a very different thing from enquiring why he "wants war," since he does not want war.

The problem could be stated in a variety of terms. Why so often do men sacrifice their economic interests under the impression that they are promoting them? Again and again one sees the people, the "common people," of a nation clamouring for a policy which runs directly counter to their interests, as when one saw American farmers voting decade after decade for a high tariff which operated to their most obvious economic detriment[1] or as when a Big Bill Thompson can induce a Chicago electorate to forget the state of the City

[1] See the author's *The Public Mind: Its Disorders; Its Exploitation*, particularly the chapter entitled "Anglophabia as an Exhibit."

Treasury by talking about King George, and a Valera induce Irish farmers to think more of the tyrannies of Henry VIII than of the price of cattle. In such cases the average man wants welfare but simply does not see that his policy sacrifices it.

It is not the facts which govern our conduct, but our beliefs about them—so often false beliefs. And it is this which makes psychology important. If there is one truth in the world which hardly needs labouring, assuredly it is the truth that men have an amazing capacity for being mistaken about their interests, that there enter into the conclusions which they draw all sorts of obscure preferences, hostilities, tempers, fanaticisms, desire to impose our will, our view, our belief, our conviction; dislike of the person who has the insufferable impudence to disagree with us. All these things, pace the Marxian, enter into the framing of policy and conduct, are again and again the determining element. To reveal the nature of these obscure psychological factors, to show how they operate in explaining errors of conduct, how they explain the fact that, honestly desiring peace, we often follow policies which make it impossible, fail to see the relation between the policy and its result, is assuredly a very indispensable part of our task. It is the most useful which the science of psychology might perform. The facts dealt with in an earlier chapter suggest that education has inadequately developed the type of introspection, the particular "knack" which would enable us to weigh one want against another, to know which of the two we will go for, if the two are mutually exclusive; the knack of knowing whether our aim is welfare or a temperamental satisfaction, such as that of showing another nation that our fist is bigger than his; the habit of asking first questions: "What are governments for? Why do we organise society at all?" "What do we really want?"

That many of the motives which set up the dangerous tempers of Nationalism can be dragged from the plane of the unconscious by a conscious and logical process is certain. To say that because a motive of conduct is hidden, unconscious, it is therefore not amenable to reason, that logic can play no part in modifying it, is of course completely fallacious. The only process by which the unconscious *can* become conscious, by which motives are dragged from the unconscious, is one into which reasoning enters.

From the moment that we began to talk about the ethical or moral quality of, say, nationalism or patriotism, analyse it, inquire whether swagger, and bragging and bullying, and making other people "tremble with our might" are really good things at all, really the kind of activities decent folk should indulge in, from that moment our motive begins to be less unconscious our desires about it to change.

The only way in which values are altered, in which the thing heretofore regarded as good becomes bad, is by a process of comparison, of introspection.

Our disastrous policies are due to certain master ideas—independence, sovereignty, what not—which dominate policy because men have accepted them as good and workable, as they have often in the past accepted as good and workable perfectly monstrous ideas like those which actuated God-fearing men Holy Inquisitioners. There is only one means of altering them: to show that they are wrong and unworkable. When men see, as they can be made to see, that such notions *are* evil, they will also cease to like them.

Behind all these irrationalisms one overriding impulse seems plainly to stand out: the lust for domination, self-assertion, coercion. This impulse, sanctioned and strengthened by prevailing traditions of "mystic" patriotism, has been unguided and unchecked by any adequate realisation either of its anti-social quality, the destructiveness inseparable from its operation, or its ineffectiveness to ends indispensable to civilisation.

The psychological roots of the impulse are so deep that we shall continue to yield to it until we realise more fully its danger and inadequacy to certain vital ends like sustenance for our people, and come to see that if civilisation is to be carried on we must turn to other motives. We may then develop a new political tradition, which will "discipline" instinct, as the tradition of toleration disciplined religious fanaticism when that passion threatened to shatter European society.

Herein lies the importance of demonstrating the economic futility of military power. While it may be true that conscious economic motives enter very little into the struggle of nations, and are a very small part of the passions of patriotism and nationalism, it is by a realisation of the economic truth regarding the indispensable condition of adequate life, that those passions will be checked, or redirected and civilised.

This does not mean that economic considerations should dominate life, but rather the contrary—that those considerations will dominate it if the economic truth is neglected. A people that starves is a people thinking only of material things—food. The way to dispose of economic preoccupations is to solve the economic problem.

## Chapter III

# HUMAN NATURE AND HUMAN BEHAVIOUR

The human nature argument is usually turned upside down: It is *because* men are quarrelsome and pugnacious that we need institutions and disciplines. It is not a problem of changing human nature but human behaviour, which can be modified by new values based on new ideas, new perceptions, new institutions; as the daily life of the world around us abundantly proves. The way in which our emotions are stirred and our nature behaves depends largely upon the way in which we read facts. One man's fear may be a wiser man's hope and vice versa.

THAT man is quarrelsome and irrational, with fight in his bone and blood, a bundle of strange pugnacities, obscure emotions, elusive resentments, unavowed desires and fears, subject to panic, quick to unreasoning and unreasonable behaviour, ready at times to fight for a word or a sign—all this must be painfully plain to anyone who troubles to note the daily conduct of men and women in the world about him.

And that, replies the internationalist, is precisely why it is so urgent to devise a League or some international constitution; to do for the relations of national groups what man, ever since he had a civilisation at all, has been busy doing for the relations of individuals. Such device is the more necessary since the contacts of nations are now so close and frequent, and the consequent causes of quarrel so much more numerous and the weapons so appallingly more destructive than heretofore.

The unruly character of man is fundamentally the only reason for attempting to create either international or national institutions, for devising rules, laws, disciplines. If man were by nature peaceful and socially minded, always reasonable, always reflective, always able to see the other's point in a dispute, never losing his temper, never subject to national prejudices and dislikes—then, of course, we should not want international agreements or conventions, or Leagues. But then, if he were like that, we should not want most of the national institutions either. Most of our laws, courts, police, churches, ten commandments, would be superfluous. These are all conscious efforts to deal with the short-comings of human nature. It is the process of civilisation by which instinct is made subject to a social intelligence, the first savage impulse to the second, more civilised thought, the process without which human nature would destroy human society. With the shrink-age of the world the time has come to add to these traffic rules on humanity's highway.

Men don't like rules, as already noted. They like to drive as the mood takes them, to "step on the gas," particularly after the second bottle of wine at lunch. *Therefore* argues the militarist, traffic rules are a mistake.

Thus a writer in the *Aeroplane*:

> "The Disarmament Conference will almost certainly end without any agreement to disarm—which will be the best end it could have. . . . Man is by nature a predatory and combative animal."

Which is exactly equivalent to saying:

> Men are apt to get fighting drunk. The right policy therefore is to see that when in that condition, they have weapons as dangerous and murderous as possible.

And that is precisely how most men apply the fact

of human pugnacity to their choice of policy when confronted by the problem of war.

Let a discussion about the League or peace start in any ordinary company of men and women and go on for any length of time, and it will be strange indeed if one in the company, with that air of assured finality, of man-of-the-world realism which usually accompanies that kind of observation, does not remark:

> Well, I'll back old human nature. Man's a fighting animal. There always have been wars and, if you ask me, League or no League, there always will be. The world isn't a Sunday School and the old Adam isn't dead yet.

Whereupon, as a rule, very general agreement; a feeling that a vital point has been made against the League, against international institutions, against Disarmament. In so far as the position of this critic is challenged, it is likely to be by the "idealistically minded" as opposed to the "realists." A protagonist of the League will probably take the line that human nature is not necessarily warlike, cite recent anthropological investigations tending to show that war is a comparatively recent habit of man's, that while the primitive savage may have been a bit indiscriminate with his club, he did not indulge in mass killing, in "forming fours" for the purpose of doing it; will attempt, in other words, to challenge the assumption of innate pugnacity upon which the critic of the League bases his case. Both sides thus add to the confusion of the real issue.

That the innate pugnacity and irrationality of man is the first and last argument *for* international institutions and agreements, is, in any ultimate sense, the only argument for them, is certainly quite inadequately realised. It is a truth to which some pretentious writers dealing with this subject remain, it would seem, oblivious.

Suppose we were in the habit of arguing: "Men like to drive dangerously; therefore traffic rules are a mistake," and that argument so affected policy as to stand in the way of getting any rules of the road accepted. The main problem then would be far less to find out why men liked to drive dangerously than to find out why they regarded the fact as a reason for having no rules.

Of recent years the literature dealing with the psychology of war has become very large, often technical and obscure, sometimes controversial and confusing. One psychologist calls for heavy endowments for research, suggests that it will take fifty years to find out what psychological treatment would really make peace secure. But if we draw utterly wrong conclusions from the facts of psychology which we already know, about which there can be no doubt, it will serve no purpose to discover further facts: we shall be able to draw wrong conclusions from the new knowledge, just as easily as we draw wrong conclusions from the knowledge which we already possess.

This primary fallacy touching the relation of human nature to social and political institutions engenders, of course, other misconceptions. The very fact that the active Pacifist agitates for these new political institutions is proof that he feels their necessity, feels that without them our nature will certainly lead us to war. I, for one, am a Pacifist, not because I think men naturally peaceable and war unlikely, but because I believe men to be naturally quarrelsome, and war extremely likely unless our institutions are so shaped as to avert it.

But those who oppose the internationalist's efforts usually impute to him the exactly contrary attitude. "The Pacifists lie," declares a popular General, "when they tell us that the days of war are over." I suppose I am as familiar with Pacifist thought and literature as most men, and I know of no Pacifist who thinks that without our doing anything about it wars will simply cease of themselves.

If Pacifists really felt that the day of war was over their activities would have no meaning. Why should they busy themselves to prevent something which they believed was not going to take place?

This inversion is, of course, related to the feeling that "you will never get over human nature," that "man is what he is," that we are the helpless puppets of emotional forces which render experience, knowledge, ideas, of no avail.

Of course, men who profess this view really believe it only to the extent that it furnishes an excuse for doing what they want to do, which is to stay in the old beliefs, to avoid new pathways, to evade the responsibility of thought, of new decisions difficult to make, possibly wrong when made. The fatalism implied in "You cannot change human nature" saves all trouble, is a complete excuse for doing nothing, avoids all responsibility. We need do nothing because nothing that we could do would surmount human nature. We search naturally and constantly for means of evading our responsibility—which is why, mainly, these pages insist upon it so much.

Except as an excuse for not doing what they don't like, men don't really believe that their intellectual activities have no effect on the course of events, or the Admiral would not be addressing a Navy League meeting and talking nonsense in an attempt to popularise additions to the navy. He believes that you *can* change human nature to the extent of overcoming man's natural dislike of high taxes, if you sufficiently awaken his still stronger dislike of foreign invasion. He obviously believes that he can alter the inertia which is so large a part of human nature and which will cause the people of this country to neglect the needs of the navy. He proposes to deflect the emotional current, to turn dislike away from the tax collector to the foreigner, to do so by a process of reasoning, such as it is, by "words" which, "as a man of action" he so despises, by "talk and theories" (as to the right method of national defence and the right treatment of foreigners) of which he is habitually so contemptuous. "Nothing," he tells us, "can ever eradicate man's natural fighting instinct." But during the war he clamoured for the suppression of all pro-German or stop-the-war writings, on the grounds that they undermined morale, because they *did* tend to nullify "the fighting instinct," as he now wants Sedition Acts to prevent the spread of Communist ideas in the army, for fear that those ideas will alter very materially the desire of at least some of the soldiers to fight the particular enemy that the government may designate. So strongly did he believe during the war that ideas *could* modify conduct, "human nature," that he was in the habit of describing conscientious objectors, putting forth obscure pamphlets, with no weapons but ideas, as a "public danger," which description he now applies to

[260]

Communists, who only represent a microscopic proportion of the country's population. He thus gives most forceful testimony in contradiction of his professions that you cannot change the course of human conduct or behaviour by "words" and "notions." It is the only way you can change it.

§

Here again words betray us. If the incantation, "You cannot change human nature," had been phrased "You cannot change human behaviour," it could not have survived ten minutes. For daily experience would have shown it to be false.

Take a quite common occurrence. Some years ago in a theatre one of the audience suddenly yelled "Fire." The audience, obeying the profoundest instinct of human nature, that of self-preservation, rose in a mass and rushed the doors, which were closed, and ten people were trampled to death. There was no fire, it was a false alarm.

A few days later in another theatre, the same cry was raised. The manager happened to be present, and was determined that the tragedy of a few days previously should not be repeated. At the moment that the cry was raised, he jumped upon the stage and in the loudest and most dramatic voice he could command, shouted: "Keep your seats. There is plenty of time and you all know what you have to do. Now, rise. Stop. Look for the nearest exit. WALK. No one runs." That theatre was emptied in perfect order, no one was hurt, though this time there was a fire and the place was burned to the ground.

run for land and harbour, rock-strewn though he knows them to be. Every "instinct and feeling" of the experienced sailor prompts him to run for the open sea and ride out the gale. Have they different instincts, a different biological make-up? They have not. They have a different experience which prompts them so to read external facts that what provokes fear in one provokes little fear in the other, what one fears greatly, the other fears not at all.

The case is not different in social and political behaviour. Here are two neighbours of mine, both members of the same profession, both of about equal incomes, both of about the same degree of education. One is an ardent protagonist of an immense increase in the British air forces, of withdrawal from the Disarmament Conference, withdrawal from the League, denunciation of the Kellogg Pact, Locarno and all similar treaties. Only so can his country be made secure and war averted. The other regards these measures of security as pregnant with the gravest possible danger, certain to provoke war, certain to betray the country's safety. Why does one draw from the facts a conclusion diametrically opposed to the conclusion drawn by the other from the same facts? The economic determinist would say that it is accounted for by some difference of interest. But that simply is not true in this case at least. In so far as considerations of interest, the welfare and security of himself or his class or nation are motives at all, one reads his interest, or his nation's interest, in one way and one in another, and it is again necessary to point out that it is just as possible for men to be mistaken as to the best way to promote their own welfare or their nation's as it is for men to be mistaken as to the best way to save their lives in a shipwreck at sea, or in a theatre fire. We see members of the same economic class, actuated by the same forces of human nature, having before them the same problems and the same facts, deeply divided on this issue of the right method of defence. Why is the same instinct of self-preservation so differently expressed in action?

Plainly difference of intellectual method, of interpreting experience, enters into the explanation. In the case of the two men in the boat, a life-long experience had proved to the professional that gales in the open sea were much less dangerous than they looked, and sunken rocks, that you could not see, much more dangerous. The amateur did not possess the experience necessary in order to carry home this truth to his mind. It is common knowledge that some men can learn the lesson of facts more quickly than others, learn to be more afraid of the real dangers than the apparent ones, and vice versa. Again, that is as true in the case of political systems as in the case of yachting. In the case of my two neighbours of such different views of the best course in national defence, one, owing it may be to some early experience difficult afterwards to discern, to some educational influence, an accidental choice of early literature, or what not, acquires what one may term the bilateral habit of thought, the habit, that is, of thinking in correlatives. He thinks of a market, not merely as a place where things are sold, but also as a place where they are bought, and realises that there cannot be one operation without the other; that a "favourable balance of trade" for one nation must mean an unfavourable for another, that defence based on being stronger than the other means that that other is deprived of defence, and so on. But my other neighbour, just as able in his way, and, it may be, quicker in decisions (an advantage in personal affairs if not too outrageously wrong), quicker perhaps just because his reflection is more limited in scope, never seems to have acquired the trick of bilateral thought, but always thinks in unilateral terms. For him it is and remains obvious, incontrovertible, that if you are stronger than your potential enemy you are safe; if he is stronger, then you are not, and that is all there is to it. When he quotes one half of the verse about the strong man armed he forgets the second half, mainly because, even if he reads it, he does not take it in. That means considering two facts together, and "one fact at a time" is enough for him. He is what you might call a "one fact at a time" man. Such a man can, even when he is the author of books on the beauty of war, declare in one sentence that the desire for peace is an evil and degenerate and anti-Christian thing, and in the next declare that we ought to increase our forces, because that is the only way we may make sure of peace. He can thus write and be utterly unaware of self-contradiction.

That these differences of intellectual habit do exist is beyond question, that they account in part for differences in interpretation of experience is extremely probable. The man who says: "We must be stronger than any likely to challenge our rights in order to get justice," and fails to see that that claim is itself a denial of justice, is not necessarily the victim of some psychological abnormality which calls for psycho-analysis; his mind is, unfortunately, an entirely normal one suffering probably under a grave, though very common, educational defect; the defect of unilateral thinking, which prompts him to see a situation made up of two parties or two sets of factors, in terms of one only. Plainly until this tendency is corrected it won't help him to give him more facts, learning. It is not the quantity of facts, but the quality of thinking which matters.

The fact would seem to indicate that psychology can play its useful role in making clear why we do not realise the self-evident; in making us conscious of what we really want of organised society; of the motives we are obeying in our jingoisms; why we cling to political condition which makes war inevitable when we don't want war at all. The case has really been put by Professor Trotter in his *Instincts of the Herd in Peace and War* in these terms:

> The only way in which society can be made safe from disruption or decay is by the intervention of the conscious and instructed intellect as a factor among the forces ruling its development. . . . There is no responsibility for man's destiny anywhere at all outside his own responsibility, and . . . there is no remedy for his ills outside his own efforts."

## Chapter I

## THE ROAD OUT

The practical issue is finally reduced to a choice between two courses: to employ force for the purpose of defence by placing it collectively behind law; or to use it by the old competitive, individual method. Collective defence can be expressed in actual policy in many different ways. It need not be a cut-and-dried plan with ironclad commitments, but a gradual shaping of day-to-day international policy. How the present world situation bears upon the development of such policy; what is essential to it; some of the arguments usually urged against it.

WHAT does it all amount to? What must the plain man do or refrain from doing, and, by his votes, encourage his Government to do or refrain from doing?

First as to his personal part, he has to make a choice between two mutually exclusive courses; a choice which he cannot evade; a choice between policies, not ends. He cannot, that is, make the decision merely by saying "I am in favour of peace." That is no choice at all. We are all in favour of peace. He has to choose between two methods of getting peace, between two sets of counsellors, both equally sincere, it may be, in their desire for peace.

At this moment of writing, in Britain (and the same situation is broadly duplicated in America) there stand on the one side powerful groups made up of newspaper proprietors, journalists, certain eminent politicians, even authors, who tell John Smith insistently that if he wants peace he must refrain from mixing up in the affairs of foreign nations, from giving any pledges to co-operate with them, must get rid of the League, or reduce it to a mere conferring body; must liberate the nation from treaties of the Locarno type, trust to our own power for defence, increase it, make it greater than any other. The sincerity of these counsellors need not be questioned. But on the other side are men who, to put it at its lowest, are of equal authority, of greater knowledge of foreign affairs, of greater experience in the field of international politics, who urge the exactly contrary course of rendering more definite our commitments under the League, of multiplying arrangements like those of Locarno, and urge that we must hold on to the collective system and its principle as the very life line of peace.

As an earlier chapter has pointed out, both courses cannot be right. If one road leads to peace, then the other leads to war. The whole issue boils down to a choice between the two. Which direction is John Smith to take? On his decision depends the direction in which the policy of his Government will develop.

To the plain question, What must John Smith do in order to eliminate war from the world, the facts here discussed give a plain answer. He must take the second of the two courses outlined above; he must encourage his Government to co-operate with other Governments in building up, in all ways possible, perhaps gradually, but in any case steadily, a system of collective, co-operative defence as a substitute for the old method of defence by competitive power, of "each his own defender."

By collective defence is meant this: that when a nation refuses peaceful settlement of its dispute and prepares to go to war, that step shall be made as hard and unprofitable as the common action of other nations can make it, without undue cost to themselves.[1] Collec-

---

[1] "The real danger arises when there is no dispute about the facts, but when the law is felt by one party to work intolerable injustice.

tive defence means any method by which the general or collective power of civilised nations—power which may be diplomatic, political, economic, financial, as well as military or naval—shall stand for the defence of each member of the community of States by resisting in common the war-maker. Then each will no longer be dependent solely upon his own power for defence, and thus compelled to be stronger than others, and, by that fact, deprive those others of the defence he claims. We must somehow end a system which necessarily means, however we may dodge or disguise the fact, that "my defence kills yours"; which is based upon denial of the most elementary human right: the right of others to the means of self-preservation (i.e. preponderant power) which we claim. The only way of ending it, so long as the nations retain power at all, is by the collective method, the placing of common power behind a law or rule which shall afford to each a measure of security. It is the choice between what Wilson called the "Community of Power," (which assures equality of the right of security), as against Competition of Power between rival parties to a dispute (which denies security to one of them).

The difference between the two methods is surely simple enough for the least instructed citizen to grasp. Yet the understanding is often made unnecessarily difficult and confused by certain current misapprehensions.

Such are those frontier questions which, owing to the intermingling of races, must leave a racial minority on one side of the boundary or the other, draw the frontier where you will. In such cases there is only one guarantee for peace; it is that the aggressor should know beforehand that if he seeks a remedy by war he will find massed against him such overwhelming force that he cannot hope for success."—*Sir Austin Chamberlain*, December 19th, 1934.

§

The collective method is not necessarily synonymous with the League of Nations though it must involve in practice some machinery of common action, third party judgment and representation of interests involved. It can be expressed in actual policy in a dozen different ways, as the principle within states may be expressed by numberless different constitutional forms.

But whatever the forms, the process must involve the principle of "power behind the law" instead of behind the rival litigants. In order to build up such common power it is not all necessary that every nation should immediately intervene in every dispute of every other nation. The first care should be to apply the principle to all existing international power combinations; to see that all alliance-forming is aimed at supporting, first of all, arbitration or third party judgment. The "other side" can then join the alliance. Our problem is primarily to prevent a misuse of power by the great states that hold power. Street brawls are not important if the nation's courts can carry on and protect life and property as a whole and power does not pass from the national government to rival political parties within the nation.

§

A curious situation is revealed in British opinion. One great group of popular newspapers, bitterly hostile to the League, also consistently advocates a military alliance with France; but it is also the group that is in favour of certain drastic revisions of the Treaty of Versailles. In its view that we must remain in close military association with France it is supported by Mr. Stanley Baldwin, who tells us that our frontier is on the Rhine—an exceedingly plain indication that we still stand for the defence of France as part of our own defence. But how in the name of common sense are you to combine a military alliance with France of the old order with revisions of the Treaty, with the maintenance, that is, of competition for power? The unjust features of the Versailles Treaty are due mainly to the desire to get power preponderance as the only defensive alternative to the collective system. Destroy the League, as Lord Rothermere would have us do, and maintain the alliance with France, as equally he would have us do, and you have got the old iron encirclement of Germany. (And the same fundamental objection inheres in an Anglo-American combination, released from all League obligations, for "imposing peace.") You offer Germany no protection against the abuses of our preponderance. Under such a system, Germany (or one of her potential allies, say, Hungary) knows that if one of our allies—Roumania, Czechoslovakia—is guilty of gross aggression we cannot afford to restrain that ally. (One recalls how pathetically Sir Edward Grey, after the catastrophe, recognised that, in order to have stopped German mobilisation, he would have had to give a promise to use his influence to restrain Russia; which he could not give.) Germany has, under the competitive system, no recourse but to oppose the whole combination by a similar one, if she can manage to create it by offering bribes to Poland, to Japan, to Hungary, or anyone else. The one alternative promising peace is to say to Germany that we will all stand in common for the principle of arbitration or peaceful

[275]

settlement, and invite her to come in and co-operate, to invite her to co-operate with us against former allies, if needs be. Such collective method does not deprive Germany of defence, it is a standing invitation to her to come in and join the club, and to add to the strength of the law which will defend her quite as much as ourselves. It is, indeed, this one fact, of offering to the potential enemy means of defence if he will observe the law, which distinguishes the collective from the "balance" system.

§

The present world situation lends itself to the formation of just such a preponderance in support of international law and order, and for this it waits mainly on the diplomatic leadership of Britain.

On the Continent, France, Russia, Czechoslovakia, Roumania, Jugoslavia, Belgium, Denmark, the Baltic States (possibly Poland) have common interest in opposing an increase of Germany's power, while the tendency of Germany's potential ally, Japan, to become master of four hundred million Chinese runs directly counter to the interests of the United States, Canada, Australia, New Zealand, the South African Union, the British Asiatic Empire. Here is the nucleus of a world combination against war by the two states most likely to disturb the peace.

One acid test will determine whether the alliance is to be as futile as the pre-war combinations, or one that can secure defence and peace: Will it offer to the other group the same defence against attack it attempts to achieve for itself? Or will it be on the old lines by which "My defence kills yours?" Will it stand by the principle, or law, that the peace-breaker, the nation refusing arbitration or peaceful settlement, is the common enemy, whether he belong to "our side" or not?

If so, it is not a combination against either Germany or Japan, because both can join it to help work the principle "All against the peace-breaker."

To say: "We stand by France," merely gives France a blank cheque for obstinacy or provocation towards Germany, and gives the latter no hope save in war.

To say: "We stand by arbitration and its institutions," compels Germany (and France) to surrender, not rights, but war as a means of getting them; makes it more profitable for both to put as much energy behind the non-military means of redress as heretofore they have put into the instruments of war.

But if the interests of lesser states (which may not always coincide with those of the greater states) are to be properly respected and represented, something in the nature of the League will inevitably be called for. The method means risks and obligations. We should be justified, perhaps, in refusing to assume risks if the only alternative were free from them. But it is a choice of risks. How do those of the collective system compare with those of the old method? Curiously enough, the costs of the collective system are very seldom presented in that relationship.

Take the first objection which usually arises. Here is a "peace" system, say the critics, which starts with the assumption that in certain circumstances we shall go to war. But does not the system of individual arming imply that we shall in certain circumstances go to war? The very fact that the present system demands the retention of our armies and navies means that we should fight "if we are attacked"—as in 1914.

"The collective system means that we may be dragged into disputes with which we have no direct concern."

Yet, somehow, under the old system a single murder in a Balkan village, a "remote quarrel" of Austria with the Southern Slavs, seems to have involved us.

"The collective system means that we hand over to foreigners the decision as to whether we fight or not?"

Then could we have stayed out without danger in 1914? Was it not the action of foreigners which compelled us to go in?

"The collective system might compel us, under the Locarno type of agreement, to fight for people whose political system and outlook we dislike—e.g. for Germany as against France, if France were the aggressor."

Did we then agree with the political system of Czarist Russia, have any intense admiration for the Serbia with which, a year or too previously, we had broken off relations because of its method of "government by assassination"? Did we fight for those countries as against tolerant and civilised Austria because we preferred their civilisation and outlook to the Austrian?

"A system based on 'resistance to the aggressor' can never work because you cannot tell who is the real aggressor, which party has attacked."

Don't we, then, under the old system, have to decide who is the aggressor? Under the old method we have to decide suddenly, in all the excitement and confusion of a complicated diplomatic dispute, when war is lurking on the horizon, whether a state—the state, that is, with whom we are quarrelling—has committed, or is about to commit, aggression; whether he has "upset the

[ 278 ]

balance" or is intending to do so, which we are told by responsible authorities would constitute attack upon us. If we believe it quite easy to determine when our rival —a state involved in a dispute to which we are party— has become an aggressor, why is it quite impossible for us to determine when one of two parties in a dispute in which we have no direct interest has been guilty of aggression? If there is such a difficulty of deciding between aggression and defence, the difficulty is certainly not solved by leaving it entirely to one of the two parties directly concerned in the dispute, leaving it, that is, until some panic and muddle comparable to that of August 1914 has arisen.

The truth is, of course, that it is easier to determine the aggressor under the collective system than under the old. In the minds of those who emphasise this objection is obviously some idea that, in order to determine what is aggression, one has to pass upon the merits of the dispute. Under a system of law, that is not the case. Will a nation party to a dispute arbitrate, accept third-party judgment—accept, that is, the principle of law at all? If not, and it takes measures to go to war in order to "take the law into its own hands" by being judge of its own dispute, then it is the aggressor whatever the ultimate merits of its case.

The difficulties of acting with justice under this rule are certainly less than under the old. If a nation's case is obviously sound, it can afford to arbitrate; if it is doubtful, it should be induced to.

"The collective system compels you to rely upon the word of foreigners instead of your own strength."

Could we, then, have managed without Allies in 1914? We seemed to need them. Under the system of competitive alliance you have to take the risk of your ally letting you down.

"The collective system involves a cumbersome international action, always difficult to organise in view of national jealousies and divergences."

Did not the old system, in 1914, involve just that? The last great war involved on the Allied side the co-operation of twenty-two states—towards the end, a most elaborate international co-operation covering the whole world in the ramifications of its economic and financial restrictions, its naval and military operations. We had to ensure the military co-operation of Portugal and the naval co-operation of Peru. Whatever difficulties there may be in the international sanctions, they all had to be met and overcome as an indispensable part of the pre-War method.

"Under the collective system, it is impossible to agree on an 'ultimate authority,' or ultimate decision. . . . The difficulties of unanimity . . . Who is to press the button?"

Who "pressed the button" in 1914? Had Great Britain much control of the matter? A shot fired in a Balkan village immediately took the control of events out of the hands of Britain, as of the other members of the Grand Alliance. Our soldiers had to go into every corner of the world—literally from the Arctic to the Antarctic circle. Difficulties arose between the Allies, not only over military and naval questions, but over those of supply—shipping, coal, foodstuffs, loans. Inter-allied boards had to face, in the midst of the hurried improvisations of war, all the problems which we declare are too complicated to be decided in peace time. The war-time improvisations have to settle whether decisions between allies shall be by majority rule or by unanimity; to devise some means of deciding between conflicting parties. All those problems have to be faced under the old method of co-operation between ten or fifteen or twenty allied states such as those who fought in common against Germany. The old method only postpones to the moment of crisis the difficulties which are advanced as making impossible collective arrangements for defence, though made at leisure in peace time.

"Collective action would bring us into conflict with America."

We should be much *less* likely to be brought into conflict with America in defending ourselves through the collective system than by individual defence. The American administration has repeatedly made clear that it would not embarrass any common action of nations to restrain the peace breaker. But our bitterest conflicts with America have arisen over the operations of our Navy when acting individually for our defence. The incidents of our naval warfare led to one war with America, and nearly to several others. The American doctrine of "the freedom of the seas" would embarrass us enormously in the event of war taking place under the old conditions, but America has made it clear that she would waive that doctrine in the case of collective action. This fact alone, especially in view of the great increase of the American Navy, which renders it the most powerful in the world, and in view of the fact that our defensive action must be mainly naval, makes defence of Britain by the collective system immeasurably more effective than it could be under the method of individual action. The fact that other states would not insist upon "neutral right" because our action would be "League action" would give to our naval power a freedom and effectiveness which it could not now possess under the old system. The co-operation of minor states in those economic pressures which were so large a part of the naval power of the past is to-day of very great importance. The defensive effectiveness of our naval operations would often depend very largely upon the attitude thereto of a large number of lesser states. Their League position now ensures that any defensive operation on our part involving blockade or embargoes would not be rendered negatory by a "neutral" world.

§

It would be true to say that there is not a single valid objection to the collective system which does not apply with infinitely greater force as against the old system. Yet the usual argument against "international sanctions" is made as though international sanctions, compulsions, are something new, a leap into the unknown, ignoring the fact that *any* defensive policy must commit us to international (i.e. Allied) co-operation in the employment of force; to international sanctions, that is, of an elaborate kind.

The case against the League is often argued as though, once the clumsiness, cost, uncertainty and risk of international action—international co-operation in the employment of economic or military pressure against an aggressor state—had been demonstrated, we were free to choose an alternative instrument which did not possess those disadvantages, although fully determined to retain a strong defensive position; as though the issue were as between force and no force, boycott or no boycott, commitment to international co-operation or no commitment. But plainly from the moment that we have decided to base national defence upon power at all, those are not the alternatives. For the decision to defend ourselves will involve us in the use of international force, economic pressure internationally organised boycotts, embargoes, blockades, commitments of an inevitably entangling kind. From the moment that we decide to defend the nation, the nation's rights, that is, by power stronger than that which may be put behind any challenge to those rights, we face sooner or later nearly all the problems of international sanctions, the difficulties which opponents of League commitments habitually advance. These critics argue as though we were starting with a clean slate and had to decide whether our international constitution had better have sanctions or not. If that were indeed the case, I for one would oppose any proposal to create machinery for the forcible coercion of a whole nation. But, assuming that we are discussing practical politics at all, that is not the issue. We have all, in fact, decided upon the coercion of the aggressor state—the state which we deem to be the aggressor against us—and will certainly not hesitate to enter upon all the international co-operations necessary for that purpose. The issue which post-War conditions put to us is whether we can devise an international policy making sanctions (which we shall employ anyhow) more effective for defence, less likely to be used at all than they were under the old method.

The preceding pages have attempted to make clear what the difference between the two is. An alliance under the old method offered no protection to the other side; one side sought superiority and the other just had to accept inequality or fight. Under the collective method an alliance offers others the rights of arbitration and their protection it attempts to secure for itself, and is an alliance which is always open to the others to join on equal terms.

§

A further word may be added concerning one or two of the criticisms just discussed.

The objection that the collective system "tends to drag us into quarrels with which we have no concern" disregards the method of that system, which is to take such measures in peace time that quarrels will never reach a stage which demands military or naval intervention. Whereas under the old method, the international situation was allowed to drift until an explosion, from the effects of which it was too late to extricate ourselves, occurred, the collective system gives us some chance of so guiding the peace-time development of events as to render the chances of an explosion as remote as possible. If the *peace-time* operation of the system, alike on the technical and political side, is successful, armed conflicts do not arise, and there is no question of our being involved. The fundamental feature of the collective system is to create such conditions throughout the world that a State never reaches either diplomatically or technically a condition which makes war for it feasible or advantageous; to create conditions, economic and political, which make it more worth while, more realist for each state, to keep the peace than to break it, to observe the rule of peaceful settlement, arbitration or what-not, than to challenge it. That means a peace-time organisation to prevent things reaching the stage of armed conflict between two States, not sudden incursions into that conflict when it has arisen. This primary misapprehension usually vitiates the popular conception of what the collective system really is.

Let us look for a moment at its possible mechanism.

Assume that we have achieved a Disarmament Convention of some kind—not very successful, if you will, but at least ensuring limitation; and that there goes with it mutual agreement for control and inspection and "guarantees of execution." If the provisions are adhered to, no one State could ever be in a position to challenge a combination of several states, because any hope of such successful challenge would depend on great accumulations of war stocks. If the provisions were not adhered to and such accumulations began, to any dangerous extent, the provisions for international inspection and control would soon reveal the fact, and the other nations would then begin to apply what one authority has called the "mineral sanction"—such withholding of indispensable raw material as would make the continuance of war preparation extremely difficult. Over ninety per cent of the world's supply of nickel, which is quite indispensable for munitions, comes from the British Empire; most of the remaining ten per cent comes from the French Empire; so that there should be no insuperable difficulty in securing a stoppage of supply to a state that was building up its armament stocks beyond the permitted degree. If you group together the British Empire, the United States and France, they have a virtual monopoly of asbestos, gold, mica, monazite, nickel, strontium. "If those nations are firm," says General Smuts, "in refusing to export mineral products to those countries that infringe the Kellogg Pact, no war can last very long"; or in any case would be so hazardous and uncertain in its results that no nation would find it good politics to undertake it. And incidentally, this withholding of material by the consent of two or three principal states of the world disposes of many bogeys about the danger of blockade which are so frequently urged as certain to make the economic sanction dangerous. Blockade would not be necessary. It would be replaced by embargo at the ports, and the dangers and difficulties of patrolling the seas by an inadequate British Navy would be in large measure eliminated.

In conjunction with these *peace-time* measures for securing observance of a Disarmament Convention would go others even easier of application: discrimination against the imports of the offending country, a discrimination which is often made now in the form of quotas on the basis of authority *now* possessed by the nations. When we consider that ninety per cent of the chief export of Japan is taken by one country—the United States; that, in the Sino-Japanese crisis, the most serious which has arisen in the League's history, the United States was even more ready than Great Britain to apply sanctions; when we remember that action by the City of London in discriminating in the discounting of Japanese bills of exchange could have intensified the exchange crisis which would have confronted Japan as the result of American prohibition of Japanese imports, one sees how powerful these peace-time sanctions could be made, if behind their organisation were a determina-

tion to make them effective. There has been of recent
years some prolonged and careful examination of the
possibility of this type of sanction, and general agreement that it is entirely feasible. One of the greatest
economists in Britain has declared that if the economic
sanction had been applied to Japan even as late as 1931,
it would have been entirely effective. But for reasons
which are touched upon below, there was not in fact
the will to apply these sanctions. We thought it more
worth while to avoid the momentary risk and difficulty
than to make the sacrifice necessary to vindicate the
collective system. We bought peace to-day at the probable risk of war to-morrow.

The main point is that power on behalf of order does
not operate by virtue of its actual, but its potential
might and the certainty in the minds of those proposing
to challenge it that it would ultimately be invoked. It
is certainly within the power of three or four great
nations, at the cost of no sacrifice which they could not
bear, to set up in peace time a mechanism of economic
sanctions which would make war so obviously unprofitable that no state would attempt it. If the economic
sanctions did provoke military retaliation, then the
combined power of two or three states—the British Empire, the United States, France—would certainly be in
a position to withstand that retaliation. If it is argued
that they are not, then indeed has armed isolation
proved itself effective. For if the military and naval
power of a whole group of great states could not resist
military action by a single state like Japan, then what
becomes of the power of, say, Great Britain, limited to
its own resources, to defend, say, India or Australia at
any moment that it may please Japan to challenge the

Empire's position? The argument that Britain could not have resisted the military retaliation of Japan, does indeed point a case for the international co-operation of Britain with other states for common defence.

We must keep in mind, of course, that with that sanction would go the diplomatic sanction, that is to say, the knowledge on the part of the offending State that it could find no allies. The two forces go together. The wars which really threaten civilisation only arise when a certain diplomatic situation has been created, a situation like that of 1914, where two great groups confront each other. Indeed, perhaps the main advantage of clear commitment to law—the law that all shall keep the peace—is that commitment to this principle makes commitments of the old diplomatic type impossible. If we are bound first to stand by the law, we cannot stand by allies intending to defy that law. Clear understanding by the people at large that we are committed to support *law*, "playing no favourites," in President Wilson's phrase, will make impossible secret understanding by governments in contravention of the principle. If the mass of men and women understand that any undertaking to support an ally who refuses arbitration is a betrayal of that primary law against war, it is difficult to see how any Government could depend upon the support of its own people in entering such a war.

We usually discuss sanctions as though the chief sanctions were an undertaking to fight; but the main sanction, and the most effective one, will be an undertaking not to fight; not to fight, that is, as the ally of any State that has refused arbitration or violated its covenants. For if there is general observance by

Governments of that not-to-fight obligation, a violator, an aggressor, has no allies; and without allies, no war endangering civilisation can ever be fought.

§

Let us take another criticism. A Liberal writer of quite the front rank (who ought to know better) says:

> How many Englishmen are there who would really be prepared to submit the British Empire to an international authority empowered to say that it was too big, that its occupation of large spaces with sparse populations was contrary to world interests, that its administration of certain parts was bad and must be reconstituted according to an international model?[1]

To appreciate the value of such criticism, one should put it side by side with other criticisms of the collective system which are perhaps even commoner, e.g. the following:

> The League, or any similar method, is bound to fail because it tends to stereotype the *status quo*. It is indeed at this moment a French instrument for sitting upon the spoils of victory. Its maintenance creates a situation in which one group is determined to maintain the Treaty of Versailles, and the other group to upset it. Explosion must come sooner or later.

The assumption seems to be that the explosion should come sooner, and that when it does, the revision of the *status quo* which the new war will give would be more satisfactory than one given by peace methods. But as we have already noted, revision of the *status quo* made

[1] *These Times*, by J. A. Spender, p. 103.

by the power of one of the parties to the dispute does *not* correct injustices; it merely puts them on the other side of the frontier, to be revised again by the other party when he gets a chance—*da capo, ad infinitum*.

But the point about the two criticisms is that both are made commonly as being an obvious defect or disadvantage of the collective system, although clearly if one is sound, the other cannot be. If in fact, the collective system is going to stabilise too rigidly the present state of things then it cannot possibly contain the risk of such enormous and profound changes as those which Mr. Spender fears: changes which would give Britain, under the League, far less autonomy than the Dominions have under the Empire. The Imperial Government, with all its power, with all its weight of tradition, is not able to dictate to Australia whether it shall receive British citizens or not. (Indeed, most British citizens, like those of India, are rigidly excluded, as also often are those coming from Great Britain.) But the League, somehow, is going to acquire power over its constituent members that Great Britain does not possess over its Dominions. If there is any validity at all in one of these criticisms, then the other must be fantastic; but both are made usually as though they were quite obvious dangers. If one is a danger, the other cannot be.

There is a fundamental confusion in this connection. Our collective guarantees do not guarantee the *status quo;* they guarantee that the *status quo* shall not be changed by war. This is a vital difference. Once you forbid war, men will set about means of change other than war. The citizen of the Central American Republic thinks first and last of revolution, armed force, as the means of redressing a grievance against the

§

At the moment of writing those who in England are sceptical of the League of Nations are usually advocates of an Anglo-American combination "for the keeping of the peace of the world." Their criticism of the League is usually based on the charge that it is an instrument by which France will insist on maintaining the Versailles *status quo*. But if we are to forbid war, we must forbid war to change the *status quo*. Or shall we, Britain and America, make ourselves sole judges of what changes in the *status quo* be permitted and what not? The problems which arise from injustices of the Versailles settlement—which Anglo-American power alone made possible—will remain and have to be dealt with. Plainly, unless the Anglo-American combination is to be an international dictatorship, and unless we are to appoint ourselves the supreme judges of the quarrels of others, there must be some organised system resembling a League to represent the respective interests. All American politicians of every shade of opinion were only a few years ago the advocates of a "League with teeth," and those who have analysed the change of opinion ascribe it to what Professor Irving Fisher of Yale summarises as "politics."[1] But American politics seem to be reversing the tendency and we may once more find the weight of American opinion in favour of American co-operation in the world task of doing consciously what the less conscious forces of history did for the States of the Union a hundred and fifty years ago.

But indeed it is not the mere joining of the League which is the vital question. The United States might

[1] See particularly, Professor Irving Fisher's book, *League or War*.

have joined the League and then have adopted a policy which would have made it impotent. The mere fact of League membership may well be an empty gesture unless it carries with it a change in the policy and conditions which produce war. If, after joining, the political conduct of each member in international relations is to remain unchanged, why should we expect the results of that unchanged conduct to differ from the results of the pre-League past? A number of drunkards do not, by the mere fact of forming themselves into a club or society, become sober.

The common habit of talking of "The League" as though it were an entity apart from the members who compose it, has led us apparently to believe that it may properly be expected to have power to do this, that or the other, though none of its members furnish power. One gets such questions as "What has the League ever done? Why did not the League act to stop Japan?" Never in the form, "Why have we failed to accomplish more by our membership? Why don't we co-operate more actively? Why did we not manage to act together in restraint of Japan?" If half a dozen men forming themselves into a club then proceeded to quarrel each with the other, to cheat, fight, disagree, we should think it strange if they began asking each other "Why doesn't the club stop us?"

Some villagers in one of the vineyard districts of France once decided to make their priest a present of a barrel of wine. Each parishioner was to contribute a bottle. A Sunday was set for the ceremony; the bottles were poured into the barrel; the priest went forward to draw ceremoniously his first glass of wine. Turning the tap, there came from the barrel pure water. In the subsequent explanations it was discovered that no one was to blame. "For," argued each villager, "if only the others had done their duty, my bottle would have made no difference."

§

There are very many, particularly in England, who would be ready to pledge the country to co-operation with others in common resistance to the peace-breaker, but would not subscribe to any method like that of an international air force, where final decision for action has to be taken by some international authority to whom responsibility is delegated; the last word being said by that authority and not by us. What is the real distinction between these two methods?

This ultimate reservation of freedom for each partner appeals particularly to the English mind, because British constitutional practice is based so much more upon the expectation that everyone concerned "will do the right thing when the time comes" without too rigid a commitment beforehand. But two points about that method have to be considered. Despite the history of the Italian case in 1914, experience shows clearly that the freedom for national decision which the method apparently preserves is usually quite illusory; and for the sake of this illusory freedom the confidence necessary if the collective system is to work at all may well be sacrificed and the whole thing become a sham.

That the freedom *is* illusory, the history already outlined clearly shows. If a State in the position of America that had no commitments of any kind could not avoid being drawn into a war that arose out of the murder of an Archduke in the Balkans, reservations to commitments that would in any case have to be pretty entangling would not seem to be of much value. And the fact of making that reservation creates the situation out of which war, and the necessity for action at all, arises. Note the effect of the reservations. A member of the collective system doubts, in view of the reservations, whether the others really will come to its support if attacked. So it refuses to disarm, and makes special alliances, thus creating suspicion in the others, causing them to do the same. The system thus collapses and there is general reversion to competitive arming. Without clear commitment to such common action against the aggressor as will give to each member of the community of nations some means of defence other than its own individual power, there can be no getting away at all from the old competitive anarchy. That is clear. If nobody is obliged to do anything the collective system simply won't work, and war prevention will be impossible. If each is really free, then we don't achieve our purpose. If we insist upon freedom, we don't get it, because we are certain to be drawn in.

If full weight is given to these considerations, it will be seen that it is not the degree of surrender of sovereignty which really makes the difference between the two methods of individual commitment to common action and general delegation of authority to act, but questions of organisation and effectiveness in view of the psychology of nationalism. The proposal for the creation in peace time of a police force internationally organised is so remote from familiar conceptions, and at first sight runs so counter to nationalist prepossessions, that the proposal is more likely to add to the average man's distrust of international arrangements than to increase his faith in them. In addition to these psychological difficulties are real difficulties of organisation. Except in the case of an international air force which ought now to be created if abolition of national air forces demand it, the line of least resistance, alike from the point of view of nationalist psychology and of actual organisation, seems to be a clear and unmistakable commitment of each to the single purpose of preventing aggression, leaving the forces to be used for that purpose national forces under national authority. Having secured the enthronement of that principle of action in European politics, it may be possible, confidence once having been established, then to go on to the creation of an international force properly speaking.

Meantime let us decline to be frightened by words. A small international air force designed to prevent the use of civil aircraft for war purposes would not be a world state or anything near it. We are not in danger assuredly, these days, of moving too quickly towards international organisation. And a small international air force may well be the only means by which an air competition destructive of European civilisation can be avoided.

§

The "collective system" is much less a cut and dried scheme of iron-clad commitments (the sanction clauses of the Covenant, for instance, are extremely elastic) than it is the introduction of a new principle of association into international affairs; a process of constitutional development comparable in part to the slow emergence of order out of the welter of feudal rivalries which gave us modern England or modern Germany or Italy, in part comparable to the process by which, in disorderly States like certain of the Latin-American Republics, order seems to be emerging out of the military chaos. Its steady development will largely depend, as the growth of order in those republics depends, upon a clearer sense of "where force belongs"—belongs as an instrument of order and justice, a sense which so much of Europe, in its arming of rival parties, seems, for the moment, to be losing. The essential is that we should be aware, in modifying the principles which determine the use of force, of the direction in which we move, whether away from order or towards it; that in this trial and error development we should be able at each stage and as each crisis arises, to choose wisely between two types of risk; to know whether, for instance, it is better to reserve the right to bomb tribes on the north-west frontier at the cost of sacrificing an agreement for the complete abolition of military aviation, or vice versa. We cannot make such decisions unless we face squarely the real nature of the competitive method which the preceding pages have attempted to make plain, and unless we realise the misconceptions involved in some of the commonest objections to the alternative collective system.

The Sino-Japanese incident illustrated the difficulty which the public found in weighing one risk against another. No one doubts that Japan was guilty of aggression. Her guilt was indeed proclaimed by the whole world (including Britain) in Congress Assembled, by the First Parliament of Man that man has managed to devise. The verdict had in it nothing of sudden passion or prejudice, and in the case of most of the sixty-odd states that gave it, no direct partisan interest. It was pronounced by third parties not directly concerned in the dispute, but only concerned to prevent aggression. They represented human society as a whole, and no verdict could have been more responsible, involving graver issues for the peace of the world. Associated with the League was the United States, which had announced at the outset its intention of standing with the League in that crisis. The co-operation of Russia was assured by reason of her special strategic position. Our dominions of Canada, Australia and New Zealand had particular interest in checking successful acts of aggression by Japan.

Seldom can there have been, or could be, so great a grouping of states having an interest in the restraint of aggression. The action first called for under the League obligations in such a situation is political and economic, and Mr. Stimson, on behalf of the American Government, made a variety of proposals.[1] The American proposals were very coldly received by the British government and British public, who soon made it clear that they would not associate themselves in any action of any kind in restraint of Japan. Indeed, the Foreign

---

[1] On 9th October 1931, the American Secretary of State sent to the Secretary General of the League a message approving the action of the Assembly, and adding:

"The American Government, acting independently through its diplomatic representatives, will endeavour to reinforce what the League does and will make clear that it has a keen interest in the matter and is not oblivious to the obligations which the disputants have assumed to their fellow signatories in the Pact of Paris as well as in the Nine Power Pact should a time arise when it would seem advisable to bring forward those obligations. By this course we avoid any danger of embarrassing the League in the course to which it is now committed."

Secretary, despite the action of the Assembly, despite our obligations under the League Covenant in such a situation, announced officially in the House of Commons that the Sino-Japanese dispute was a distant quarrel with which the British Government did not intend to concern itself. One member of the House declared, amidst cheers: "I am for Japan." Very nearly the whole Press of Britain took the line that Japan ought not to be "nagged" by the League, and even when Japan did what no Power, Asiatic or European, has ever before done with impunity, shelled in peace time a city which was partly British, the same newspapers found excuse, urged that nothing must be done, that we should, as one anti-League paper put it, "Clear out of the League, so as not to become entangled in any anti-Japanese movement." As these lines are being written a "mission" sent by the Federation of British Industries is in Japan seeking orders, its members have discussed a British loan to Japan for the development of Manchukuo, the recognition of that state, and one of the principle members of the Mission, Sir Charles Siligman, announces in a Press interview that "practically every thinking Briton is in favour of a revival of the Anglo-Japanese Alliance." These reports are published in British papers quite casually, often warmly approved, seldom condemned— by papers that tell you repeatedly that Britain has done everything possible for peace and the League, and that if either fails it will be the fault of foreigners who won't co-operate or do their part in any system of collective defence.

The casualness with which the press and public accepted the failure to discharge Covenant obligations, the failure to make any real effort to render the collective system effective showed that there had been no real understanding of the issues at stake. No other nation—neither the United States nor the other League members —treated the Treaty obligations involved so lightly as British opinion seems to have done. Yet the attitude which in Britain one encounters more frequently than any other is something like this:

How do you expect us to believe in the League as a political reality when it shows impotence such as that revealed in the Sino-Japanese affair?

The fact being that it is mainly the line taken by British public opinion which made effective action impossible. Not bad faith, but bad understanding was to blame.

§

The foregoing implies that the particular type of constitution by which a principle is worked is less important than a real understanding on the part of the people involved of the essential nature of the principle itself. There are Balkan and Latin-American states that possess far better constitutions from the legalistic point of view than the one possessed by Britain. But those others don't give better results in terms either of order or justice. The constitutional points are not unimportant, but the underlying understandings come first.

There is little realisation of the need of corresponding understandings in peace preservation. The public continually ask for "plans" by which peace may be preserved. Yet ever since men began to see the need of peace, "plans" in the sense of constitutions for the governance of international relations, have been as plentiful as blackberries in autumn. The world this last fifteen years has been discussing an infinite variety: various revisions of the League Covenant, Peace Acts, Plans for Mutual Assistance, Protocols, Pacts of Non-Aggression, a United States of Europe, a Pan Europe, a World State, International Disarmament, an International Police Force, Air Police, Economic Sanctions, an Alliance of English-speaking Peoples . . . The problem is not to find the Perfect Plan (which, if perfect to-day, would be imperfect to-morrow) it is to find out why the nations won't accept any workable plan, but cling instead to unworkable ways of international life.

"Tell us what to do to get Peace," says the Average Man, "and you can depend upon our doing it." He is told, and whereupon, in four cases out of five, angrily rejects the advice, quite sure that he knows better.

The usual procedure is then to give him a new plan, which, if it gets at the root of the trouble at all, means that it will ask of him certain sacrifices, the revision of unperceived injustices, treasured habits or prides or prejudices. And when he discovers that these sacrifices *are* asked of course he rejects the new plan as vigorously as he rejected the old until finally there is presented a plan which asks no sacrifices at all, the revision of no habits, the correction of no injustices, abandonment of no prejudices, no pride of place, no limitation of independence, or freedom of action or sovereignty. To this plan he agrees. And that plan, of course, leaves the situation exactly where it was, accomplishing nothing whatever.

That is the history of the Peace Plans of the centuries. For such plans are as old as the Areopagus of the Greeks, with numberless medieval adaptations (usually emanating from the Papacy, like "the truce of God") and post-medieval adaptations like that of the Grand Design of Henry IV (of which a fellow monarch said: "It is perfect, flawless, save for one thing—no earthly prince will ever be persuaded to agree to it."). We had spates of "arbitration fever" before the War, during the nineteenth century, with world conferences at the Hague. Everyone sang the praises of arbitration, but everyone also said, when it came to making treaties: "Of course we must exempt honour and vital interest; and we ourselves must be the judge of what they are—in fact we must in each case decide whether a given dispute is one suitable for arbitration or not." Which did not profoundly alter the situation.

The "abstractly perfect" scheme of international government, which would certainly solve all difficulties if mankind were only wise enough to accept and abide by it, may well be in practice the worst, the most hopeless, because the most remote from the familiar, asking from the ordinary man so big a step into the unknown that he simply refuses to take it. The problem is to find, not so much "plans" as a general policy which will result in international relations developing in the right direction, a policy which, in the actual conditions of jealously guarded national independence, mutual suspicion and fear, will nevertheless be adopted and worked in good faith; which is non-committal enough for acceptance, committal enough to bind to right courses, which, by gradually improving international relations, will make possible more comprehensive plans later. Such must always be a compromise between what the more far-sighted would like and what will be accepted by less far-sighted governments and peoples in existing conditions of public opinion and national feeling, remembering always that those conditions are not fixed and unchangeable things for which no one is responsible and which no one can alter, but things which all of us help to make and which can be modified in response to our efforts.

It serves little purpose for the expert to indicate the way of escape if the layman refuses to believe that it is the way. The problem for the expert is not only and not first to find the way of escape, it is first to enable those for whom the way of escape is designed, and who are travelling in the other direction, to see that it is indeed the right road.

For these reasons, this book has not included a detailed examination of the various proposals for League revision, nor discussed the way in which disarmament might be accomplished, or an international air force made effective. They are all important questions well worth discussion; each well worth whole books to itself. The common need of all of them, however, is steady public support of the principle which underlies them. It is precisely that steady support which the whole history of the various plans which have been brought forward in the last fifteen years shows to be lacking. Professor Einstein, among others, has pointed out the astonishing oscillations of public opinion, at one moment clamouring for a League to Enforce Peace (with the emphasis on the force) and then when presented with one containing even modified sanctions, reject it because it has any at all; at one moment protesting that peace must not be based upon the hegemony of any group, and in the next breath proposing an Anglo-American hegemony to ensure peace. These confusions must be cleared up if any plan is to work. Which is why this book has concentrated upon making the underlying principles and the underlying alternatives clear to the ordinary man.

## Chapter II

# THE SHORT ANSWER

This chapter is designed to help the ordinary man in dealing with arguments most current in the daily talk of train and club and dinner table bearing on the following points: "War is inevitable," "Human Nature is naturally quarrelsome," "You cannot change Human Nature," "War is a Spiritual Cleanser," "War will continue so long as Man is selfish," "What would you do if a Brute attacked your Sister?" "Would you leave Houses unlocked, or refrain from resisting the Burglar?" "The Strong Man armed," "Arms are for defence," "Armaments mean Peace" (Lord Rothermere), "Defence demands that we should be stronger than any Probable Enemy," "Defence must rest upon a Balance of Power," "Isolation is the best Peace Policy," "Our Policy is Defence, so our Armaments need disturb no Foreign Nation," "Conflict of Ideals, Religion, Race, produce War," "Marathon . . . the Armada . . . War as a last resort," "Expanding Populations need Food and Space," "Capitalism, the Need of Disposing of Surplus Goods is the Cause," "Some Capitalists would benefit by War," "Armament Makers cause War," "Peace would perpetuate an unjust *Status Quo*," "Avoid War by removing the Grievances which cause it," "Armies and Navies are Police," "The Policy of Commitments failed in 1914," "The League is impotent—a Talking Shop," "The League places British Policy under Foreigners' Control," "The League costs too much," "What Security have we that Foreign Nations will keep their Word?" "Only Britain is pacifist . . . it is dangerous to preach Peace in England when Foreigners prepare for War . . ."

To a certain number of the propositions or questions enumerated at the beginning of this book, "short answers," useful perhaps in the general discussion of this subject, are given below as a supplement to the more exhaustive treatment in the body of the book.

I

*War is inevitable*

Which war? Any war proposed at any time by any irresponsible newspaper about anything? Plainly, some wars which might take place if the silliest or more panicky elements were unrestrained, can be prevented.

[ 306 ]

Further, militarists don't believe that all wars are inevitable, because they urge more armament, on the ground that that will help to preserve peace—stop war.

Disease is inevitable, but we have eliminated ancient pestilences like the Black Death, bubonic plague, leprosy, cholera, by better sanitary measures. The measures sometimes fail; we don't thereupon abandon them; we stiffen them. Our national constitutions sometimes fail to prevent civil war, but we nevertheless know that constitutions are better than making every election a civil war. The League, which is as yet a baby, may not be able to stop every war all at once; but unless we just give up the ghost and let civilisation go to the devil, some constitution like the League must sooner or later be established.

## II

*Human Nature is naturally quarrelsome*

That is why we must have a League of Nations, or institutions of restraint and discipline. The only reason. If human nature were perfect, most of our regulatory institutions would be unnecessary. The "human nature" argument is usually turned upside down. See pages 255-267.

## III

*You cannot change Human Nature*

You don't need to. But you can certainly change human behaviour, conduct, which is what matters: Cannibalism, human sacrifice, slavery, polygamy, heretic burning, legal torture, the duel, are cases in point. These changes of behaviour are brought about mainly

[307]

by changes of ideas; ideas of what is workable, right, wrong, pleasant, desirable. Our very desires change. See pages 255-267.

## IV

### War is a Spiritual Cleanser

But the militarist who uses the argument tells us that the increase of armament which he urges will preserve peace, deprive men of the spiritual benefits of war. Which does he want? War or peace? See pages 13-33.

## V

### War will continue so long as Man is selfish

War demands of men the greatest possible unselfishness, the greatest sacrifice of all, life; destroys prosperity; wealth, trade; brings the utter disorganisation of finance, investment; produces bankruptcy, poverty. If men were more intelligently selfish, war would not take place.

## VI

### What would you do if a Brute attacked your Sister?

"Give him a sock on the jaw." But if conditions were such that women were liable to violence, I should not be content with brothers being handy at the moment of attack, but would co-operate in organising a system of police, magistrature, courts, which is precisely what those who use this argument as analogous to the restraint of violence in the international field refuse to do internationally. See pages 13-33; 160-178.

## VII

*Would you leave Houses unlocked, or refrain from resisting the Burglar?*

By all means lock your door, and take a poker to the burglar. But if each householder had to depend solely upon his own strength, with no reliance upon the power of the community, the help, that is, of his neighbours represented by police, magistrature, then any bandit gang which was more powerful than a single household would have the country at its mercy. When blunderbusses were commonplaces of household furniture, highwaymen were much commoner than they are now when not one household in a thousand has a firearm on the place. It is not the prowess of individual householders which gives security, but the better organisation of the community for mutual defence. The true analogy as between household defence and national defence is indicated, not by the question whether you will take a poker to the burglar, but whether you will pay your police rate to protect others as well as yourself. If no one would make sacrifices for the general defence, police, there could be no general defence. Defence must be collective and co-operative or fail.

## VIII

*"The Strong Man armed"*

The end of the verse is never quoted. "When a stronger than he should come upon him and overcome him, he taketh from him his whole armour wherein he trusted and divideth his spoils" (Luke xi, 21), which is the whole case for the collective system of defence, implicit in arrangements like those embodied in the Covenant of the League. So long as each householder —or nation—has to depend purely upon its own power, it is overcome immediately some single individual is stronger. If the householder—or nation—is part of an organised society, then the burglar, bandit aggressor, has to meet the power of not one individual, but that of the whole community, and every individual is more secure. That is the meaning of St. Luke's parable, and we might well apply it to the international situation. See pages 160-178.

## IX

*Arms are for defence*

Then, as heretofore used, they have accomplished their purpose very badly. They did not defend the million who died in the war nor the millions maimed; the prosperity which was ruined, the trade that has vanished; nor the democracy war was to make safe for the world, for there is an epidemic of dictatorship; nor freedom from Prussian militarism, for the post-war militarism is more ruthless even than the pre-war brand; nor our own political security, since it is, we are now told, more endangered than ever. If we have to burn down our house to prevent its being burgled, and then have it burgled, it is time we found a better method.

## X

*Armaments mean Peace* (Lord Rothermere)

The armaments of other powers? Of Germany, Japan, Russia? Then why do we worry about them? Would "armaments mean peace" if each of the political parties in Great Britain, following the example of certain foreign countries (which we are invited to imitate) got an army? If Sir Oswald Mosely had one, the Labour Party another, the Co-operative Societies another, the Small Traders Association another and the Trades Unions still one more? What is true of the political groups we call parties is true of the political groups we call nations.

## XI

*Defence demands that We should be stronger than any Probable Enemy*

Then what of his defence? Is he to go without? General security by that method would only be possible if each could be stronger than the other. It defies arithmetic.

## XII

*Defence must rest upon a Balance of Power*

How do you know when two nations are equal in power? One has more men, another more industrial resources. How do you equate them? American experts once argued that a six-inch gun cruiser was of more value on this side of the Atlantic than on the other because its advantage came out in foggy weather, when ships had to operate at close quarters, and demanded that this factor should be taken into account. How many ships to how much fog?

And if you *could* get equality, it is all upset if one of the parties makes a new alliance. The technical element in defence is subordinate to the political, to the consideration of who is going to be with us and who against us.

## XIII

*Isolation is the best Peace Policy*

Isolation plus competitive armament is impossible. Suppose, having built up our strength to that of the probable enemy, he makes an alliance, so that you have no longer armament equivalent to the armament it would have to meet, what do you do? You make an alliance too. Britain had over twenty allies in the Great War, and needed them. If we go in for "maintaining our armaments at a level with possible enemies" we cannot go in for isolation. An alliance is a source of power, like submarines or an air force. If the enemy adopts that arm, we must adopt it too or drop out of the race.

## XIV

*Our Policy is Defence, so our Armaments need disturb no Foreign Nation*

Defence of what? Our soil, the protection of our homes from the foreign invader?

Every war we have fought since the Norman conquest has been fought in someone else's country. The fact does not make them aggressive. They may all have been defensive wars, but plainly defence consisted of something more than defending our soil. Isolated America has landed her troops on foreign soil nearly a hundred times in her short history. National defence means defending the nation's interests, which may collide with the interests of other nations anywhere in the world. But if, in a dispute with another, in a case where the question is whether he is or you are right, you ask power to be in a position to be the judge, then you claim a right of judgment denied to him, deprive him of the very defensive rights you claim as so indispensable to yourself. Your power automatically deprives him of the means of defending *his* rights.

## XV

*Conflict of Ideals, Religion, Race, produce War*

Differences of religion used to produce the worst wars of all, the religious wars. It was not inevitable they should continue, for they have ceased. The feeling of nationalism need no more produce war than the emotions of religion. Welsh, Scots, English who once fought now live together in peace, French and English in Canada, English and Dutch in South Africa. But this peace would be impossible if both sides excused their temper by calling it "race patriotism" and declaring war between them to be "inevitable."

## XVI

*Marathon . . . the Armada . . . War as a last resort*

The folly of men and the bad organisation of the world may well produce situations in which war becomes unavoidable, as famine may push men to cannibalism. The fact is not an argument against the desirability of so improving agriculture as to make cannibalism unnecessary, nor against so improving international policies and political methods as to make war unnecessary.

South American revolutionaries, confronted by tyranny, say: "Civil war is better than slavery." Yet while easily aroused to the need of fighting, they are with much greater difficulty aroused to such constitutional improvements and better political method as would make civil war unnecessary. The question is not whether war is to be the last resort, but the first. Means of organisation not possible to the Greeks or sixteenth-century Englishmen are possible to us, and we should use them. We have abolished famine, once endemic, and prevented that excuse for cannibalism. We can abolish political anarchy and that excuse for war.

## XVII

### Expanding Populations need Food and Space

Every nation in the world is attempting, not to seize the food and goods of other nations, but to keep them out, by tariffs, quotas, etc. The problem of the modern world is not scarcity, but over production, that is to say, maldistribution, difficulties connected with such adjustments as the machinery of exchange, the monetary apparatus, etc. These adjustments can only be made by agreement, international organisation.

Conquest does not solve these problems. They are as severe in countries possessing great territories, like Britain, as in countries which possess small, like Sweden, Denmark, Switzerland. Japan *has* a severe population question, but she has not begun to use the colonies she already possesses, because, if emigration is to succeed, the emigrant must be able to find a market for his product, and the world is direly glutted with the kind of products produced by emigrants. A better economic organisation of the world as a whole would give Japan a much better chance of solving her problem than could conquest of new territories, especially in view of the fact that she does not use the colonial territory she already

[314]

possesses. Japanese militarists do not realise these economic truths any more than other militarists.

## XVIII

### *Capitalism, the Need of disposing of Surplus Goods is the Cause*

When the Capitalist, having gone to war, has secured his victory, how can he use that victory for the purpose of disposing of his surplus? Britain had victory in 1918 over its most redoubtable commercial rival. Are British Capitalists more able to dispose of their surplus than they were before the war? They are less able. Capitalism, even in the victorious countries, is in a much worse position after war than it was before, profoundly shaken, faced by social revolution, the breakdown of money, banking, finance, many Capitalists utterly ruined. Another war would about finish off the whole system. If in face of this Capitalism as a system is using its influence towards war it must be from motives of suicide.

## XIX

### *Some Capitalists would benefit by War*

Some Capitalists would benefit by a new Great Fire of London; all industries related to the building trades would boom. It does not make arson a Capitalist interest.

## XX

### *Armament Makers cause War*

Fifty armament makers may tell the nations to go to war. But why do the nations obey? Building firms would doubtless like us to burn our house down. We should not do it to please them. Why should we burn our child alive to please armament firms? To discover what really gives the armament maker his power we must discover what are the motives in Mr. John Smith to which they so successfully appeal.

## XXI

### Peace would perpetuate an unjust Status Quo

Would another war in which the vanquished of the last were victors give a better *status quo* than the present one? A victorious Germany would not make a treaty more just than the one we made in 1919. It would be more unjust, but the injustices would be on the other side, and we should be the victims, compelled then to fight against injustice and make a new treaty, which would necessarily be worse than the present one, because of there being more to avenge, which would therefore give more cause for German resentment. . . . Settlement made by the victors after a war can never correct the injustices of the *status quo,* only alter their character. The argument that without war you cannot change a fundamentally injust situation is the stock argument for evolution in Spanish American republics. But much more fundamental changes in political structure and social conditions have been made in Britain this last hundred years than have resulted from all the civil wars of South and Central America. Once rule war out, and means of change other than war are discovered: the claims for rights which in the eighteenth century produced war between Britain and the thirteen colonies are accorded to Australia and Canada and other

Dominions, not merely without war but without bitterness. The granting of Dominion status to Ireland followed upon bitter resistance during two generations to the much less sweeping demands of Gladstonian Home Rule.

## XXII

*Avoid War by removing the Grievances which cause it*

We had no treaty of Versailles to resent in 1914; nor had Italy, nor America, nor had most of the Allies that fought against Germany. They fought because German victory would have created such preponderance of power in the world against them that they would have been defenceless. But their victory made Germany defenceless—defenceless against judgment delivered by the rival party to the dispute, and so did not remedy the fundamental difficulty at all.

## XXIII

*Armies and Navies are Police*

Answers XIX and XX show that armies and navies are instruments by which one of the parties to a dispute becomes its judge. But the purpose of a police force is to prevent the individual from taking the law into his own hands, to restrain the litigant from becoming the judge, the exactly contrary purpose of national forces as they operate for defence under the old system. The problem in the international field is to transfer power from the litigants to the law. The only way by which general defence can be secured is for all to support a rule or law, like that of submission to third party judgment. When most great states support that law by making common cause against the state that defies it, then defence will be secured by the preponderant power of civilisation as a whole.

## XXIV

### *The Policy of Commitments failed in 1914*

Most of the states drawn into the war against Germany (e.g. America, Italy, Roumania, Japan) were not committed beforehand. That freedom did not prevent them from being drawn in. Commitment would have prevented it. If Germany had known to a certainty that by following a certain line of policy she would cause a score of states to take the field against her she would not have followed that line, and there would have been no war.

## XXV

### *The League is impotent—a Talking Shop*

The League can only have power if those who are its members give it power. Where else would the power come from? The French have always wanted to give it power, so have most of its other members. It is we in Britain who have been disposed to hold back. It hardly lies with us, therefore, to talk of its impotence.

The failure in the Sino-Japanese case was due to the failure of the national governments which compose the League to take the same risks for the collective system of defence which they readily take for the individual system.

Since co-operation is impossible without interchange of ideas, talk is inevitable. When misunderstandings arise, there is only one known means of clearing them

up—"talks." If there is not talk before a war there will
be talk after.

## XXVI

### The League Places British Policy under Foreigner's Control

Nothing like as much as the old anarchy and the
Balance of Power did. The Southern Slavs quarrelled
with Austria, and we were helpless to take any steps; an
archduke was murdered and a million Englishmen had
to give their lives in the resulting quarrel. Had a
League existed before 1914, so that these disputes could
have been dragged into the open, and so that we should
have known more precisely what the commitments
were, we should have had far greater control of policy
than in fact we had. An Isolationist paper in a leading
article wrote not long since: "Britain should resolutely
refuse to enter any international conference the
majority of which were foreigners."

## XXVII

### The League Costs too Much

Britain's contribution to the League bears the same
proportion to the nation's total income that a contribution of 3d. a year would to the income of a man with
£350 a year. Can a man with £350 a year afford a
farthing a month to insure the safety of his house? The
interest on the cost of one battleship would pay Britains
contribution to the League for ever, without asking the
nation for another penny. In other words, if we can
save *one* battleship we have saved the whole cost of the
League. The League actually costs our people about

a penny farthing per head; the war system about ten pounds per head.

## XXVIII

*What Security have we that Foreign Nations will keep their Word?*

Keep their word to do what? To refrain from attacking us? We should under the collective system have every guarantee that we have at present, and very considerable ones in addition which we do not now possess. Our national armed forces would be relatively as powerful after all-round disarmament as now: reduction of the forces that might be brought against us would have taken place concurrently with reduction of our own. The security against secret arming would be better under the new system, since any plan of disarmament would provide for supervision, mutual inspection of armament *in peace time,* and would arrange for the cutting off of supplies of armament material to any State arming itself in violation of the terms of a Disarmament Convention. This constitutes a check against making ready for attack, which the present system does not provide. Further, combinations of power against us would be much more difficult under the collective system than they are now, for they would all be formally pledged not to side with the aggressor.

These advantages would accrue, in some measure at least, even though foreign nations did not fulfil their obligation to come to our aid in the case of attack. But we have to depend on their so doing just as much under the old method as under the collective method. If we had been compelled to wage our war single-handed against Germany, we should have been beaten. We had, and needed, twenty allies.

Moreover, it is not a question of "trusting to the good faith" of foreigners from the moment that it is to their plain interest to adhere to the collective system. It then becomes a question whether they see their interest or not.

## XXIX

*Only Britain is pacifist . . . it is dangerous to preach Peace in England when Foreigners prepare for War . . .*

All these objections arise from confusion as to what the issue is and the debate about. It is not a debate as between arms and no arms, defence or no defence, but as to which method of armed defence is likely to most be effective: the method which attempts to defend one side by automatically depriving the other of defence, or the collective method which would secure equal rights of defence for all by pooling power for the defence of law —the first law being that no one shall go to war.

It is not true that foreign nations as a whole are less in favour of this method than we are. France, the greatest military power in Europe, has always favoured it, Russia favours it, all the lesser states favour it. In crises like that of the Japanese aggression upon China, the United States favoured it. It is Britain mainly that hangs back.

# BIBLIOGRAPHY

The area outlined in this book has been covered in greater detail by the present writer in his other works as follows:

## THE GREAT ILLUSION 1933
Relates the theme of *The Great Illusion* first published in 1908 to the present situation. The book undertakes to show that the advantages, particularly the economic advantages, usually attributed to victory are illusory. It is not a "balance sheet" but an analysis showing that certain assumptions concerning military power and economic advantage, the need for the political expansion of nations with increasing populations, all commonly accepted as "axioms" are in fact nonsense. The book discusses the relation of the economic to the moral motives in war; states the case for co-operation as the basis of civilisation.

## THE FRUITS OF VICTORY
A sequel to *The Great Illusion*, of less value than *The Great Illusion* being a survey of the world in 1920 showing how the war's results had borne out the general propositions of *The Great Illusion*.

## THE UNSEEN ASSASSINS
Is mainly an inquiry into the question: "Why don't we see the self-evident?" the extremely simple truths about human society which, if acted upon, would enable us to avoid such catastrophes as war. The unseen assassins of our peace and welfare are the unrecognised implications of the policies which we follow, often with the best intentions. It discusses education in relation to this problem and illustrates the theme by discussion of current international and imperial problems.

## THE MENACE TO OUR NATIONAL DEFENCE
Discusses the problem of collective defence particularly in relation to the air arm and the technical nature of air warfare and its particular dangers; considers the possibility of the abolition of national air forces, and the internationalisation of civil aviation.

## THE MONEY GAME
Many of the economic fallacies which embitter international relations, which set up tariffs and economic warfare have their root in

what the economists call the "mercantilist illusion"— a misunderstanding of the nature of money. It lies at the root of the reparations difficulty and the present difficulty with America over the debts. Explanations of currency problems however rapidly become very confusing for the layman—as would explanations of bridge to anyone who had not played it. *The Money Game* is an attempt to do for currency what the cards do for bridge—reduce its explanation to visual demonstration. It consists of special cards as well as book.

Among the authors whose work will be found most useful in the preliminary study of the subject are the following:

## STUDIES OF PRE-WAR CONDITIONS LEADING TO WAR

G. LOWES DICKINSON, *The International Anarchy, 1904-1914*. London, 1926. And any of his other work related to this subject.

A historical survey of the events which led up to the Great War. The author is careful to lay the blame on the "international anarchy" rather than on any particular power.

ARNOLD J. TOYNBEE, *A Study of History*. London, 1934 (3 vols.). A comparative and analytical study of man's efforts to rise above the primitive level during the last five or six thousand years. Other volumes to follow.

LUIGI STURZO, *The International Community and the Right of War*, translated by Barbara Barclay Carter. London, 1929.

A historical critique of the origins of war. The author's theme is the eliminability of war, which is the child of a particular form of political and social organisation.

KIRBY PAGE, *National Defense*, a Study of the Origins, Results and Prevention of War. New York, 1931.

A careful examination of the causes of the World War and of the events that led up to it, comparing them with the situation at the present day.

PARKER T. MOON, *Syllabus on International Relations*. Macmillan, 1925.

A comprehensive guide to the study of the economic, geographic, sociological and other aspects of international relations. Invaluable to both student and teacher.

## THE ECONOMIC ASPECT: INTERNATIONAL CO-OPERATION

R. G. HAWTREY, *Economic Aspects of Sovereignty*. London, 1930.

The theme of the book is economic expansion or exploitation as a

# BIBLIOGRAPHY

cause of war. The author looks for a cure within the existing social system.

H. J. LASKI, "The Economic Foundations of Peace," a chapter in *The Intelligent Man's Way to Prevent War*. Gollancz, London, 1933. A statement of the Marxian case that "capitalism is the Cause of War."

WALLACE McCLURE, *World Prosperity*, as sought through the Economic Work of the League of Nations. New York, 1933.
A study of Internationalism from the economic point of view. There is a useful section on the economic aspect of War and Disarmament.

PARKER T. MOON, *Imperialism and World Politics*, New York, 1927.
A comprehensive history and analysis of contemporary imperialism and its effect on international relations since 1870. Reveals the economic fallacy of imperialism.

LEONARD S. WOOLF, *Economic Imperialism*. London, 1920.

PAUL EINZIG, *The Economics of Rearmament*. London, 1923.
A critical survey of the effects of rearmament or disarmament upon the economic life of the nations.

FRANK H. SIMONDS, *Can America Stay at Home?* New York, 1932.
An American journalist discusses the traditional Isolationism of America, pointing out that "the profits of international peace can only be shared by peoples prepared to pay the tax of international responsibility." All his work is useful and significant.

ARTHUR SALTER, SIR, *Recovery*. London, 1932.
An analysis of present day problems, financial, commercial and political, showing the need of international co-operation in all three fields.

SECRETARIAT OF THE LEAGUE OF NATIONS, *Ten Years of World Co-operation*. Geneva, 1930.
An official record of the progress made in every aspect of the League's activities during the first ten years of its existence.

## THE WAY TO PEACE

LEONARD S. WOOLF, *International Government*. Allen & Unwin, London, 1923. Editor of *The Intelligent Man's Way to Prevent War*. Gollancz, 1933.

F. S. MARVIN AND OTHERS, *The Evolution of World Peace*. London, 1933.
A collection of essays tracing throughout history from early times to the present day the steps, ideals and mistakes which have marked the path towards Peace. Each essay is the work of an expert on the particular period.

[325]

# PEACE AND THE PLAIN MAN

CECIL, LORD. Notably his chapter "The League as a Road to Peace" in *The Intelligent Man's Way to Prevent War*. Gollancz, London, 1933. Anything he writes is certain to be useful and significant owing to long first hand knowledge of negotiations between the governments at Geneva, war-time membership of the British Government, etc.

G. P. GOOCH, *In Pursuit of Peace*. London, 1933.

A selection from the addresses delivered at the National Peace Congress at Oxford in July 1933. Three of these are concerned with the definition and implications of Pacifism.

NICHOLAS MURRAY BUTLER, *The Path to Peace*. Essays and Addresses on Peace and its Making. New York and London, 1930.

In the course of these essays the author considers the various Pacts and Instruments which have attempted in recent times to substitute arbitration for War.

J. W. WHEELER-BENNETT, *Information on the Renunciation of War*. London, 1928.

A history of the Kellogg proposals for the renunciation of War, collecting and commenting upon all the documents relative to the negotiations.

HANS WEHBERG, *The Outlawry of War*. Washington, 1931.

A series of lectures delivered before the Academy of International Law at the Hague and in the Institut Universaire de Hautes Etudes Internationales at Geneva. Special attention is given to the Covenant of the League of Nations, the Geneva Protocol and the Kellogg Pact.

A. A. MILNE, *Peace with Honour*. London, 1934.

An amusing and extremely readable discussion of the pacifist issues.

GILBERT MURRAY, *The Ordeal of this Generation*. London, 1929.

All his pamphlets are worth reading as also his article on "Revision of the Peace Treaties" in *The Intelligent Man's Way to Prevent War*. Gollancz, London, 1933.

C. M. LLOYD, "The Problem of Russia," a chapter in *The Intelligent Man's Way to Prevent War*. Gollancz, London, 1933.

STORM JAMESON, "The Twilight of Reason," a chapter in *Challenge to Death*. Constable, 1934.

PHILIP NOEL-BAKER, "Peace and the Official Mind," a chapter in *Challenge to Death*, a very useful symposium covering much of the whole field. Constable, 1934.

# BIBLIOGRAPHY

## SPECIALISED STUDIES RELATING TO SPECIFIC PROBLEMS

### THE LEAGUE OF NATIONS

C. Howard-Ellis, *The Origin, Structure and Working of the League of Nations.* London, 1928.

A full, careful and detailed text-book, strictly limited in scope to the internal organisation of the League.

C. K. Webster and Sydney Herbert, *The League of Nations in Theory and Practice.* London, 1933.

A critical survey of the development and activities of the League, with special reference to the organisation of World-Peace and the growth of International Co-operation.

Felix Morley, *The Society of Nations*, its Organisation and Constitutional Development. Washington, 1932.

A record of the events which led up to the formation of the League and a careful analysis of its subsequent development and history.

Florence Wilson, *The Origins of the League Covenant*, documentary history of its drafting. London, 1928.

An exact report of the proposals and discussions which accompanied the drafting of each Article of the Covenant.

T. P. Conwell-Evans, *The League Council in Action.* London, 1929.

A study of the methods employed by the Council of the League of Nations to prevent War and to settle International Disputes.

### THE PEACE PACT OF PARIS

David Hunter Miller, *The Peace Pact of Paris*, a Study of the Briand-Kellogg Treaty. New York and London, 1928.

The history of the Pact from its earliest origins to its conclusion. All the relevant documents, including the Pact itself, are transcribed and collected in the appendix.

James T. Shotwell, *War as an Instrument of National Policy, and its Renunciation in the Pact of Paris.* London, 1929.

An account of the diplomatic steps in Europe and America which led up to the Pact of Paris, with an explanation and discussion of its terms.

### DISARMAMENT

Philip Noel-Baker, *Disarmament.* London, 1926.

The greatest living authority, perhaps, on problems of disarmament and the constitution of the League possessed by virtue of a wide contact with events at Geneva and first-hand knowledge of disarmament negotiations.

SALVADOR DE MADARIAGA, *Disarmament*. London, 1929.

This book remains a standard text-book on the subject. It contains not only a detailed history of the question but proposals for the application of its principles to particular problems.

J. W. WHEELER-BENNETT, *Disarmament and Security since Locarno*.

A history from 1925-31 of the preliminary work and events which led up to the Disarmament Conference of 1932.

ZEITSCHRIFT FUR POLITIK, *Disarmament and Equal Rights*. Facts and Problems dealt with in the negotiations on Disarmament and Equal Rights 1933-34, edited and translated into English by Richard Schmidt and Adolf Grabowsky. Berlin, 1934.

The German point of view on Disarmament, well-documented.

## ARBITRATION

W. ARNOLD-FORSTER, *The Victory of Reason*. The Hogarth Press, 1926. A plea for arbitration; also his chapter on "Arbitration, Security, Disarmament" in *The Intelligent Man's Way to Prevent War*. Gollancz, London, 1933.

JACKSON H. RALSTON, *International Arbitration from Athens to Locarno*. London, 1929.

The general principles, early history, development and methods of International Arbitration. A standard work on the subject.

## THE PRIVATE MANUFACTURE OF ARMAMENTS

H. C. ENGELBRECHT AND F. C. HANIGHEN, *Merchants of Death*, a study of the International Armament Industry. London, 1934.

A history of the Arms Traffic from the Middle Ages to the present day. The authors discuss in detail the leading firms and personalities of modern times and their influence on World politics.

OTTO LEHMANN-RUSSBULDT, *Die blutige Internationale*. Hamburg, 1929.

The author discusses the connection between the Armament firms of the various countries of Europe during and after the War and criticises the League of Nations for its inaction.

LOUIS LAUNAY AND JEAN SENNAC, *Les Relations Internationales des Industries de Guerre*. Paris, 1932.

An account of the power, ramifications and inter-relations of the Armament firms, principally in France.

UNION OF DEMOCRATIC CONTROL, *The Secret International*, Armament firms at work. London, 1932.

A short pamphlet filled with useful information.

# BIBLIOGRAPHY

BEVERLEY NICHOLS, *Cry Havoc*. London, 1933.

A passionate attack on the forces that make for war, with special reference to the Armament Trade.

## SANCTIONS, INTERNATIONAL POLICE AND AIR

D. MITRANY, *The Problem of International Sanctions*. London, 1925.

A concisely written, critical discussion of the problems of sanctions in relation to the Covenant of the League. The theoretical arguments are useful, though their application is already out-of-date.

DAVIES, LORD, *The Problem of the Twentieth Century*. London, revised edition, 1934. *Force*. London, 1934.

A study of the place of force in human society with special relation to international problems. The author here elaborates the case in favour of an International Police Force.

MAXWELL GARNETT, *The Freedom of the Air*. London, 1933.

This little pamphlet, reprinted from the *Contemporary Review*, develops the argument for a League of Nations Air Force, whose sole function would be protection against air-raids.

JONATHAN GRIFFIN. A series of useful pamphlets on the Air Police and aviation, etc.

THE COMMITTEE ON ECONOMIC SANCTIONS, *Boycotts and Peace*, edited by Evans Clark. New York and London, 1932.

A report of the findings and recommendations of the Committee on Economic Sanctions, with supplementary chapters to indicate their applicability to particular countries.

ALEC WILSON, *World Security*, an Essay on Sanctions. London, 1931.

A booklet devoted to the discussion of the possible forms which sanctions might take and to their justification and expediency.

LEON BLUM, *Peace and Disarmament*. London, 1932.

An interesting chapter is devoted to the arguments for and against an International Army for Police Work.

PHILIP NOEL-BAKER, "A National Air Force No Defence" and "The International Air Police Force," chapters in *Challenge to Death*. Constable, London, 1934.

# INDEX

# INDEX

# INDEX

# INDEX